MINNESOTA HISTORICAL SOCIETY

Public Affairs Center Publications

RUSSELL W. FRIDLEY

Editor and Director

JUNE DRENNING HOLMQUIST

Managing Editor

TEN MEN
OF MINNESOTA
AND AMERICAN
FOREIGN POLICY
1898–1968

By Barbara Stuhler

MINNESOTA HISTORICAL SOCIETY • ST. PAUL • 1973

Copyright © 1973 Minnesota Historical Society
International Standard Book Number: 0-87351-080-1

Library of Congress Cataloging Data:

Stuhler, Barbara.
  Ten men of Minnesota and American foreign policy, 1898–1968.

  (Minnesota Historical Society. Public Affairs Center. Publications)
  Includes bibliographical references.
    1. United States — Foreign relations — 20th century. 2. Minnesota —
Biography. I. Title. II. Series.
E744.S956   327.73 [B]   73–15967

For my father

G. RUSSELL STUHLER

CONTENTS

ILLUSTRATIONS

PREFACE

IT SEEMS only fair to the reader to explain my motive and define my purpose. Like many not native to the state, I have been impressed with the integrity and strength of the Minnesota political experience. I confess to being a fascinated observer of a tradition that Abigail Q. McCarthy has termed "issue politics and participatory democracy." For more than two decades, I have also been engaged in the task of educating Minnesota citizens on the compelling issues of American foreign policy. The pages that follow are witness to my interest in bringing Minnesota politics and United States foreign policy together. No effort is made here to describe the totality of this relationship. Such an undertaking would embrace a much more complete inventory of ideas, issues, and individuals. My purpose was not to write a definitive or even a comprehensive treatment of the foreign policy attitudes of ten representative Minnesotans but rather, by attempted judicious selection, to indicate the main threads of their interests and concerns. Nevertheless, it is my hope that this volume may justify the proposition that public men of Minnesota have contributed significantly to the nation's foreign policy, perhaps more so than those in some sister states. The final proof of this thesis would lie, of course, with a series of comparable studies.

These ten men of Minnesota were not necessarily heroes or villains. They were ordinary mortals given to certain views by reason of environment and experience. Understandably, their impact on the foreign policy scene was diverse both in influence and attitude. There is no single, simplistic Minnesota view of the world.

In any accounting of the debits and credits of an undertaking such as this, the author customarily assumes responsibility for the debits — and I do. The credits go particularly to those institutions which made this research possible: initially the graduate school of the University of Minnesota which granted me a leave of absence in the winter of 1969; later, the Minnesota Historical Society from which I received a Public Affairs Center research fellowship in 1971; and to the society's Louis W. and Maud Hill Family Foundation revolving fund which covered a portion of the publication costs. I cannot begin to measure the contributions of the staff of the society to my efforts. They were well informed, instructive, co-operative, and afforded me both intellectual challenge and good companionship. A series of graduate research assistants who have worked for the World Affairs Center added more to my pleasure than my pain in this task, especially Rolf N. Sigford whose scholarly skills were a special joy. My colleagues in Continuing Education and Extension at the university were sympathetic and encouraging. William C. Rogers, director of the World Affairs Center, cheered me on and asked me hard questions, the *sine qua non* of a collaboration which has lasted more than twenty years.

Finally, I thank those with whom I have served on the state and national boards of the League of Women Voters and my friends who have put up with the vagaries of authorship. Their expectations have moved me to achievements beyond my belief.

St. Paul, Minnesota   *Barbara Stuhler*
August, 1973

TEN MEN AND THEIR MILIEU

THE POLITICAL HISTORY of Minnesota has been noted for its diversity. Indeed it has been described as suffering from "political schizophrenia," for its citizens have been tenaciously traditional as well as rigorously radical.[1] Out of the rich political lode of Minnesota history from 1898 to 1968 have come men whose views of American foreign policy were marked by varying degrees of introversion and extroversion. This state in the Middle West has provided noteworthy spokesmen for four points of view — imperialism, isolationism, internationalism, and interventionism — which in various forms were important to the nation's foreign policy during the seventy-year period covered by this book. The ten Minnesotans who are the subjects of the chapters that follow have been selected because of their intimate involvement with the state's political experience, and because that involvement in each case concerned the principal foreign policy issues confronting the nation at the time. They viewed the shifting tides and rode or deflected the currents of American foreign policy as members of Congress (where no fewer than five of them sat on the Senate foreign relations committee), as secretary of state, as presidential assistant, as vice-president of the United States, and, in several instances, as aspirants to the presidency.[2]

The earliest of these ten Minnesotans was CUSHMAN K. DAVIS, a Republican who served as United States senator from 1887 to 1900 and who represented the imperialism which peaked in the debates and decisions surrounding the Spanish-American War in 1898. Davis has been included because he was a member of the foreign relations committee from 1891 to 1900 and a prime mover in the decisions leading to war with Spain, the annexation of the Hawaiian Islands, and the acquisition of the Philippines.

The roles of three men — CHARLES A. LINDBERGH, SR., HAROLD KNUTSON, and HENRIK SHIPSTEAD — will be discussed against the background of isolationism, a complex phenomenon which gathered momentum during the first decade of the twentieth century and continued to influence American foreign policy for some forty years. Lindbergh, a Republican who represented Minnesota's sixth district in Congress from 1907 to 1917, was later a member of the

Farmer-Labor party, a radical offshoot of the GOP which made its first appearance in the state in 1918. A controversial reformer, he opposed American participation in World War I as an unworthy diversion from domestic priorities of social justice and economic well-being. Knutson, a Republican who followed Lindbergh as sixth district congressman from 1917 to 1949, was, unlike his predecessor, a pedantic and conservative advocate of isolationism from the time of his election to the day of his defeat thirty-two years later. He earned his political longevity by accurately reflecting the vigorous isolationist sentiment of his constituency. Henrik Shipstead, a Farmer-Laborite turned Republican, represented Minnesota in the United States Senate from 1923 through 1946 and was a member of the foreign relations committee throughout those twenty-four years. A hardy political independent, Shipstead's maverick isolationism in peace and war culminated in his vote against ratification of the United Nations Charter in 1945. His defeat in 1946 pointed to the waning of isolationism as a dominant factor in Minnesota politics in the first half of the twentieth century.

Separated by two decades, four diverse spokesmen — FRANK B. KELLOGG, JOSEPH H. BALL, HAROLD E. STASSEN, and WALTER H. JUDD — reflected what might be called the postisolationist period, which had a feeble inception in the 1920s and reached a fuller internationalist flowering during the years after World War II. Kellogg, a Republican, was United States senator from 1917 to 1923 and a member of the Senate foreign relations committee from 1921 to 1923, ambassador to Great Britain, 1923–25, and United States secretary of state, 1925–29, in the cabinet of President Calvin Coolidge. A conservative internationalist in this period, he eschewed political alliances but generally supported the League of Nations, the need for commercial relations among countries, and the utility of arbitration and conciliation as means of reconciling international conflicts. He is best remembered for his coauthorship of the Kellogg-Briand Pact of 1928 renouncing war as an instrument of national policy.

Three Republicans, who came to political prominence twenty years after Kellogg, confirmed the Minnesota shift from isolationism to internationalism. Joseph H. Ball, a senator from 1940 to 1949, was a determined internationalist whose election in 1942 (following his appointment by Governor Stassen in 1940) was viewed at the time as a significant benchmark in Minnesota's break with the tradition of isolation. By legislation and public persuasion, Ball helped move the Congress and the country to the support of a postwar organization for collective security. Harold E. Stassen, governor from 1939 to 1943, delegate to the San Francisco conference establishing the United Nations in

1945, chief of the foreign operations administration from 1953 to 1955, disarmament assistant to President Dwight D. Eisenhower from 1955 to 1958, and presidential aspirant from 1948 to 1968, revitalized the Republican party in Minnesota, turning it from isolationism to internationalism. In and out of office, Stassen was an advocate of policies and programs to defuse tensions and to contain international conflict. Walter H. Judd, fifth district congressman from 1943 to 1963, was a leading spokesman for the United Nations, foreign aid, reciprocal trade, and collective security. A member of the House foreign affairs committee from 1947 to 1963, he was best known for championing the Nationalist Chinese cause and for advocating resistance to the advance of communism in any form, time, or place.

Two Minnesotans who were influential especially in the last half of the 1960s — HUBERT H. HUMPHREY and EUGENE J. McCARTHY — acted against the background of a period in which interventionism vied with internationalism as the dominant thrust of American foreign policy. Humphrey, Democratic-Farmer-Labor party senator from 1949 to 1964, Senate foreign relations committee member from 1953 to 1964, and vice-president of the United States from 1965 to 1969, was an internationalist senator and an interventionist vice-president. As the presidential nominee of the Democratic party in 1968, he voiced modest expressions of dissent with the American intervention in Vietnam. Eugene J. McCarthy, Democratic-Farmer-Labor party fourth district congressman from 1949 to 1958, United States senator from 1959 to 1971, and Senate foreign relations committee member from 1965 to 1969, was also a presidential contender in 1968. He was only moderately well known in the nation until his formal protest against the American involvement in Vietnam in 1968 contributed in no small measure to catalyzing and coalescing the country's impatience for peace.

These ten men participated in the discussion and debate — sometimes also in the decisions — concerning the principal foreign policy issues of the period, beginning with an impulse to empire in 1898, then a commitment to isolationism, a conversion to internationalism, and ending with a tortured intervention in 1968. The four concepts — imperialism, isolationism, internationalism, and interventionism which provide the framework for this study — have been analyzed intensively, and no doubt will continue to be a source of scholarly controversy.[3] The terms are chameleonlike, varying in colors as the international environment changed. One must be arbitrary, however, and choose definitions which are appropriate in the context of this work.

While numerous definitions have been applied to imperialism, the turn-of-the-century interpretation applicable to Davis implied the political domination of one people by another. Though the European imperial example helped to inspire the American replication, there were differences between the two (as there were similarities but of a lesser magnitude). American imperialism was more makeshift, more culturally insidious (except perhaps for the French), and characterized, as Robin W. Winks has said, by a desire to "make colonial societies over in the American model so they could qualify for self-government or for admission into the Union itself." United States imperialism was not motivated by the desire to annex other countries but rather to improve them for their own sake. If there has remained one enduring heritage from nineteenth-century imperialism, it has been this effort to persuade other nations to accept American values; cultural imperialism still obtains. Davis, who also argued the imperialist cause for commercial gain and political power, represents a minor chorus on the American political stage. While a kind of political and economic imperialism has been the consequence of the pre-eminent power of United States dollars, guns, and butter in the second half of the twentieth century, it has not been a conscious, articulated policy.[4]

Because of the various forms it has taken, the concept of isolationism almost defies definition. This study merely assumes that a "desire to check American participation in world affairs is central to the isolationist persuasion."[5] In the first years of the republic, isolationism was taken to mean avoiding alliances and standing back from the ancient quarrels of Europe, an attitude that persisted in the circle of public debate into the twentieth century. Pre-World War I isolationism contained economic, ethnic, and radical components, but the ethnic factor declined in the period before World War II, and isolationism acquired a more conservative cast. By the 1950s efforts to revive the old isolationist sentiment met with little public favor. The issues raised — most particularly by the war in Vietnam during the 1960s — set in motion attempts to ascribe a "new isolationism" to those who supported United States withdrawal from Vietnam, who opposed a large defense establishment, and who argued generally for a greater selectivity in defining American foreign policy. But the differences among the isolationisms of the past and present create grave doubts as to the validity of the analogy.

Many serious analysts of American foreign policy during the 1960s have repudiated the "global disengagement" argument. John M. Cooper, Jr., for example, pointed out in 1969 that the "clearest difference between the current controversy and the debate that surrounded isolationism is a shift in focus. The central concern is no longer whether the United States should be involved beyond the hemisphere but, rather, what should be the methods, directions, and priorities in pursuing such involvement." Ronald Steel insisted in 1971 that "Today's so-called isolationists have for many years been convinced internationalists: architects of NATO, the Marshall Plan, and the United Nations, ardent defenders of foreign aid, the containment strategy, and America's role as a world power. These anti-interventionists, to use a more accurate word, in no sense advocate American isolation. They favor expanded cultural, social, political, and economic ties with all the nations of the world community. Rather than seeking isolation, they call for retrenchment from commitments that have become exorbitant, unnecessary and dangerous." [6]

Internationalism, as used here, is not meant to imply the converse of isolationism because neither concept is pure or unidimensional. One political scientist has noted that "If variety has attended the definition of isolationism, confusion has been the mark of whatever it is that isolationism is not. The difficulty is that there is no single, logical antithesis to the isolationist persuasion." Another scholar, Sondra R. Herman, has asserted that the internationalists were not of one mind, that they did not hold a "unified set of beliefs." Like the isolationists, they have been both radical and conservative. [7]

For the purposes of this study, internationalism is intended to mean an acceptance of the need for some degree of American participation in world affairs and a willingness to commit the United States to programs of international co-operation. In the early part of the twentieth century arbitration and mediation in the settlement of disputes were characteristic of the internationalist persuasion. After World War I advocates urged American membership in the League of Nations and affiliation with the World Court. And following World War II, they favored the United Nations, the Marshall Plan, and other programs of economic and political collaboration. Internationalists were generally intent on building institutions and developing a sense of global consciousness; they favored commercial interplay among nations and the concept of collective security.

Interventionism, as Max Beloff noted, is "the attempt by one state to affect the internal structure and external behavior of other states through various degrees of coercion." It has been a commonplace in the history of world politics, and in all likelihood, it will continue to be so. Interventions have been praised and damned; they have been both negative and positive, and they have existed in varying orders of magnitude. During the nineteenth century and even before, intervention had been practiced in a largely nonideological context, its goal being to force a change in conduct or policy on the lesser state. Beginning in 1917, when the first communist state was established in Russia, to 1954, when the French withdrew from Asia, American interventions were frequently motivated by the perception that communism might be both an economic and a political threat to democracy. The effort in Vietnam was designed not only to contain communist expansion, but to defeat the activities of a communist party within a country. Much of the initial confusion surrounding the American commitment in Indochina stemmed from the belief that the United States was acting on behalf of the international community.[8]

In one sense "the history of imperialism is the history of intervention, although imperialism often meant outright colonization." Like imperialism, the term interventionism has been loosely used. One consequence of the war in Vietnam was a growing belief during the 1960s that every form of relations among states was tantamount to intervention — a widely exaggerated interpretation and one without foundation. What set the American intervention in Vietnam apart (and, of course, war is the ultimate manifestation of intervention) was its ideological content.[9]

Of the four foreign policy attitudes that have prevailed in Minnesota between the Spanish-American and Vietnamese wars, isolationism has been the most pervasive, both in time and temper.[10] From the day of Charles Lindbergh's election in 1906 to the moment of Henrik Shipstead's defeat in 1946, isolationism was a dominant strain in Minnesota foreign policy thought. Like that of its neighboring states, Minnesota's posture stemmed from a variety of sources. American involvement overseas had been protested by the nation's founders; isolationist ideology was nurtured by the continuing belief in the uniqueness of the American experiment and, in Minnesota, by a political tradition that accepted and reinforced agrarian radicalism.

The Middle West, combining economic protest, ethnic ties to German and Scandinavian heritages, and a party tradition of unorthodox Republicanism, was the heartland of isolationism. Its citizens shared an insular security not felt by those on the seaboards. The economic practices of eastern bankers and munitions makers had instilled a fear that these groups would lead the nation into war for personal gain. The many first- and second-generation Germans who populated Minnesota had experienced a wrench of loyalties in World War I. The Scandinavians had brought with them to the state a tradition of neutrality. Immigrants who had fled Europe to avoid war hoped that their new homeland would hold itself aloof and aloft as an example of noninvolvement. The advocates of Minnesota radicalism worried that preoccupation with foreign affairs would interfere with finding progressive solutions for the economic and social inequities of society. Their isolationism was strongly ideological in content, applying, as one observer noted, "a kind of originally agrarian progressive thinking to world affairs." [11]

The isolationist ideal, born with the republic, persisted even as the United States emerged as a world power. It was not easy to dismiss or discard a way of looking at the world that had been espoused by the first spokesmen of the new nation, had served useful purposes in an earlier time, and, accordingly, had acquired the patina of tradition. A vision of Old World corruption and New World innocence had early given the nation a sense of "differentness," which Henry Steele Commager has described as arising from "the notion that contact with or involvement with the Old World would endanger the experiment." [12]

Thomas Jefferson was especially drawn to this concept of the two worlds, and in his first inaugural address in 1801, he expressed his relief and satisfaction that the United States was "Kindly separated by nature and a wide ocean from the exterminating havoc of one quarter of the globe" and "too high-minded to endure the degradations of the others." Jefferson was joined by Benjamin Franklin, Thomas Paine, the Adamses — father and son — and, of course, George Washington in articulating suspicions of the ways of the Old World. John Quincy Adams, for example, was firm in his belief that an American could not live long in Europe "without losing in some measure his national character" and that an American abroad "breathes an atmosphere full of the most deadly infection to his morals." Jefferson concurred, writing that "an American, coming to Europe for education, loses in his knowledge, in his morals, in his health, in his habits, and in his happiness." [13]

The doctrine of separateness from the Old World found its strongest expression among men of the soil. Jefferson, who did not see a town until he was almost eighteen, believed that "Cultivators of the earth are the most valuable citizens." He claimed for them a monopoly on civic virtue: "They are the most vigorous, the most independent, the most virtuous, and they are tied to their country, and wedded to its liberty and interests, by the most lasting bonds." The ideas which made up what one historian has termed the "agrarian myth" had as its hero the yeoman farmer and its central tenet was that he was the ideal man and citizen. Since rural life held its own virtue and since agriculture was "a calling uniquely productive and uniquely important to society," government, therefore, had a special responsibility to attend to its interests and concerns.[14]

One of the nation's first political divisions was the result of rural-urban conflict. Alexander Hamilton, as Washington's secretary of the treasury, pursued policies which, it was argued, favored the mercantile and investing classes at the expense of the planters and farmers. The establishment of the first bank of the United States, a Hamiltonian innovation, gave Jefferson a symbol for Eastern urban wealth and domination. In a later period Wall Street would serve the same purpose for the progressives. Jefferson's party, formed in opposition to the Federalists, defended the propertied interests of the farmers; its appeal was to their moral primacy. The political strength of the Jeffersonians was grounded in support from small-scale farmers, craftsmen, and rural debtor classes, and its geographic orientation shifted westward as these groups moved beyond the Appalachians. The Hamiltonians were the affluent, commercial classes of the Atlantic seaboard cities whose prosperity depended on a flourishing commerce with Europe. Paul Seabury stated that as a consequence the East "remained a more internationalist region of America, its manners and morals attuned more closely to those of Europe and, in contrast to that of the American West, its cultural and political leadership less fascinated by the image of a wholly self-contained America."[15]

Thomas Jefferson's foreign policy endorsed frugality in military spending, protectionism in trade, and a sphere of influence that was hemispheric in dimension. While admitting the need for a militia and a navy sufficient for defense, he was wary of military expenditures which "will grind us with public burthens, & sink us under them." During the Napoleonic Wars, Jefferson imposed a fifteen-month embargo on American shipping to retaliate against French and British preying on American commerce. The Embargo Act of 1807 brought economic paralysis not only to the trading cities of the Northeast but to the farms and plantations of the West and South. Still Jefferson was adamant that if the United States were to be at peace, it must be self-sufficient and end its dependence on foreign goods and overseas trade.[16]

In Jefferson's view it remained for America to secure freedom for the western hemisphere. This concept surfaced in the 1820s at the time President James Monroe considered joining with Britain in a manifesto designed to prevent possible interventions by European powers in the New World. Monroe, establishing a precedent which has since been frequently followed, consulted with his two immediate predecessors in the White House before coming to a decision so crucial to the interests of the United States. With the blessing of both Jefferson and James Madison, Monroe in 1823 proclaimed that the American continents "are henceforth not to be considered as subjects for future colonization by any European powers," and that any such efforts would be viewed as "the manifestation of an unfriendly disposition to the United States." In turn, the United States affirmed its policy of nonintervention in the affairs of Europe. Thus was born the doctrine that bears Monroe's name, a doctrine designed to protect the New World from European rivalries and greedy European ways. Washington's prescription to avoid permanent alliances and Monroe's proclamation were the components of American foreign policy thought in the nineteenth century.[17]

As late as 1885 President Grover Cleveland reaffirmed the faith in his inaugural address: "The genius of our institutions, the needs of our people in their home life, and the attention which is demanded for the settlement and development of the resources of our vast territory, dictate the scrupulous avoidance of any departure from that foreign policy commended by the history, the traditions, and the prosperity of our republic. It is the policy of independence, favored by our position and defended by our known love of justice and by our power. It is the policy of peace suitable to our interests. It is the policy of neutrality, rejecting any share in foreign broils and ambitions upon other continents, and repelling their intrusion here. It is the policy of Monroe and of Washington and of Jefferson."[18] But Cleveland was articulating an innocence soon to be lost. Events would conspire, as the twentieth century appeared, to effect a drastic change in American foreign policy.

The tradition of isolationism was compromised by the determinations of Cushman Davis and others during the Spanish-American War in 1898 to extend America's "civilizing" mission across the Pacific. This compromise, because it was in Asia and not in Europe, was fraught with less trauma (though the decibels of debate were high) than the issue of American involvement in World War I, so vigorously protested by Charles Lindbergh. Woodrow Wilson's stated purpose of making the world "safe for democracy" collapsed in the aftermath of war because decision-makers were reluctant to extend the Jeffersonian ideal of example-setting to a working model of collaboration. The bankruptcy of Europe in the interwar period intensified the reversion to isolationism as the nation turned its back on the League of Nations and returned to a "normalcy" soon to be obsolete. Frank Kellogg's modest efforts in the 1920s to halt that retreat proved fruitless.

The isolationist rhetoric of the period between 1918 and 1941 bespoke an economic self-sufficiency and a political neutrality. What the proponents of isolationism — Henrik Shipstead and Harold Knutson among them — either failed to recognize or refused to admit was that a significant rearrangement of economic power had made non-sense of the notion of self-sufficiency. The United States had moved from a debtor to a creditor nation, and American private investment abroad had skyrocketed. Isolationist sentiment in this period between the wars demanded that the nations of Europe pay their debts and insisted on the erection of the highest tariffs in United States history. Both policies intensified the world's financial troubles and culminated in international chaos. Economic distress in Germany brought Adolf Hitler to power, and as his appetite was apparently unsatisfied by aggressions and territories, nations neither knew how to respond nor felt that they had any responsibility to do so. In the United States neutrality was the order of the day.

One study measuring foreign policy sentiment by seventy-three congressional roll call votes from 1933 to 1950 concluded that Minnesota was definitely isolationist during that period. Foreign policy votes in the House of Representatives put Minnesota sixth from the top among the most isolationist states. In the Senate Minnesota varied between seventh and twelfth, probably due to the election of internationally minded senators for the later period of the survey. The study also revealed that Republicans were considerably more isolationist than Democrats, rural areas more so than urban regions, and predominantly German communities more so than those of other national backgrounds.[19]

In that seventeen-year period Minnesota elected to Congress nineteen Republicans, seven Farmer-Laborites, two Democrats, and seven members of the Democratic-Farmer-Labor party organized in 1944. The state's population was predominantly rural, and persons born in Germany or of German parentage constituted 23 per cent of its ethnic composition in 1930. There were more Germans than there were Swedes (19 per cent) or Norwegians (18.8 per cent).[20]

When war broke out in Europe in 1939, fresh voices sounding new sentiments began to be heard and noted in Minnesota. A few political leaders, segments of the press, and certain organizations marshaled their forces to persuade citizens that their fate was intertwined with the nations fighting the Axis powers, and that the Atlantic and Pacific oceans did not immunize the United States from the consequences of aggression. That the efforts, most notably of Joseph Ball, Harold Stassen, and Walter Judd, had some effect was evidenced by a story in the *Minneapolis Star-Journal* of November 6, 1941, recording reporter Mathew W. Halloran's impression that whereas the citizens of southern Minnesota had previously been isolationist, they were now strangely silent. Most effective in point of impact was the Japanese attack on Pearl Harbor in December, 1941, which shocked all Americans into a realization that their possession had been reached by sea and air power. While the "day of infamy" did not transform Minnesota overnight, it diffused the nostrums of invincibility and isolation.

The world after the second great war was a very different place. The United States was the only principal to emerge relatively unscarred; the nations of Europe were in distress, their empires in disarray. Determined not to repeat its post-World War I error, the United States accepted the principle of collective security in its affirmation of the United Nations. There was no difficulty in 1945, as there had been in 1918, in persuading the Allies not to be vindictive against the aggressors in peace settlements. There was minimal opposition to American leadership, either at home or abroad, in establishing the United Nations. There was little partisan dissension over the need for international co-operation, but in the high hopes that the United Nations would keep the peace, there was very little understanding that the weaknesses of other nations, previously great powers, were so acute that additional responsibilities would accrue to the United States. Arthur M. Schlesinger, Jr., writing in 1949, observed that "No nation, perhaps, has become a more reluctant great power. Not conquest but homesickness moved the men of Bradley and Stilwell; Frankfurt or Tokyo were but way-stations on the road back to Gopher Prairie." [21]

With countries the world around struggling to recover from the devastation and deprivation that accompanied war, the Soviet Union, even though it, too, suffered enormously, emerged as the only other nation with residual strength. When the wartime collaboration between the United States and the Soviets did not continue in peacetime, and when the threat of Russian hegemony extended into the Middle East, the Mediterranean, and Eastern Europe, the United States determined to confine these ambitions. Out of this decision emerged a host of policies, programs, and commitments which divided the world philosophically, politically, and economically into East and West — a division with more than geographical connotations. The so-called Iron Curtain clanked down and "containment" became the name of the foreign policy game.

America's acts to rehabilitate Western Europe were unprecedented gestures of generosity and in clear contrast to American penuriousness of the interwar period. For a nation which had earlier eschewed entanglements, the United States indulged — some say overindulged — in a global feast of defensive alliances with more than forty nations. The arms race escalated as each side saw the other stocking its nuclear arsenal, and confrontations of greater or lesser peril occurred between the Soviet Union and the United States in such disparate places as Greece and Turkey, Berlin, Korea, the Middle East, Cuba, and Indochina. The Cold War, as it came to be called, was critical in its intensity during the late 1940s and throughout most of the 1950s.

Indicative of the measure of Minnesota's commitment to the new look of American foreign policy was its support from 1949 to 1960 of United States participation in the United Nations and other international programs, foreign trade, economic and military aid, and participation in collective defense arrangements. As a 1961 study showed, the state's congressional delegation approved of larger overseas obligations by a ten-to-one ratio. In this switch from its previous isolationism, Minnesota was not alone.[22]

The United States, in its enthusiasm for its new internationalism and in its efforts to counter the appeals of communism, once again became messianic. This time the impulse did not take the form of territorial expansion as it had in 1898 nor, as some would insist, was it solely motivated by dollar imperialism. Rather it was a revival of the attempt to convert other nations to the value systems of democracy. It was a new form of "civilizing," motivated by an older fear of state socialism and a newer worry over Russian imperialism, heightened by the recent memory that failure to counter Hitler's aggressions at an early stage had embroiled the world in war. Adherence to the concept of collective security, in certain instances, led to exaggerated interpretations. Unilateral intervention, for some, seemed an appropriate extension of America's international commitment to serve as the world's policeman to prevent aggression and secure peace. Unfortunately no individual or nation has yet produced a satisfactory definition of aggression. Invasion of one nation by another is a gross example, but the subtleties of revolt, civil strife, and indirect aggression have continued to confound the experts. Efforts to construct an enduring peace have been exasperatingly unsuccessful.

The American involvement in Vietnam in the 1960s was accepted initially by most citizens as a necessary intervention — either to stop aggression from the North against the South, to make the People's Republic of China more cautious about its ambitions in Asia, to prevent southeast Asia from joining the communist orbit, to live up to United States treaty commitments, or to establish credibility of the American promise to aid friends and allies. But in the late 1960s sentiment began to change, as the majority swung with the minority challenging the ideological and strategic assumptions that underlay the undeclared war in Vietnam. The 1968 presidential contest, from the snow and sentiment of New Hampshire in March to the sticks and stones of Chicago in August, was a climactic period in the evolution of American foreign policy. A major irony of American politics in that fantastic and fateful year was that two Minnesota men — Hubert Humphrey and Eugene McCarthy — identical in party and contemporary in experience, forged the debate.

The men of Minnesota who appear in these pages were actors on the foreign policy stage from 1898 to 1968. The drama in which they played both starring and supporting roles underscored the hard truth that the United States, like other nations, could not remain insulated from the world. The relatively painless conflict with Spain in 1898 seemed to justify imperialism, the extension of America's messianic impulses, economic power, and political ambitions. Yet the imperial experiment also denoted a declining of the American sense of uniqueness. It took two wars to shed the mantle of isolationism: World War I and its aftermath undermined America's sense of economic and political insularity; with the end of World War II the United States was moved to conscious world leadership and committed to the concept of internationalism. The Cold War created what some might term an overinflated perception of responsibility. Military technology and nuclear weaponry both enhanced and removed any feeling of invincibility. In the 1960s, interventionism triumphed over internationalism, again raising serious doubts about America's ability and integrity in the exercise of power and provoking questions about the nation's role in the world community — as model or missionary or something in between.[23]

It is perhaps pretentious to suggest, as Sinclair Lewis once did, that in order to understand America, it is necessary to understand Minnesota.[24] Nevertheless, in this abbreviated account of men, ideas, and events in Minnesota and the world, a recognition of some issues, stresses, and aspirations which have been shared by other Americans may be apparent. Throughout the foreign policy convulsions and contortions that occurred during this seventy-year span, the public service of these ten Minnesotans coincided with issues of great moment — the Spanish-American War, World War I, the contest over United States membership in the League of Nations, the interwar isolationist period, World War II, the Cold War, and the American intervention in Vietnam. It may be useful, therefore, to analyze the concerns of these men of Minnesota as they played their parts in constructing, protesting, or approving America's place in the maelstrom of international politics. While they may not have had a unique impact on foreign policy in all the periods under scrutiny, they can serve to illuminate the shifting national attitudes of reluctance or enthusiasm toward American involvement in world affairs.

This seventy-year survey of ten men of Minnesota and American foreign policy confirms the diversity of the state's political experience. While there are notable similarities of style and substance, the ideas and philosophies expressed extend along a continuum embracing conservative and liberal Republicanism, third-party radicalism, and a progressive Democratic party orientation.

Conformist Republicans like Cushman Davis and Frank Kellogg shared a conviction that American leadership should be applied to world problems. Imperialism in the Davis concept of territorial acquisition and political control was a significant if short-lived foreign policy manifestation of America's westward expansion. Kellogg's internationalism was less aggressive and more modest; even so, in a different time frame, it constituted a substantial break with the isolationism that infused Minnesota's outlook on the world. Wayward Republicans like Charles Lindbergh and Henrik Shipstead shifted their allegiance to the Farmer-Labor party. Lindbergh stayed radical and helped to formulate an intellectual framework for isolationism. Shipstead strayed from his reputation as reformer and joined conservative Harold Knutson in a last-gasp effort to refute the changing role of the United States on the world scene during the interwar period. A belief in international organization and co-operation as an alternative to isolationism and the historic balance of power diplomacy fashioned the commitment and rhetoric of the latter-day Republicans — Joseph Ball, Harold Stassen, and Walter Judd. In the same vein but of another party, Hubert Humphrey and Eugene McCarthy were Democrats in the Wilsonian tradition, accepting responsibility, the inevitability of interdependence, and the need for international institutions. The trauma of Vietnam divided Americans — and two Minnesotans in particular. Yet as 1968 drew to a close, interventionism was on the wane and a new internationalism, uncertain of design and content, began to emerge.

Chapter 1

THE MARCH OF EMPIRE
IN STEP WITH CUSHMAN K. DAVIS

*"The sovereignty of the United States has been expanded
immensely by the war with Spain. I believe that for this
the American people were ordained."*
CUSHMAN K. DAVIS, 1900.

IN ITS LEAD EDITORIAL heralding the onset of the twentieth century,
the *New York Times* on January 1, 1900, accurately concluded, "The
outlook on the threshold of the new year is extremely bright." The
United States seemed secure, confident, and was flexing its muscles
in overseas adventures. The populist movement, which during the
1890s had attempted to organize the protests of agricultural America
as a political force against the growing economic power of industrial
America, had slowed down. Agitation for free silver which had given
William Jennings Bryan and the Democratic party an issue was quies-
cent. Andrew Carnegie's personal income in 1900, with no income
tax to pay, would be $23 million. John Pierpont Morgan built a tempo-
rary ballroom next to his house to accommodate 2,400 guests at his
daughter's wedding and, before the year was out, would begin negotiations with Carnegie for the formation of the United States Steel Corporation. Complacency was a fitting word for the closing years of the
nineteenth century.[1]

Yet this sense of complacency rested precariously on a time bomb
of economic inequality and social injustice. The security, confidence,
and strength of nationhood were not shared by all the people. In
the Middle West the farmers were doing well by past standards but
poorly in contrast to the industrial giants of the East. They protested
against the "unholy alliance" dominating the midwestern economy:
the railroads which hauled their produce; the banks which granted
them loans; and the tariff-protected industries which sold them goods.
Monopoly, laissez-faire economics, and Wall Street were irritants on
the soft skin of the body politic.

While Morgan and his set lived in a world of mansions and yachts,
the ordinary man and his family tried to live on an average annual

income of $651. Low wages coupled with long hours and unsafe working conditions fanned the flames of radicalism. By 1900 the labor force of the United States included 1,750,000 children under sixteen years of age. The built-in social security of the frontier disappeared as the frontier itself was closed. The influx of immigrants — 448,572 in 1900 — tended to keep wage levels depressed. The promise of American life was still only a promise to the vast majority.[2]

In the last two decades of the nineteenth century, the commercial interests of the country increasingly looked abroad for profits from trade and investment. A navy capable of protecting those interests seemed both suitable and desirable. This idea was ably supported by the arguments of the intellectual Captain (later Admiral) Alfred T. Mahan, whose famous studies on the political implications of sea power in the 1890s had made him an important theoretician of the new American imperialism overseas.[3] Mahan was both prophetic and persuasive. He had influential friends at court — Senator Henry Cabot Lodge and Assistant Secretary of the Navy Theodore Roosevelt. He also had history on his side as the festering sore in the Caribbean precipitated the Spanish-American War in 1898. For years, as George F. Kennan has said, Spanish rule on the island of Cuba had been challenged by native insurgents, "poorly organized, poorly disciplined, but operating on the classical principles of guerrilla forces everywhere and enjoying all the advantages of guerrillas operating on home territory against an unpopular foreign enemy." Spanish attempts to suppress the insurrection were "inefficient, cruel, and only partly successful."[4]

In the course of this conflict, American property holdings were damaged and public opinion was deeply shocked by the tales of violence and misery from the island. American statesmen such as Lodge, Roosevelt, and William R. Day, then assistant secretary of state, became convinced that a continuation of the situation in Cuba would be intolerable to United States interests. If Spain did not put an end to its excesses of exploitation and oppression, the United States in some way would have to intervene.

Two events precipitated the ultimate decision. The first was an indiscreet letter to a personal friend from Enrique Dupuy de Lôme, the Spanish minister in Washington, in which he spoke slightingly of President William McKinley as a cheap, vacillating politician. The letter found its way into the hands of a New York newspaper which published it on February 9, 1898. Americans reacted with indignant loyalty against this affront to their leader. The second episode was the sinking of the United States cruiser, *Maine*, in Havana harbor on February 15 with the loss of 266 American lives. It seems to be the judgment of history that these two events triggered the war with Spain as a means to an end — American expansion beyond its continental borders.

McKinley's sincere, if timid, resistance to war collapsed. The conflict extended from Cuba across the Pacific to the Philippines, and in a single day, May 1, 1898, ships of the American navy under Commodore George Dewey quashed Spanish fortifications. The Philippines, successfully wrested from Spain, were up for grabs. It had taken just ten weeks of actual fighting to win an overseas empire. From London American Ambassador John M. Hay said in an exulting letter to his friend Theodore Roosevelt, "It has been a splendid little war." [5]

In keeping with the revolutionary tradition which had attracted immigrants to the United States in great numbers, the blows struck for liberty by Greek, French, and Hungarian patriots during the first half of the nineteenth century were applauded nationwide. Similarly the Cuban struggle for independence, which predated the Spanish-American War by many years, received enthusiastic backing from the United States as a whole. [6]

At the same time, the anti-imperialist, antimilitarist tradition was also vigorous. The intellectual credentials of the opponents of war were impressive. Jane Addams, Mark Twain, Senator George F. Hoar of Massachusetts (disagreeing with his colleague, Lodge), and Andrew Carnegie were among the prestigious persons who backed the anti-imperialist cause with their names and money and pens. The Anti-Imperialist League, founded late in 1898, became the first important national foreign policy pressure group of the twentieth century. "Its stated purpose was not to oppose war as such, but to insist that . . . a war of liberation . . . must not be turned into one for empire." The league was fearful that the quest for power and prestige abroad would detract from needed reform at home, a recurring theme used by those who have deplored United States overseas involvements from the time of the war with Spain to the war in Vietnam. [7]

In Minnesota opinion over the prospect of war with Spain was mixed, but like the rest of the Middle West, the humanitarianism and missionary zeal of its people made it lean toward intervention. The press in Minnesota was generally sympathetic to the Cuban drive for independence. The *Minneapolis Tribune*, one of the state's most influential papers, was restrained in its enthusiasm and critical of the chauvinism of the *St. Paul Pioneer Press*, its rival across the Mississippi River. Still the *Tribune* favored recognition of Cuban independence, a policy which it admitted would probably bring war. [8]

The Minnesota business community included many who, like their

Cushman K. Davis,
about 1898

counterparts nationally, were opposed to war, It is a historical irony that the populists, the followers of Bryan, and those who would come to be known as progressives did not join forces with the anti-imperialists. While they were anti-imperialist, antimilitarist, and antientanglement in theory, they were in fact caught up in the crusade to free the oppressed Cubans from tyrannical Spain.[9]

Politics was another consideration. The great expansionist decision of the last years of the nineteenth century was generally, if not totally, supported by Republicans, opposed, but not universally, by Democrats. Minnesota's Republican credentials were impeccable. From 1858 to 1900 there had been but two Democratic senators (the first two) and eleven Republican senators. In that same forty-two-year period, the Minnesota delegation in the House had comprised eleven Democrats, two from other parties, and thirty-one Republicans. In 1898 Minnesota's senators and representatives (all Republican) were unswerving in their support for war. John Lind, second district congressman from 1887 to 1893 and soon to be elected governor on the Democratic-Populist ticket in the fall, was among the volunteers for military duty.[10]

Despite the debate, once war was declared Minnesota rallied

'round the flag. The state joined the march of empire by saying yes to the question, as historian Theodore Christianson put it, "Should the policy of 'expansion,' the acquisition of the Philippines, Puerto Rico and other island possessions, and the war to suppress the Filipinos, be approved?" [11]

Leading the affirmative response was Senator Cushman Kellogg Davis, a nineteenth-century man who stood, as he liked to say, "in the vestibule of the 20th century." [12] His answers to the questions of United States intervention in Cuba and assumption of an empire in the Pacific influenced American foreign policy at the highest level.

Davis was born at Henderson, New York, on June 16, 1838. He grew up in Wisconsin and attended Carroll College in Waukesha before graduating from the University of Michigan. He returned to Wisconsin, studied law, and was admitted to the bar in 1859. His brief Civil War stint, during which he served for the most part as aide to Brigadier General Willis A. Gorman, territorial governor of Minnesota from 1853 to 1857, was terminated by illness. Ex-Lieutenant Davis moved to Minnesota in 1864 in search of health and wealth. He found both. Settling in St. Paul, he engaged in the practice of law and enjoyed almost instant success — a success ensured by General Gorman's acceptance of Davis as a partner in his prestigious law firm, an association that lasted until Gorman's election to the post of St. Paul city attorney in 1869. Early in the 1880s Davis formed a partnership with Cordenio A. Severance, and in 1887 they were joined by Frank B. Kellogg, a distant cousin of Davis. [13]

Like many lawyers, Davis played with the idea of a political career. A lifelong Republican, he sought and won a seat in the Minnesota House of Representatives in 1866. In the next year at the age of twenty-nine, he was appointed United States district attorney and held that position until 1873, when he resigned after winning the Republican nomination for governor. Just as Harold Stassen in a later period had journalist Joseph Ball championing his political career in the columns of the St. Paul Pioneer Press, so too did "Cush" Davis have Harlan P. Hall. Hall, editor of the St. Paul Dispatch, launched the Davis candidacy for governor in 1873 as a trial balloon. The motives of Hall and Ball were similar: to forward the cause of the young Republicans against the old guard. In Hall's case there was in addition an element of malice. When Senator Alexander Ramsey had refused in 1870 to consent to a federal appointment for Hall, the editor determined to defeat William D. Washburn, Ramsey's candidate for governor, and ultimately Ramsey himself. Hall began writing of the "old fogies" and calling attention to Davis as the Moses who could lead a procession of young Republicans into the promised land. Hall's efforts snowballed, and in 1873 Davis agreed to seek the nomination. There is some question whether Hall or Davis was more surprised at the political success which resulted. But his two-year term as the youngest man yet to occupy the governor's chair was undistinguished. Christianson states that "few administrations have left so few milestones . . . as that of Cushman K. Davis." [14]

Failing in his next ambition to gain the senatorial nomination in 1875, Davis returned to his lucrative law practice, but he finally won the Senate seat twelve years later in 1887. It was a selection widely applauded in Minnesota. Typical of the plaudits was the *Sauk Centre Tribune's* approbation of Davis' "mental strength," and its ensuing comment that "The only really good thing the Republican party of this state has done for several years past is sending Cushman K. Davis to the U.S. Senate." The editorial appraisal was on target. Davis' intellectual prowess impressed his fellow senators and his diligence earned their respect. [15]

From the outset of his senatorial career, Davis was interested in foreign affairs — an interest fomented by his fascination with international law — but he was not appointed to the Senate foreign relations committee until 1891. He succeeded to the chairmanship in 1897 when John Sherman became McKinley's new secretary of state, and Senator William P. Frye of Maine, who was next in line, declined the post. Davis gave this account of Frye's decision: "'No, Davis,' he said, 'I am not going to take the chairmanship of that great committee. There is some question as to whether or not I am fit for it. But there is no question about you. You are the man. . . . You must take the post.'" The story minimized Frye's personal preference to continue as chairman of the committee on commerce, but Davis credited his good friend with an act of generosity. In terms of prestige and personal opportunity for Davis, it was just that. [16]

Davis was a good choice, in the opinion of one historian, because "He had been appointed to the Committee six years before and had quickly risen to prominence there, having little interest in matters other than those pertaining to foreign affairs." [17] At the time, one writer noted, "Davis is an ideal Chairman of the Foreign Relations Committee." Before going to the Senate, he had pursued the study of international law and had read extensively not only in English, but in French and Italian works as well. Later he would say, "that is the way my seemingly aimless study during those long winter evenings up at St. Paul fitted me for what I shall always look back upon as the brightest part of my career." While this may have been a rationalization by Davis to cover his disappointment at the failure of his presidential boomlet in 1896, it was a propitious time to be chairman. Sherman at seventy-four was admittedly too old to be other than a weak secretary of state, and the Davis-led committee consequently took on a new importance.[18]

When Cushman K. Davis succeeded to the chair of the Senate foreign relations committee in 1897, the foremost international issue was Cuba. Davis had no reservations about the course of action the United States should pursue. Intervention was the logical extension of his expansionist sentiments, which had first come to public notice in 1893 when he took a leading role in urging that the United States annex the Hawaiian Islands.[19] Along with others, Davis had pointed to the economic, defense, and "civilizing" reasons for securing these islands in the mid-Pacific: (1) the region was a natural center of commerce, a jumping-off place to the economic opportunities represented by China, Japan, and Asian Russia; (2) the islands could be utilized as a defensive outpost for American sea power; (3) American missionaries had pioneered in Hawaii, and it was "manifest destiny" to complete the work of converting, educating, and civilizing. "I am not in favor of a colonial system such as Great Britain has, and such as France is striving for, but I want to see my country well defended, and her hold upon the enormous commerce of the future in the Pacific Ocean assured."[20] Davis kept at the issue, but five more years were to pass before the Spanish-American War illustrated the strategic importance of the islands and Davis succeeded in his quest for annexation.

Before the war with Spain, Davis had been torn between a personal conviction that the United States should act on the Cuban situation and a partisan loyalty to President McKinley, who was exercising a fair measure of restraint in the face of party and journalistic pressures to the contrary. In Detroit on February 22, 1898, Davis gave a speech in which he spoke slightingly of Spanish "atrocity and horror" against the understandable Cuban desire for "nationality and liberty." Nevertheless, he went on to counsel moderation as he remained loyal, though not entirely sympathetic, to McKinley's efforts to pursue a diplomatic resolution of the conflict.[21]

Later in a postwar speech in Chicago on February 22, 1899, Davis would emphasize the restraints exercised by the American government "against all manner of provocation, of outrage to American property and citizenship; against the taking of the lives of American citizens, against the destruction of scores of millions of property, the American people, with great reluctance, abstained from war." The decision to go to war was made "not only for the cause of humanity but for national honor." In both oral and written communications, the senator from Minnesota reiterated his conviction that United States intervention had been clearly justified "for the protection of its own citizens, their persons, property, and interests." He documented the case by pointing to the destruction of $18 million out of America's $50 million investment in Cuba and the drop in American exports to Cuba from $100 million to $25 million. He was also concerned that "American citizens have been incarcerated in Spanish prisons, have been driven from their homes to many a place of concentration where famine and fever do their mortal work." [22]

Davis' influence at this point in history was notable. With the failure of previous efforts to negotiate, the president asked Congress for a declaration of war on April 11. Davis took the initiative by preparing the Senate foreign relations committee report on the "Affair in Cuba." The St. Paul Dispatch of April 13, 1898, commented that the report would "go into history as one of the most important papers ever presented in Congress" and that "Senator Cushman K. Davis was the central figure from the moment the senate convened today."

With the report, which "contained at once indictment, proof and verdict" were three resolutions written by Davis. These declared that the people of Cuba ought to be free and independent; that Spain should withdraw from Cuba; and that the United States would use military force if necessary to achieve these ends. A fourth point, the so-called Teller Amendment (named for Senator Henry M. Teller of Colorado) disclaimed any intention on the part of the United States to annex Cuba. The resolutions passed both houses of Congress, were signed by President McKinley on April 19, and formed the basis of the ultimatum to the Spanish government. The next day Davis wrote to his law partner, Severance, "McKinley sent his ultimatum to Spain and the next scene in the drama will be one of war." [23]

He was right. Obviously Spain could not accept the terms of the ultimatum and retain any shred of national honor. On April 25, 1898, Congress declared that a state of war had existed with Spain since April 21. Davis was especially gratified, since he had been primarily responsible for guiding the war resolutions through the Senate and bringing them to a successful conclusion in the midst of heated debates and disagreements between the two houses. In ornamental and convoluted prose, the St. Paul Pioneer Press of April 20, 1898, reported that "It was Minnesota's able senior senator who . . . drafted the ringing resolution which . . . compelled the approval of both houses of congress . . . and which . . . sounded the trumpet blast of the ultimatum. . . . he recognized . . . that the highest and wisest diplomacy was to cut the Gordian knot of diplomacy with the sword." The account gave full cognizance to Davis' leadership "from the start of his bold initiative as the framer of the resolution . . . to the finishing triumph." The Minnesota congressional delegation was unanimous in its support of the Davis resolutions. Significant assists were supplied by James A. Tawney of the first congressional district, who kept fellow House Republicans in line, and by Joel P. Heatwole of the third district, who served on the conference committee that negotiated the differences between Senate and House versions.[24]

It was shortly after this parliamentary triumph that President McKinley reportedly asked Davis whether he would respond favorably to an invitation to be secretary of state. Davis declined, presumably because he was certain of re-election to the Senate and preferred to exercise his influence there as chairman of the foreign relations committee. He had the status, if not the rank, of a cabinet member; he was a daily visitor to the White House, and McKinley depended on him for advice and counsel. The *Pioneer Press* of April 25, 1898, commented on the offer in flattering terms and concluded that Davis' choice was a wise one because "He is likely to be senator from this state so long as he wishes to serve it and the country in that capacity." Frank Kellogg wrote Davis that "Your friends here universally approve of your determination not to go into the cabinet. It is generally understood that you could have gone in had you been willing to accept it."[25]

The war with Spain was waged in the Caribbean and spread across the Pacific to the Philippine people, who were also rebellious under Spanish rule. Those islands were important because of their proximity to China, which was just beginning to fire the economic and commercial imaginations of American merchants and politicians. Senator Davis concurred with his eminent and powerful Minnesota client, railroad builder James J. Hill, who believed that trade with China would cause America to prosper and would help to populate the western states. The Minnesota senator also foresaw the day when the independent Philippines could serve to counter expanding Japanese power in the Pacific. The surprisingly efficient victory in Manila Bay prompted a thoughtful letter from Davis to his friend Severance in May, 1898, in which he remarked that the occupation of Manila raised grave questions about what to do with these conquests in the arrangement of a peace. He added that "the adjustment and conformity of China, comprising about one-third of the human race, to intercourse, political and commercial, with Western civilization is one of the most gigantic evolutions which has ever taken place in history." He concluded by expressing his satisfaction that the "elements of internal discord" were "yielding to the powerful solvent of love of country and pride in its glory." [26]

In the two-year period from 1898 to 1900, the question of "political ascendancy" over the Philippines in whole or in part fired a great foreign policy debate in the Congress and in the country. There was bitter reaction among the anti-imperialists. The philosopher William James deplored in private correspondence "the presumption to force our ideals on people to whom they are not native"; in a public letter he protested that "We are now openly engaged in crushing out the sacredest thing in this great human world — the attempt of a people long enslaved to attain to the possession of itself, to organize its laws and government, to be free to follow its internal destinies according to its own ideals." His Harvard colleague, Charles Eliot Norton, wrote that America "has lost her unique position as a potential leader in the progress of civilization, and has taken up her place simply as one of the grasping and selfish nations of the present day." [27]

Others who opposed "ascendancy" asked by what right Americans, whose country had been established on the thesis that government derived its just powers from the consent of the governed, could assume the rule of empire over other peoples. More particularly American control over a distant land with a diverse and alien population fitted neither expansionist thought nor tradition. Republican Senator Hoar of Massachusetts summed up this argument to Congress by drawing a distinction between expansion (Hawaii) and empire (the Philippines). The first was an invitation "to willing and capable people to share with us our freedom, our self-government, our equality, our education, and the transcendent sweets of civil and religious liberty." The second was the type of colonial domination "held out to us in the Far East and the West Indies as the result of military conquest" which had been "the ruin of empires and republics of former times." Hoar insisted that "dominion over subject people and the rule over vassal states" were "forbidden to us by our Constitution, by our political principles, by every lesson of our own history and of all history." The American rule, he said, should be to acquire no territory "except where we can reasonably expect that the people we acquire will, in due time and in suitable conditions, be annexed to the United States as an equal part of a self-governing Republic." [28]

In Minnesota, too, there were sounds of dissent. Charles E. Towne, who was later appointed by Governor John Lind to the Senate upon Davis' death, commented, "The possession of the Philippine Islands

BRINGING IT HOME TO US.

Congressman James A. Tawney and Senator Davis, as pictured in a *Minneapolis Journal* cartoon, March 17, 1898

was in no way necessary to the success of the war nor within its purpose." After criticizing Davis because he proposed that the government of the Philippines follow the general line of the English crown colonies, Towne maintained, "The whole scheme of colonialism is out of harmony with our institutions. It belongs to imperialism, not to republicanism."[29]

Channing Seabury, chairman of Minnesota's Board of State Capitol Commissioners, who named several other businessmen as being of like mind, wrote Davis that the war was not popular nor was the action of Congress "in *forcing it upon the country.*" He deprecated the notion of possessions, saying "Get *a Coaling Station* at Pearl Harbor and stop there. We do not need the island nor Cuba, nor Manilla [*sic*], nor any *more* country to *protect* and *govern.*" Reporting to his partners Kellogg and Severance, Davis referred to this letter as a "curiosity of mugwumpism and literature." He was not particularly concerned about public opinion. To people who felt that the actions of the United States were without popular support, Davis replied that Jefferson did not acquire the consent of the people when he negotiated for the

Louisiana Purchase, and the same held true when the United States acquired Florida in 1819 and the territory that became California and New Mexico from Mexico in 1848.[30]

But Davis had support in Minnesota from Republican leaders who held in favor of empire, both from a sense of duty to the Filipinos and for the sake of commercial and political advantages which would come to the United States as the result of possessions in the Far East. In 1897 James J. Hill had said, "When we built the Great Northern Railway to the Pacific coast [in 1893], we knew that it was necessary to look to Asia for a part of our traffic." Though Hill had opposed the war with Spain, he favored the annexation of the Philippines. "If you go back in the commercial history of the world," he said, "you will find that the people who controlled the trade of the Orient have been the people who held the purse strings of nations."[31]

Following the "splendid little war," Cushman Davis was appointed one of five American delegates to the Paris Peace Commission which negotiated the conditions of its settlement. The other commissioners were William R. Day, who resigned as secretary of state to head the commission; Senators Frye of Maine and George Gray of Delaware; and Whitelaw Reid of the New York Tribune. Gray, the only Democrat, represented the anti-imperialists; Day was a moderate, and Reid, Frye, and Davis were expansionists.[32]

Before Davis' appointment to the commission, Henry Cabot Lodge had written to Theodore Roosevelt expressing his concern over the administration's hesitancy with respect to the Philippines. He thought it essential that at a minimum the United States keep Manila, "which is the great prize, and the thing which will give us the Eastern trade." In his view, the character of the peace commission would be the determining factor, and "if Davis goes, as reported this morning, all will be well."[33] Lodge was right, from his point of view. Senator Davis proved to be a hard-nosed negotiator, who played a major part in the settlements which were made in Paris.

President McKinley's initial charge to the commissioners sought only sovereignty over the island of Luzon and a guarantee of equal rights for American commerce on the other islands comprising the Philippines. On October 25 Davis, Frye, and Reid telegraphed Hay, who was then secretary of state, their preference for total acquisition. They were persuaded that taking only part of the Philippines would be impracticable and dangerous, politically and commercially. Day dissented from this view, calling for adherence to the president's more modest course, and Gray objected vehemently: "We should . . . not follow in the selfish and vulgar greed for territory which Europe has inherited from mediaeval times." The presidential response ultimately approved the Davis-Frye-Reid position. Davis was jubilant over McKinley's acquiescence as evidenced in a letter from Paris to his friend, Henry A. Castle, who had been promoted from the postmastership of St. Paul to serve as auditor for the post office department in Washington. "We take up the Philippines tomorrow," wrote the senator. "It is [a] matter of gratification and just pride to me that my views as to them have finally prevailed here and *Elsewhere*." The "Elsewhere" was, of course, the White House.[34]

Another issue in the commission's deliberations was the question of compensation to Spain. Only Davis held out for none. In another letter to Castle, he said, "I advised the Prest. by cable against this offer and against paying Spain a dollar. Each of the Comm's wired his individual opinion on this point and, in mine, I stood alone." Davis failed to win his way, and $20 million was paid to Spain as a face-saving compensation for its loss to the United States of Cuba, Puerto Rico, Guam, and the Philippines. Whitelaw Reid recorded in his diary after the treaty had been agreed to on December 8, 1898: "The first man to arrive in my room this morning was Senator Davis, who said he came down early that he and I might express congratulations alone. We were the two in whom there had been no variableness or shade of turning, and we at best had a right to regard the triumph as entirely unmixed." As the historian Julius W. Pratt neatly put it, the United States had "utilized the war with Spain to acquire an island empire in the Caribbean and in the Pacific."[35]

After two and a half months of negotiation, the treaty was signed on December 10, and the commissioners sailed from Southampton on the *St. Louis*. On board during a night of "jollification and entertainment," Senator Davis was selected as spokesman for the commission and reportedly said, "We got all we were sent for, and more, too." President McKinley received the Paris peace treaty from his commissioners on the day before Christmas, 1898.[36]

Davis was credited with being one of the two strongest and most effective men in the group. A fellow commissioner later said that he was "our magazine, our bulwark." His knowledge of international law and his facility with languages "reinforced the scholarship of our commission and proved of special use to us in documentary references."[37]

The treaty now faced the process of ratification. Senator Davis had many skills. He was scholarly, literary, personable, and a proven diplomat. In the face of vigorous opposition, however, he was not a master of the fine art of steering legislation to a successful conclusion. He was, according to one account, "a Republican thunderer and the best of good fellows," but "the big senator from Minnesota was not gifted as a manager." In the matter of ratification, Davis was most assuredly not in the driver's seat. Dominating the scene were the president and Republican senators such as Lodge, Nelson W. Aldrich of Rhode Island, and Stephen B. Elkins of West Virginia. Davis, apparently aware of his shortcomings, told McKinley, "When you see Senator Elkins, have him tell you about the struggle. I do not believe we could have secured ratification without him." [38]

The basis for the determined opposition to ratification was clearly stated in a Senate resolution introduced by George G. Vest of Missouri. It said that "under the Constitution of the United States, no power is given to the Federal Government to acquire territory to be held and governed permanently as colonies." Protest against the acquisition of the Philippines was the intent of the resolution and debate was lengthy. Finally Davis, under great pressure and uncertain of votes, set February 6, 1899, as the day for decision. The Republican pressures on the Democrats were rather unexpectedly assisted by William Jennings Bryan's call for ratification. The result was that fifteen Democrats, Populists, and independents joined the Republican majority. On the Republican side only Hoar of Massachusetts and Eugene Hale of Maine voted against ratification. The final tally was 57 to 27, or a margin of one vote over the necessary two-thirds majority. [39]

Secretary of State Hay complained about the six-week ratification process, saying that "A treaty of peace in any normal state of things ought to be ratified with unanimity in twenty-four hours." Lodge confided to Roosevelt, "Davis, who is the best fellow in the world, cannot make a canvass and is no manager. He would ask me every morning how the vote stood, and I think that is about all he knew about it." Historian Henry Adams commented in a letter that "the whole executive crowd . . . [was] furious because Cush Davis let himself be bluffed in the Senate by an impudent assertion that the opposition had thirty-six votes" and consequently had "lost reputation as a leader by his waste of very precious time." But to others and probably to Davis himself, ratification of the Treaty of Paris on February 6, 1899, may have been the capstone of his political career. Later he would refer to the treaty as "one of the most complete diplomatic triumphs recorded in the annals of international negotiation." [40]

Following the war, Davis was re-elected in 1898 by the Minnesota legislature to an unprecedented third term as senator. His popularity had never been greater and had he chosen this moment (and had the opportunity been present) to seek the presidency, he might have found the support that was lacking in 1896. Henry Castle related that in the early months of 1898, there had been some "mutterings of hostility" to Davis, but the events of the Spanish-American War which had propelled him into prominence as Senate leader and presidential adviser ("the actual arbiter of national destiny") served to replace constituent antagonism with pride. Nor did the unqualified endorsement of the popular President McKinley hurt his chances for re-election.[41]

Though his documentation and deliberation gave him a commanding presence in debate, Cushman Davis was not an effective speaker. Rather he was a philosopher and an implementer. He had other foreign policy interests, but none so absorbed his intelligence and his energy as the march of imperialism. Part of the influence he exerted stemmed from his scholarship. His successor, Senator Towne, who had disagreed with Davis' expansionist beliefs, acknowledged that "no contemporary statesman excelled him in acquaintance with the literature of international law, or in the ability to state its principles and to argue their application." Towne related as an example an incident in which Secretary of State James G. Blaine relied on a certain diplomatic precedent told him by Davis from his reading of a French authority that "in all probability avoided the extremity of war with a South American State."[42] Furthermore, as chairman of the Senate foreign relations committee, he was in a powerful position to translate thought into action.

To Davis economics was the important force which controlled governments and dictated the fact of war or peace. "To buy, to sell, to build, to lend — these are the modern purposes of which governments have become the instruments," he said. The people of the United States must not become "mere spectators in the evolution of commerce, conquest and civilization." As a devotee of Admiral Mahan's thesis that it was America's destiny to be a great naval and military power, he articulated the themes of expansionists who looked toward the Pacific. But he stood firm in the tradition of isolation from Europe: "With all this the United States will, as always heretofore, stand for peace. . . . We shall not entangle ourselves in the controversies of European States."[43]

Davis rationalized the Spanish-American War by terming it just, brief, and humane, pointing out that its results "went far beyond expectation or prophecy." He equated expansionism with progress, which he defined as the extension of sovereignty by civilized states over "the barbarous or rudimentary or decaying nations." "The good old word for this was 'growth'; 'expansion' is a later term, and 'imperialism' is a word of still later misapplication used to excite prejudices by an epithet," he said. He believed that peace would be made possible by power and that the United States should stand as "the great armed Neutral of the world." Finally, he perceived a commonplace of today, that nations "touch one another," that "relations of all kinds . . . occur with hourly frequency," and that "Under such conditions, the interest of any state in its international affairs becomes exceedingly important." [44]

Cushman Davis died on the battleground of politics while stumping for McKinley during the campaign of 1900. An injury to his foot progressed from bad to worse, involving operations and amputations. Kidney infection compounded the problem, and after a painful illness he died on November 27, 1900. His last words were reported to be, "Oh, that I might live five years more for my country's sake!" [45]

Davis had lived long enough to see his dream come true. With the Spanish-American War and the Treaty of Paris which closed that war, the United States had chosen to participate in the affairs of the Pacific world, while maintaining the doctrine of isolation from Europe. [46] The ideology of continental isolation had been sullied by enthusiasms for military and economic power and for the extension of America's "civilizing" influences overseas.

The Jeffersonian notion of New World virtue had been transformed into a somewhat more active concept of New World mission. The United States had warred with Spain to free Cuba from Spanish tyranny and acquired Hawaii and the Philippines "to spread the blessings of liberty, democracy, and equality to other peoples of the earth." The next few years would see the nation entering enthusiastically into Asian affairs with the declaration in 1900 of an open door policy for China, active participation in the suppression of the Boxer Rebellion, and a prime role as peacemaker between Japan and Russia in 1905. In making what was a partisan Republican decision, the Middle West reflected its partisanship by pressing for and endorsing the westward expansion. By a coincidence of politics and power, Cushman K. Davis had the opportunity — and took it — to exercise leadership in the cause. By his opponents, he was called "jingo"; by his supporters, he was called "statesman." [47]

Davis received the highest accolades of his state and nation. He was buried in Arlington National Cemetery. Mrs. Davis received messages of condolence from President McKinley, Senators Mark A. Hanna and Henry Cabot Lodge, Secretary of State John Hay, Secretary of War Elihu Root, ambassadors and ministers, and from many others of great or less renown. The *Pioneer Press* of November 28,

1900, devoted two three-column headlines on page one to his death: "Senator Davis Dies" and "Loss to the Nation."

A memorial service conducted by the Ramsey County Bar Association extolled him for foreseeing "the great commerce that was to spring up on the Pacific ocean between this country and oriental nations," for engineering the acquisition of the Hawaiian Islands, for consolidating "public sentiment of this country in favor of the Spanish War," and for his part in negotiating the concession by Spain to the United States of "so many of her colonial possessions." His closest political ally, Henry Castle, would later say, "Peace and war waited on his words." [48]

Cushman Kellogg Davis was the first Minnesotan to exert significant influence on American foreign policy. He played a tenacious part in the battle for the annexation of the Hawaiian Islands, composed the ultimatum which resulted in war with Spain, and participated in the decisions that won an empire for the United States. At the height of the imperialist period in the nation's history, Davis was a certain advocate of America's manifest destiny.

Chapter 2

CHARLES A. LINDBERGH:
RADICAL ISOLATIONIST

*"Our own affairs must be made to accord with justice
before we can exercise much international influence."*
CHARLES A. LINDBERGH, 1923.

IN 1907 seven years after the death of Cushman Davis, Charles A.
Lindbergh, Sr., went to Congress from Minnesota's sixth district. The
United States was settling into its new role as a world power. The
long tradition of nonentanglement with Europe did not stand in the
way of involvement with South and Central America or the Pacific
Ocean nations. The Panama Canal was begun amidst a flurry of Canal
Zone diplomacy, much of which smacked of imperialism; the Open
Door policy of John Hay was receiving acclaim; and in 1905 the United
States mediated the brief war between Russia and Japan waged
largely for Manchurian territory.[1] It was a foreign policy scene that
Davis had helped to shape and Minnesota's new congressman was
to criticize throughout his career.

Superficially Lindbergh and Davis had much in common. Both were
well read, both were respected in their communities, both had prospered from the practice of law. But they were worlds apart in their
political attitudes. While both wore the same party label, the senator
represented the "reliably Republican" school, the congressman the
"rigorously radical." As the United States became increasingly attentive to the outside world, the politics of the two men dictated their
responses; Davis had been eager for outreach, Lindbergh was reluctant to get involved.

Ironically as imperialism peaked, the anti-imperialist forces were
assisted by domestic crises. Reform movements coalesced around the
plight of the farmer and the urban worker. Foreign policy concerns
were viewed as unwanted and unwarranted diversions from this
central issue, and there were few who surpassed Charles Lindbergh
in his zealous efforts to convert Minnesotans to the primacy of domestic
economic policy. Although Lindbergh had approved of the Spanish-
American War, he had done so in keeping with the populist rather

than the expansionist-imperialist rationale. He considered the war just by virtue of America's freeing the oppressed Cubans, reimbursing Spain for her territorial losses, and promising eventual freedom to the Philippines.[2]

Minnesota's new man in the House, much more than Senator Davis, had been shaped by the rural pioneering tradition of mid-America, a region not immune to the fever of protest. He had absorbed as part of his growing up the ideas and concerns of Ignatius Donnelly, the Granger movement, the Farmers' Alliance, and the Populist party.[3] Economic oppression and social privation lay at the roots of a series of these reform movements, which began in the 1860s with the National Grange, moved through the 1870s with the Anti-Monopoly and Greenback parties, the 1880s with the Farmers' Alliance, and flourished in the 1890s with the People's party and populism.

With the turn of the century — which witnessed a return to prosperity, the ending of a war that had shifted attention from domestic to foreign policies, and the defeat of Bryan by McKinley — internal unrest had no organized outlet for expression. Populism had run its course as the nineteenth century closed, but agrarian discontent still simmered under the surface and the spirit of protest was by no means dead. Thirty years of agitation in the nation's farm belt had laid the foundation for what was to come: the politics of progressivism, which took its most dramatic form in the contention for the presidency in 1912. The Progressive, or Bull Moose, party with Theodore Roosevelt at the helm was badly defeated in the election that brought Woodrow Wilson to the White House and with him, in one of the many oddities of politics, many tenets of progressivism to the country. World War I suspended and fragmented the movement, but it would be revived under other auspices such as the Farmer-Labor party in Minnesota. Throughout these years Lindbergh was part of the regional and national "middle-class rebellion," as William Allen White termed it.[4]

In Lindbergh's maturity, the grievances of farmer and worker would be articulated by the Nonpartisan League and would be bonded by the organization of the Farmer-Labor party. Their positions were affirmed in Lindbergh's mind by his own background, observations, and experience. He also found himself at home with the dissident Republicans who formed first the National Progressive Republican League in 1911 and later the Progressive party.[5]

Lindbergh's father, Ola Månsson, was a conventional Swedish farmer and an unconventional parliamentarian, a reputation he earned in the Riksdag for championing the cause of the underdog in Sweden. His political enemies engineered trumped-up charges of embezzlement (he was a director of a loan office of a local branch of the Bank of Sweden), forcing him to change his name to August Lindbergh and to start a fresh life in the New World. He immigrated in 1859 with his second wife and their recently born first son, who was destined to follow in August's footsteps as a radical parliamentarian in the American Congress.[6] To his son August passed on a sense of compassion for the poor and unfortunate. Throughout his life Charles Lindbergh (or "C. A.," as he was called) was sensitive to the needs and aspirations of those who earned their livelihoods by tilling the soil or working with their hands.

The Lindberghs settled in Stearns County, Minnesota, near what would become the village of Melrose. There they lived in a log cabin with a dirt floor, sustaining themselves by farming and hunting. After first attending a local school his father had helped to establish, Charles earned his way through Cogan's Academy near Sauk Centre by shooting and trapping game. He went on to the University of Michigan, where he studied law and graduated in 1883.

In 1884 Lindbergh opened his own law office in Little Falls, Minnesota. He was honest, he was kind, and his practice prospered. He branched out into real estate, an equally successful venture. Marriage to Mary La Fond in 1887 was a happy union which produced two daughters. After Mary died in 1898, Lindbergh married Evangeline Land in 1901. Their only child was a son, Charles, Jr.[7]

The senior Lindbergh's career has been overshadowed by his son's dramatic solo flight across the Atlantic Ocean in 1927. The younger Lindbergh was to stay in the limelight because of the tragic kidnapping of his son, the literary talents of both him and his wife, and the leadership he brought to the anti-interventionist cause in the period before World War II. As his father's son, the flier came by his isolationist sentiments honestly, for C. A. Lindbergh was a premier, if unusual, isolationist of his own time.[8]

The congressman was opposed to World War I largely for economic reasons; he was not an advocate of liberal trade policies, and he was unsympathetic to overseas adventurousness. He was an intellectual advocate of the school of thought which insisted that an active or responsive foreign policy was an unwanted diversion from the problems needing solution at home. His prime concern was to structure the economy in such a way that it would make exploitation by the few impossible and thereby gain well-being for the many. The Lindbergh stance is an important strain in Minnesota political history; it symbolizes a theme in midwestern politics of the era which one writer has described as the "culture area of political discontent."[9]

In 1905 Lindbergh found a forum for his developing ideas in *Law of Rights*, the first of several magazines he started, published, and edited, and all of which failed in their infancy. Much of Lindbergh's economic thought was straight out of Jefferson whom he called "the greatest of the great": "Agriculturalists are at the fountain head of the world's energy. All that exists in a social way has grown from the soil and centers upon it." After the farmer in importance, "the mainstay and the balance wheel of humanity," came the laborer and then the small businessman. But the exploitation and enslavement of these three classes by profiteers resulted in a "crushing domination of property interests over human rights." In order to maintain their powerful position, the profiteers employed their resources to buy the press, to pressure government to pass laws favorable to their cause, to elect sympathizers to public office, and to manipulate the economy through "scientifically created" panics. At fault was the system, not individuals, and it was necessary, therefore, to reform the system so that "the natural demands of commerce and trade" would be "divorced from personal favor or property reference."[10]

The changes Lindbergh considered essential were the establishment of a federal financial system independent of private monopoly control and federal ownership of communications and transportation. Although he urged what were then regarded as radical revisions in the established economic order, he did not subscribe to revolution because he feared that the resulting confusion would defeat the goals of reform. In Lindbergh's view, there was nothing wrong with the American political tradition of self-government that an enlightened populace could not cure. Educated and organized, the farmers, the workers, and the "legitimate" businessmen could eliminate the profiteers and purge the government of representatives serving special interests. (It was this coalition, although with less than total small business support, that would catapult the Farmer-Labor party to victory in 1922 and establish it as the state's second party.)[11]

Lindbergh first ventured into national politics in 1906 when he was persuaded by friends and local party leaders to challenge Clarence B. Buckman, the unpopular incumbent in the sixth congressional district.[12] The view of Buckman as a "political manipulator" was expressed in newspapers such as the *Elbow Lake Herald* which indicated that support was waiting for "A vigorous clean, able man . . . to insure Buckman's defeat." From afar the *Minneapolis Journal*, which would drastically change its opinion over the years, agreed that Lindbergh was "a man of ability and culture." The hotly contested Republican primary was essentially a battle of personalities rather than issues.

But Lindbergh did not neglect the opportunity to parade his major theme that special interests serving selfish purposes "take the earnings of the people." Like the populists before him, he particularly singled out the railroads for their discriminatory rates, the trusts and combinations for their manipulative powers. Buckman, argued Lindbergh, should not be returned to office because he sided with the gigantic corporate interests of the state and nation and was indifferent to the needs of the common people.[13]

Lindbergh defeated Buckman and won easily over Merrill C. Tifft, a Democrat, in a quiet general election contest.[14] His political career began with five successful elections and ended with five successive defeats, the last defeat by death before the outcome of the 1924 gubernatorial primary was known. Although nominally a member of the Grand Old Party (GOP), Charles Lindbergh became an active participant in the new, progressive politics of his time.

"The central theme in Progressivism," wrote historian Richard Hofstadter, "was this revolt against the industrial discipline: the Progressive movement was the complaint of the unorganized against the consequences of organization." One such form of organization was the trust. Between 1898 and 1904, 234 of them — with a capitalization of over $6 billion — had been organized, arousing the indignation of consumers on farms and in factories who blamed rising prices on the trusts' conspiracy of power. On this issue Lindbergh gained some national notoriety. During his third term in Congress in 1911, he introduced a resolution calling for an investigation of financial institutions and corporations to see whether they were operating in restraint of trade and violating the law. Nothing came of it until the next year when Democratic Representative Arsene P. Pujo of Louisiana, chairman of the committee on banking and currency, stole Lindbergh's thunder by introducing a nearly identical resolution, and the "Money Trust" investigation was under way. The facts that emerged from the so-called Pujo investigation impressively confirmed Lindbergh's suspicions. The Morgan interests, which dominated the big business scene, held 341 directorships in 112 corporations with aggregate resources of over $22 billion. This incomplete inventory represented more than three times the assessed value of all real and personal property in New England, more than twice the assessed value of all the property in the thirteen southern states, and more than all the property in the twenty-two states west of the Mississippi. Though Lindbergh was vindicated, he lamented the resulting remedial legislation which he thought insufficient for the task.[15]

While Lindbergh, like other progressives, viewed foreign affairs as an intrusion on domestic reform, international issues and crises would not vanish at a reformer's wish. Lindbergh's response to the Mexican incident of 1914 sheds light on his foreign policy outlook. In 1910 Francisco Madero had begun a three-year revolt against the long-entrenched dictatorship of Porfirio Diaz. Diaz was overthrown, but Madero's liberal government in turn was toppled in 1913 by the reactionary Victoriano Huerta. President Wilson refused to recognize Huerta on the principle that he did not enjoy the consent of the governed. Friction between the United States and Mexico increased to such an extent that Wilson allowed munitions to be supplied to Huerta's enemies, and stationed American naval vessels off Veracruz to prevent Huerta from receiving war supplies from Europe. The Wilson blockade in 1914 led to an incident in which American sailors, replenishing supplies in Tampico, were arrested but quickly released. Admiral Henry Thomas Mayo declared that a twenty-one gun salute to the American flag would constitute a necessary apology. Huerta refused and Wilson, protesting that American rights had been continually scorned by Huerta, asked Congress to sanction the possible use of force.[16]

The Mexican resolution passed the House on April 20, 1914, but the next day — before the Senate could act — Wilson, aroused by news that a German ship bearing arms was about to land there, telephoned orders to seize Veracruz. Wilson's pressure was one of several factors that forced Huerta to flee to Spain. The succeeding Mexican government of Venustiano Carranza was recognized by the United States in 1915.[17]

In his response to the Mexican affair, Lindbergh singled out special interests at work in Mexico exploiting the people and the natural resources as the provocation for United States involvement. By 1913 there were over 50,000 Americans in Mexico, and their investments, concentrated in the rich oil fields, totaled about $1 billion, or more than those of all other foreign nations combined. According to Lindbergh, these interests were clamoring for United States intervention "in order to establish what they consider a stable government in Mexico. They do this in order to exploit Mexico and the Mexicans." While the Mexicans were fighting for freedom, he argued, certain American business concerns were waving the flag to arouse fervor for a cause that was no more than a money-making venture. He also recalled the Spanish-American War, saying that the Philippines had become "a burden on our hands." In Lindbergh's view, the Stars and Stripes should be unfurled only in the cause of justice. He insisted in a letter to his daughter that "We cannot run the domestic affairs

of other countries without paying dearly for that sort of fiddling."
Lindbergh thought that the president's support of Admiral Mayo was
a stupid blunder to meet a frivolous demand and that it had resulted
in an unwitting admission of the legitimacy of the Huerta government.
Despite Lindbergh's disapproval of the motive and the methods he
voted for the resolution that supported the president, believing that
a rebuke of Wilson by the Congress might incite Huerta to further
action and make war inevitable.[18]

Lindbergh was to follow the same pattern in World War I. He
condemned what he regarded as essentially economic inducements
to war; he opposed United States involvement; but once the nation
was at war he stood behind the effort to bring peace to the world
as soon and as equitably as possible. His position adhered to a long-
standing tradition of avoiding the bellicose activities of Europe. In
the Middle West this tradition was reinforced by an alliance of ethnic
interests with the forces of economic protest. The 1910 federal census
had shown that 35.2 per cent of the total population were "new"
Americans, either immigrants themselves or born to immigrant parents. Of these only 9 per cent were German and less than 3 per
cent were Austrian.[19] In Minnesota, however, 26.2 per cent were
foreign born and 45.3 per cent had foreign-born parents, making a
total of over 70 per cent who were new Minnesotans. The ethnic
composition of this group was also strikingly different from the national
picture: over 25 per cent were from Germany and nearly 40 per cent
from the Scandinavian countries of Sweden, Norway, and Denmark.
If one adds Minnesota's Irish population of close to 5 per cent, with
its anti-British bias, a demographic composition of citizens with understandably neutral or pro-German sentiments emerges.[20]

While most German-Americans in Minnesota (and in the United
States) chose to support their adopted nation once the two countries
were at war, the choice was not absolute, and there were some new
Americans who remained loyal in varying degrees to their homelands.
The National German-American Alliance, founded in 1901 to promote
good citizenship, protect the German element against nativistic attack,
and foster amicable relations between Germany and America,
advocated a neutral attitude by the United States. According to George
M. Stephenson, the Scandinavians were divided; the majority of the
Norwegians were probably pro-Ally, but the Swedes were largely pro-
German. This included the influential Swedish Lutheran clergy for
whom Germany was the bastion of Protestantism and the protector
against Catholicism and Slavic domination. Russia, not Germany, was
Sweden's traditional adversary.[21]

Yet the response of the Middle West, as has already been suggested, was more than ethnic, encompassing a radical economic bias that fulminated against "evil men in black coats deceiving the people at the behest of bankers and manufacturers." The inheritors of populist protest agreed with Lindbergh who told Congress that "lords of special privilege" conspired to push America into World War I for profit. The economic reformers were angry at Britain because in their eyes it was the central manipulator of international finance contrary to their interests. This feeling was sustained by admiration for the Germans who had led the world in enacting enlightened social legislation.[22]

The outbreak of war in Europe in the summer of 1914 surprised Americans. When the Austrian heir to the throne was murdered in Sarajevo, Austria-Hungary used the event as an excuse to quash Serbian nationalism. A relatively obscure event in a remote Balkan province hardly seemed reason for a major European war. After the initial shock, Americans were both angry and relieved — angry that European quarrels had once again caught fire, relieved that this was apparently none of their business. The *Plain Dealer* of Wabash, Indiana, put the sentiment succinctly: "We never appreciated so keenly as now the foresight exercised by our forefathers in emigrating from Europe." On August 16 the *New York Times* depicted the war as the "full fruit of ruin and savagery" of the "European idea." President Wilson asked the American people to be "neutral in fact as well as name . . . impartial in thought as well as in action."[23]

The national reaction and the presidential assessment were shared by Minnesotans. Newspapers in the state characterized the war as absurd, futile, and dictated by racial fights centuries old, greed for territorial aggrandizement and industrial expansion, and the outworn militaristic policies of European autocracy." The *Duluth Herald* of September 2, 1914, termed the conflict "barbarous . . . a hell's broth . . . a noisome mass of anachronisms, a denial of Christianity, a betrayal of civilization." On September 13 the *Minneapolis Journal* said, "The people of the United States do not believe in war. They regard the awful happenings in Europe as the crime of the century."[24]

Events, however, began to outrun principles. Slowly there came a realization that it might not be easy for the United States to resist the tugs of war. American public opinion was assaulted on all sides. There were leagues to enforce peace, defense societies, associations against militarism, and organizations for preparedness. The dichotomy was exemplified by Cyrus Northrop, president emeritus of the University of Minnesota. In 1915 he was head of the 70,000-member Minnesota Peace Society which had been founded in 1913; he also lent his name as honorary president of the state branch of the National Security League, an organization which advocated strong military and naval forces as preparation against war. (Northrop stated he saw no inconsistency in holding offices in both groups.)[25]

The issue of war or peace became highly charged with the sinking of the *Lusitania* on May 7, 1915, by a German submarine, causing the loss of 1,198 lives, 128 of them American. Opinion in the United States was outraged. Only two midwestern papers defended the action, the *Milwaukee Free Press* and the *St. Louis Times*, both in cities with exceptionally large concentrations of Germans. President Wilson responded with restraint, saying "There is such a thing as a nation being so right that it does not need to convince others by force that it is right."[26]

When the question of Americans traveling on belligerent ships was raised, the Gore-McLemore resolutions were debated in Congress in March, 1916, warning citizens not to travel on the armed merchant ships of the Allies. All ten of Minnesota's representatives and one of its senators voted affirmatively, but the resolutions were defeated. The president was gratified by the decision because he believed that if the German U-boat could keep American nationals off the sea lanes, the respect of other nations, the confidence of American citizens, and the nation's prestige before the world would be lost. He endeavored to keep the United States out of war and to gain a German promise not to fire without warning. The second objective he won for a time; the first he ultimately lost.[27]

Wilson was trying to secure accommodation between the belligerents, but his efforts at mediation failed. The basis of his argument was for "a peace without victory" as the only way to bring about a permanent settlement. As part of this agreement, he envisioned a world community based on the equality of all nations, upon freedom of the seas, upon a general reduction of armaments — "a peace made secure by the organized major force of mankind."[28]

Neutrality became more precarious when Germany announced the resumption of unrestricted submarine warfare in 1917. The president went before Congress to request the arming of American merchant ships. In the midst of the congressional debate and filibuster over this issue, the famous Zimmermann telegram was made public. Intercepted by the British and delivered to the Americans, the message revealed a proposal by Arthur Zimmermann, foreign minister of Germany, to invite Mexico into an alliance as a belligerent. In response the House passed an armed ships bill with only fourteen negative votes. Minnesota's representatives Lindbergh and Charles R. Davis of the third district accounted for two of those fourteen votes. Lindbergh argued that freedom of the seas was but a rationalization to protect commerce and, while he admitted that the freedoms of trade and travel were abstract rights, "they are not the rights that lead to the exercise of civilization but the rights that lead to barbarism." In the Senate the Zimmermann telegram was used to try to influence stubborn holdouts (among them Moses Clapp, Minnesota's lameduck senator), but a filibuster was instigated, thus preventing a vote before adjournment of the Sixty-fourth Congress on March 4, 1917.[29]

Nevertheless, the telegram's content provoked a stormy public response. As a proposed assault on United States territory, it convinced Americans of German hostility. In Minnesota the press and the public had become increasingly critical of Germany's conduct. The Minnesota legislature had communicated its support for the president's position to arm merchant ships. City and village councils, educators, and scores of organizations echoed this sentiment. Newspapers castigated the Minnesota congressional trio for their votes and filibuster in opposition to the armed ships bill and charged that they had misrepresented the state. The Patriotic League of St. Paul termed the Davis and Lindbergh votes "un-American, unjustifiable and cowardly." But "peace with honor," the slogan of the loyalists, was still contending with the opposition's "peace at any price." In Minnesota groups such as the German-Americans, organized labor, and a portion of the congressional delegation continued to resist the possibility of United States participation in the war.[30]

Economic opposition to the war in Minnesota was defined most clearly by the Nonpartisan League, which had been conceived in 1915 in the protests of North Dakota farmers against the financial domination by the millers, bankers, and railroad men of Minnesota. It was weaned on the organizational genius of Arthur C. Townley, matured in the heat of wartime controversy, and finally gave rise to the Farmer-Labor party. The group called for state ownership of packing plants, terminal elevators, flour mills, munitions factories, mines, and communications. It urged fixed prices for the necessities of life, and, to match conscription for the armed forces, proposed that large fortunes be confiscated for the war effort. Like Lindbergh, league spokesmen opposed United States entry into the war on the grounds that it served only the interests of the profiteering few. The league's antiwar attitude mirrored the thinking of its members. The combination of radical economics and foreign policy attitudes provoked a score of epithets hurled at league members — revolutionaries, red socialists, free lovers, agitators, anarchists, atheists, un-Americans, disloyalists, communists, and pro-Germans.[31]

Throughout the trauma of this time, Lindbergh's attitude on the war remained constant. In December, 1916, he introduced a concurrent resolution calling for the regulation of business and industry to relieve the people of the burdens of war. The next year he sponsored a bill that would have established an advisory referendum by the people before a declaration of war by Congress, an unsuccessful tactic again used by isolationists in the late 1930s. Although he supported legislation to increase the efficiency of United States military forces, recognizing the need for hemispheric defense preparations, Lindbergh opposed bills for naval appropriations. His oratory was as intense as his legislative efforts to halt the drift toward war. Time and again, the Minnesotan insisted that the causes of war were economic; he called for government-owned production of all munitions to stop profiteers in their quest for war. According to the congressman, the "maelstrom of hell" that was war would lessen America's power and "destroy for a time our ability to conquer the world by the establishment of an economic system that will appeal to all humanity and be accepted for its justness." The failure of "existing civilization," he said, was documented by the "battered continent of Europe." It was America's task, not to imitate "misguided nations," but to "establish the economic system that will make war unnatural." As he was winding up his congressional career in March, 1917, Lindbergh voiced the hope that "somehow, some place, somewhere, sometime a nation will have to take a step toward civilization" and expressed his disappointment that his time and his nation had not fulfilled this aspiration.[32]

When the vote on the fateful issue of war and peace was cast on April 6, 1917, Lindbergh's political career had taken another turn. During his five terms in Congress, the issues he stood for — opposition to big business, for labor, for farm and industrial reforms, against political bosses and party control, for financial reform, for woman's suffrage, for conservation, and later for prohibition — had received widespread constituent support.[33] In five successive elections he had no trouble in trouncing his opponents. Yet he was apparently dissatisfied and frustrated with his efforts in Congress and sought a wider constituency for his views.

He filed first in the 1916 Republican gubernatorial primary from which he withdrew. Then he entered the Republican senatorial primary, where he ran a poor fourth to Frank Kellogg's first.[34] Lind-

Charles A. Lindbergh,
about 1920

bergh's enforced (and temporary) retirement from politics in March, 1917, gave him time to attend to his personal affairs and to complete his most controversial book, *Why is Your Country at War and What Happens to You after the War and Related Subjects.*

This slim volume contains the most complete and expressive presentation of Lindbergh's economic philosophy, especially as it related to the issues of World War 1. Written long before the fighting ended, it could well have become the Bible for the disillusioned revisionists of the interwar period to come. The ideas set forth in this book were almost identical to those which would nurture the Farmer-Labor party. Lindbergh wrote that while "ours was the first government to make a proper start . . . the doctrine of so-called 'reasonable profit' to the owners of capital, without taking into account the necessity for a reasonable compensation for the industry and production of toilers" had undermined justice and was destroying civilization. War — and American participation in it — had been the consequence of speculative intrigue. Lindbergh could only hope that the conflict would "develop into a war against the old order of things." [35]

This small book with its big title turned out to be explosive. Issued as it was in 1917, the year the United States went to war, it was not "kindly received," as one observer said in understatement. A few days after Lindbergh, who had again decided to run for governor, gained the endorsement of the Nonpartisan League for his candidacy, federal agents, evidently acting under the orders of Attorney General A. Mitchell Palmer, entered the plant where *Why is Your Country at War* and an earlier Lindbergh book, *Banking and Currency*, were being printed and ordered the owner to destroy both copies and plates.[36]

The Nonpartisan League was similarly attacked. Once the United States went to war, the league formally but not uncritically backed the war effort. Because many league leaders spoke out against conscription, they were charged with treason — charges which stunned Scandinavian members and helped to attract to membership German-Americans who were antipathetic to the war and who were persecuted in the name of patriotism.[37]

When Lindbergh and the league came together in the Republican primary of 1918, the liaison shook Minnesota to its political foundations. The *New York Times* on June 18, 1918, called it "one of the most spectacular campaigns in the history of the state." Lindbergh had entered the race for the Republican gubernatorial nomination on his own initiative. In order to achieve political power in Minnesota, the Nonpartisan League originally intended not to organize a third party but to seize the machinery of the Republican party to which most of its members belonged. The league's endorsement of Lindbergh was a move to that end, and the natural union between them was cemented by their opposition to the incumbent Republican governor, J. A. A. Burnquist, who was in their judgment perpetrating a police state upon the people of Minnesota. By legislative fiat and administrative implementation, individual liberty was at issue in Minnesota. The question of loyalty was the central theme of the Burnquist-Lindbergh contest.[38]

The Minnesota legislature, which was in session when war was declared, had passed a series of laws giving voice to its fears of so-called foreign-born disloyalists and economic radicals. Chief among these acts was that establishing the Minnesota Commission of Public Safety, consisting of the governor, attorney general, and five appointed members. Backed with an appropriation of one million dollars, the commission was endowed "with the most sweeping powers probably ever accorded any state agency to that time." In addition to broad general power to "do all acts . . . necessary or proper for the public safety and for the protection of life and public property or private property of a character as in the judgment of the commission requires protection" and to use "all necessary power not herein specifically enumerated," the commission was given five specific powers. Among these were the power to acquire property considered "necessary or desirable"; the right to "seize, condemn or appropriate" such property; and the power to subpoena persons and documents, with punitive measures authorized if resistance was met. The commission engaged in a wide range of activities. It closed saloons and motion-picture theaters; directed a census of alien land ownership; boosted the sale of Liberty bonds; and took other actions to bring conformity and ensure all-out support for the war.[39]

Aware of the prewar divergence of opinion in Minnesota, the commission was especially concerned with suspected disloyalty, alleged pro-Germanism, potential dissent, and possible efforts to evade the draft. Through its publicity department and its contact with all the newspapers in the state, the organization launched an indiscriminate attack against Germans, stressing the barbarism of the "German race" and the existence of dangerous German enemies lurking within Minnesota's borders. When German-Americans were not being attacked as barbarians, they came in for strenuous exhortations to "Proclaim your loyalty! Cut out the protests. Cease being sorry for yourself. . . . Get right into the game!" Loyalty meetings were held in "disaffected" counties throughout the state.[40]

Concern was also expressed over the textbooks used in teaching German in the schools. Some thirty books were ultimately banned after commission investigation. Another inquiry revealed that English was not the primary language of instruction in about two hundred parochial and private schools. Accordingly a resolution was passed stating that it was the patriotic duty of schools and teachers to use English as the exclusive medium of instruction.[41]

The safety commission removed from office certain county officials who had been outspoken critics of the war. It prevented the People's Council of America for Democracy and Peace, an organization opposed to conscription, from holding its national convention in Minneapolis. And it helped in the successful elimination of the Industrial Workers of the World (IWW or "Wobblies") as a significant force of radical labor protest through federal court indictments.[42]

The Nonpartisan League, with its radical economic ideas and growing political clout, was a prime target for the slings and arrows of the conservative safety commission. Harassed by the constant criticisms and charges of disloyalty and sedition, the league unintentionally gave the commission an opportunity to disrupt its efforts. At the league-sponsored Producers' and Consumers' Conference in mid-September, 1917, Senator Robert M. La Follette gave the closing speech. The theme of the convention was patriotism and protest, and the St. Paul Auditorium was jammed on the night of September 20 to hear the foremost protestor of them all. He did not let them down. The *Minneapolis Journal* of the next day reported critically that "The crowd . . . burst into a frenzy of enthusiasm at every La Follette attack on the justice of the war." [43]

The tragedy of the convention was its aftermath. La Follette, taunted by hecklers, forgot his promise to the league leadership to tread softly on the war issue. This lapse was compounded when he was misquoted in the Associated Press news report of his speech as having said, "We had no grievances" against Germany. In fact he had said that "we had, at the hands of Germany, serious grievances." The error, which the AP finally admitted nine months later, was to result in a Senate investigation of Senator La Follette, an investigation of the Nonpartisan League by the safety commission, and an even more vigorous prosecution of dissidents. It was Senator Kellogg who introduced the resolution to expel La Follette from the Senate, but he voted against it after the AP recanted. [44]

The intensity of the safety commission's antagonism toward the league is revealed in the testimony of its acknowledged leader John F. McGee, a Republican lawyer from Minneapolis, as he complained to a congressional committee that Minnesota law enforcement officers had been too lenient with the "treasonable" league. In the same statement before the Senate committee on military affairs in April, 1918, he charged league leaders and organizers with being "seditionists and, I think, traitors." McGee was concerned also with the ethnic composition of the nation and worried that the birth rate among Germans and others "of foreign extraction" exceeded that of "what we call Americans." He predicted that the United States would fall as had Rome when those of foreign birth or extraction outnumbered the Romans. Finally, the former judge offered his own formula for dealing with dissidents — firing squads! [45]

The effort by the safety commission to equate the Nonpartisan League with disloyalty was in large part politically motivated. The league's crime was not sedition but economic theory. As a writer for the *Public* put it: "The 'essential truth' [was] that the inspiration and the dominant motive is the desire to protect the established economic order." [46]

It was in a climate where conformity was the mark of loyalty that the Republican primary campaign of 1918 was waged. The press took up the cudgel with a vengeance. The *Minneapolis Journal* of March 21, 1918, called Lindbergh a "confirmed pacifist" and asserted that the league desired a "Bolshevist victory." On May 22 the paper maintained that the election was a test of loyalty for Minnesota and that Lindbergh "has a public record of disloyalty and demagoguism." Five days later the *Journal* made the point again, saying "There is no middle ground in this contest. Those who are not for America and her fight for civilization are against her. The issue is drawn. On which side do you stand?" Obviously the *Journal* thought one had to stand with Burnquist since Lindbergh was the "candidate of disloyalty." [47]

The *St. Paul Dispatch* in a series of editorial comments on June 3, 5, and 10, also called the election a test of loyalty and termed Lindbergh a "copperhead." The *New York Times* contributed to the vitriol on May 29, calling Lindbergh a "sort of Gopher Bolshevist," and saying that he was lucky to be out of jail. And the *Sauk Centre Herald* in Lindbergh's home county proclaimed on May 18 "that any citizen with sons in the army of freedom who supports Charles A. Lindbergh for Governor are firing a charge of buckshot into the backs of their own boys." [48]

The loyalty issue was made out of false cloth. Both Lindbergh and the league backed the war after the United States entered it. The platform of the Nonpartisan League stated that first and foremost the war must be won, and pledged its aid to the effort. In both private and public communications, Lindbergh, while regretting the stupidity of United States involvement, asserted his support of the war for the sake of peace. But the past was more vivid in people's minds than the present, and invective was not confined to words. [49]

In small towns boys were paid ten to twenty-five cents to steal Lindbergh banners from cars and buggies. Lindbergh and other league speakers were often run out of town; they were mobbed and stoned, and law officers averted their eyes or sanctioned the violence. League spokesmen sometimes dodged bullets, but they could not always escape being tarred and feathered or facing a lynching threat. With good reason one historian observed that "virtually mob rule prevailed during the campaign of 1918. . . . The period was like a reign of terror throughout the state." [50]

Lindbergh, writing to his son, admitted that he was "Having strenuous times." He told of several incidents in which he was threatened by mob hysteria and denied the opportunity to be heard. He was appalled at the intensity of feeling and although he expressed the wish the Charles were with him, he concluded that it was probably just as well he was not because "when people are so excited, [you]

Lindbergh was hanged in effigy in Goodhue County during the 1918 gubernatorial campaign.

can't tell what some one might pull off." Lindbergh warned his daughter that she "must prepare to see me in prison and possibly shot." Two weeks before the election he was jailed in Martin County, but the charges of unlawful assembly for the purpose of teaching the doctrines of international socialism and conspiring to interfere with the nation's military policies were soon dropped. He was, in fact, a prime target of his three-year-old prediction that those who had opposed American involvement in the war would suffer the "strangulation of free speech."[51]

The Minnesota election became a national issue. Congressman Clarence B. Miller of Minnesota's eighth congressional district attacked Lindbergh on the floor of the House, calling him "a man who disbelieves everything our country stands for" and questioning whether the author of such a book as *Why is Your Country at War* should be permitted to be "at large." When President Wilson sent William Kent, a federal trade commissioner, to Minnesota to investigate disloyalty charges against the league, Kent not only exonerated the organization but sent $1,000 to Lindbergh's campaign fund.[52]

Throughout the continuing vilifications and violence, Lindbergh persisted in his defense of free expression. At the outset of his campaign, he had argued that "a few would destroy democracy to win the war and the rest of us would win the war to establish democracy." He declared unequivocally that the opponents of the Nonpartisan League had prostituted the principles of freedom. Two months later in May, 1918, Lindbergh and other candidates presented a memorial addressed to Governor Burnquist which protested that the "conditions existing in Minnesota . . . [are] repugnant to a free people" and asserted, "In attempting to make your personal loyalty, aided and abetted by mob violence, intimidation and oppression, the issue in the coming campaign, you have unwittingly made Democracy the real issue." [53]

As the campaign drew to a close, Lindbergh was accused of religious bigotry. During his last term in Congress, he had introduced a resolution calling for an investigation of a controversy between the Free Press Defense League and the Catholic church. Although he seemed to imply a prejudgment with his statement that "many of the high dignitaries of the Church of Rome have been the ally of oppression," he subsequently insisted that his real purpose had been to clear the air of charges and countercharges. Nothing came of this until a week before the 1918 election. On June 8, 1918, the *Catholic Bulletin* resurrected the resolution as evidence of Lindbergh's anti-Catholic prejudices. The ensuing uproar among Catholics takes little imagination to envisage, and one local bishop even asked for public prayers that Lindbergh would not be elected. [54]

Lindbergh had expressed the hope that these unethical acts would be recognized as such and work to his advantage. Although he lost the election, his optimism was partially justified. When the dust settled and the shouting died down on June 17, 1918, Burnquist came out the winner by the surprisingly small margin of 48,699 votes. The campaign had been far more successful than the Nonpartisan League expected. Burnquist's total was swollen by Democrats who voted in the Republican primary to ensure his victory, believing that he would be the weaker of the two candidates against Fred E. Wheaton in the general election. On the other hand, Lindbergh's unexpectedly high total probably represented a backlash against the repression of Burnquist's forces, especially among the Germans and Scandinavians. [55]

The 1918 Republican primary had two significant results: it proved Minnesota to be "loyal," and it turned out to be the gestation period for the birth of the Farmer-Labor party. Despite the defeat of Lindbergh, the Nonpartisan League and organized labor, meeting separately on August 25, agreed to sponsor candidates for the general election. The name "Farmer-Labor" was adopted to fulfill the requirements of party designation on the ballot.[56]

Five months later the end of World War I wrote finis to the Minnesota Commission of Public Safety. The commission's last report of January 1, 1919, reaffirmed its bias that the disloyal men of Minnesota "formed a constituency of considerable size," that there were among them pacifists, pro-Germans, and "professional politicians of the socialist or Nonpartisan league stamp." The commission seemed satisfied that it "undertook to kindle the back fires of patriotism among the rank and file of this ilk. . . . With the leaders it used the mailed fist." [57]

In retrospect, as Theodore C. Blegen pointed out, most Minnesotans were loyal and gave "wholehearted" support to the war effort. As a matter of fact, the Germans in Germany were surprised and disappointed that their kinsmen in America were relatively indifferent to the fate of their old homeland and did not rise in arms to protest the declaration of war by the United States. A fitting epitaph for the Commission of Public Safety was provided by Theodore Christianson when he wrote, "The virtue of loyalty often became the vice of intolerance." [58]

The attention of the nation turned from war and politics to peace. Although he shared Woodrow Wilson's ideal of "peace without victory," Lindbergh's version was "an economic victory for the masses of the world." He had high hopes that a time of peace would bring equal opportunity to all and special privilege to none. He recognized that the United States could not withdraw into its earlier isolation without settling the European situation. The United States was, Lindbergh admitted to his daughter, "in the world game now." He therefore applauded Wilson's efforts to do away with secret diplomacy, to secure the rights of self-determination and freedom of the seas, but he did not believe that given the existing economic system the League of Nations could succeed in guaranteeing peace. As he pointed out in the March, 1919, issue of *Lindbergh's National Farmer*, if fundamental economic reforms were instituted, there would be no need for a League of Nations "for there will be nothing of importance to quarrel about." By the time the Treaty of Versailles was defeated in the Senate in March, 1920, Lindbergh's hostility to the league had heightened. He commented in a letter to his daughter that "Wilson has his pay now for trying to tie us to a world war machine. Nothing ever done in my judgment was so un-American as to try to hitch us to that treaty." [59]

Like many intellectuals and liberals of his time, Lindbergh displayed an intense interest in the new Russian state emerging from the revolution of 1917. At least, Lindbergh argued, the Russian revolution was worthy in motive and ought to be left to run its course. At best Russia was the first nation in the world to attempt significant economic reform. Tongue in cheek, he mimicked those who fretted at the Bolshevik goals of doing away with poverty, hunger, and ignorance by saying "The very idea!" He wrote his daughter that the "simple minded and long oppressed Russians," rather than Americans, as he had hoped, might "lead the world to democracy." [60]

Until the coup of November, 1917, the Russians had been in the war against Germany. Allied hopes that they might continue were soon shattered, and many strategists thought the only logical solution to be armed intervention in Russia so that Germany would not be relieved of the two-front dilemma. President Wilson moved moderately, cautiously, and reluctantly, so that there would be no possibility of misinterpreting America's presence as an effort to interfere with Russian internal affairs. But circumstances conspired to escalate and prolong the intervention: for one, the pressure to rescue 50,000 anti-Bolshevik Czechoslovakians slowly retreating across Siberia; for another, the concern that the 72,000 Japanese troops in the area be restrained from seizing territory in Siberia and north Manchuria; and finally the confusion generated by the mix of American emotions regarding this new and daring experiment in economics and governance. In the end fear was the conquering emotion, and American troops finally departed in 1920, two years after their first arrival on the north Russian scene. With other American radicals, Lindbergh thought it nobody's business what kind of government the Russians had just so long as "they let us alone." [61]

In 1920, still consumed by concern and commitment, Charles Lindbergh, now more than sixty years of age, ran on the Farmer-Labor ticket for his old congressional seat against Harold Knutson, who had been elected in 1916 when Lindbergh vacated the office. Knutson was well entrenched and in close touch with the views of his constituents. Lindbergh's continuing radicalism alienated him from the Republicans, and his independent attitude prevented complete rapport with the younger leadership of the emerging Farmer-Labor party. Knutson polled 47,954 votes to Lindbergh's 21,587. [62]

The veteran campaigner entered two more election contests. In 1923 there was a special election to fill the United States Senate seat left vacant by the death of Knute Nelson. Lindbergh entered the Farmer-Labor primary on a personal platform whose foreign policy planks included opposition to imperialistic wars, "self-determination of all nations," and "recognition of the new Russian Republic." During this campaign, Lindbergh's son flew him around the state. Near Glencoe while both father and son were away from the airplane, someone using wire cutters severed a cable on the plane, but neither man was hurt in the emergency landing. Despite the innovative mode of transportation, Lindbergh was old hat in Minnesota politics, and he finished a poor third to Magnus Johnson, who went on to join Henrik Shipstead in the Senate under Farmer-Labor aegis.[63]

His protestation that the 1923 senatorial primary was his last political effort was poor prophecy. Lindbergh had one final fling in the 1924 gubernatorial primary, although his daughter said later that "He was forced in . . . by selfish people . . . who knew he was ill. They even filed for him. Had he not been really ill, he would not have been in the last campaign." Poor health forced Lindbergh to withdraw, and he threw his support to a little-known but rising politician, Floyd B. Olson, who also failed to win the nomination.[64]

On May 24, 1924, Lindbergh died at sixty-five of a brain tumor. At the funeral services held in the First Unitarian Church of Minneapolis, Reverend John H. Dietrich said that honor, justice, and love of his fellow man marked the public career of Charles A. Lindbergh. Other post-mortems assessed him as a man of courage and principle. Thomas Pederson, a close and devoted friend, said that Lindbergh was "a generation ahead of his time . . . a man who could neither be bribed or bought" and who "died with the conviction that he had been a failure." Lindbergh would not have judged his failure in personal terms but rather in his inability to effect change.[65]

Reform politicians of the Lindbergh era were not often men of wealth. Lindbergh once had both money and property. Before 1921 he was estimated to be worth a quarter of a million dollars, money earned from his prosperous law practice, from his land holdings in Minnesota and Florida, and from his interests in several banks. He claimed that he could have made an even greater fortune by exploiting those who, unlike himself, were ignorant of the inner workings of the American financial system. Instead he spent his life trying to reform the institutions from which he prospered but which, in his judgment, denied prosperity and even security to others. He thought the world was filled with the numberless victims: "The whole social system has seared my soul." For someone with this sensitivity, it is little wonder that money had very little meaning for him, and he gave away most of his fortune in the extensive loans he made to friends in the 1921 depression. He spent the last two years of his life practicing law in Minneapolis and living in a cheap room in a church-run hotel.[66]

Lindbergh espoused Jeffersonian agrarianism and isolationism, and repeatedly voiced his suspicions of financial interests. Many of the reforms he proposed were radical, and it was his consistent radicalism that brought him scorn and abuse. In describing the House Republican rebels of the early 1900s, Russel Nye observed, "Charles Lindbergh of Minnesota was a direct political descendant of Donnelly and Populism, a lone wolf in politics, the most leftish of the group, and a bitter hater of trusts and privilege." Another scholar made the point that no congressman went as far as Lindbergh in ascribing war to the economics of the system.[67]

His persistent efforts on behalf of civic education, through publication and politics, stand high on his record of personal and public concerns. He was a man of pride — "The Money Trust contest was instituted by me" — and was pleased that the "leading progressives have gleaned many of their ideas" from studying his speeches and writings. Of himself he wrote, "With the exception of La Follette, no man in public life has forced the fight against special privilege with such courage and so heedless of personal interests."[68]

Lindbergh was one of those who gave to the Nonpartisan League and later to the Farmer-Labor party an intellectual base by relating a dominant theme of American life to the times and temper of the World War I period. The "one great compelling duty of America," he wrote, "is to put its own house in shape, and to stand upon an economic system that will make its natural resources available to the intelligence, industry and use of the people. When we do that the way to world redemption from the folly of present chaos will stand out in our country so clearly, honestly and usefully that we shall be copied wherever peoples do their own thinking."[69]

Charles Lindbergh gave Minnesota a gospel of radical isolationism that would be resurrected and preached by latter-day disciples who recognized him as their preceptor. Though Harold Knutson and Henrik Shipstead followed in his footsteps, their motivations had more conservative foundations. He may have been a lone fighter in his congressional time, but there were many enlistments in his cause in the years that followed. It is as a forerunner and political pioneer that he merits our attention — a man who was indeed, as his friend said, "a generation ahead of his time."

Chapter 3

HAROLD KNUTSON AND HIS CONSTITUENTS: A TRUSTED ALLIANCE

> *"They said I was against rural electrification, old age assistance, price support for farm commodities, farm cooperatives, and aid to Europe. They said I was for isolation – whatever that means."*
>
> HAROLD KNUTSON, 1948.

HAROLD KNUTSON succeeded Charles A. Lindbergh as congressman from the sixth district of Minnesota in 1917. Initially Knutson's ideology was consistent with that of his predecessor. Unlike Lindbergh, however, he ultimately settled into a domestic conservatism, rarely veering from the isolationist line. His beliefs exemplified the body of isolationist thought which had a substantial impact on the turgid movement of United States foreign policy toward internationalism in the period from 1920 to 1940. On foreign policy issues he was overshadowed by more colorful and powerful personalities such as Henrik Shipstead, George W. Norris of Nebraska, and Gerald P. Nye of North Dakota. Knutson's contribution to the nation's public affairs must be measured, not by legislation bearing his name or by parliamentary effectiveness, but rather by his remarkable longevity and the loyalty of the voters of his district who elected him to office for sixteen consecutive terms. Part of that district — Stearns County — was described by Samuel Lubell in 1951 as "in many ways the classic isolationist county in the whole United States." For four decades its congressional seat was occupied by two isolationists, one a radical, the other a conservative.[1]

Knutson, who came easily and unobtrusively to national politics (having never held previous office, though he once served as a page in the state legislature), was a member of Congress for the period spanning pre-World War I isolationism to post-World War II internationalism. Until his defeat in 1948, he was never out of touch or out of favor with his constituents. He kept close watch over his district, and his stand on major issues mirrored its will. This was the measure

Harold Knutson, 1946

of his political success. In successive election contests from 1916 to 1946, he never had a serious challenge.

Harold Knutson was born in Norway on October 20, 1000, and emigrated to the United States before he was ten years old. He was raised on a dairy farm in Sherburne County, where he was exposed to the agrarian ideology — "I have said on more than one occasion that I consider . . . the agricultural Midwest to be the backbone of the country" — and where he claimed to have learned from his mother "the great lesson of Americanism." Her evening prayers always included, Knutson remarked, "a note of thanksgiving to Providence for having permitted our family to come to this wonderful country where each and every one is free to carve out his own career." Yet Knutson in adulthood was unwilling to share that opportunity, devoting much of his congressional energy to efforts to limit immigration.[2]

The young Knutson, after attending public and agricultural schools, became a printer's devil and subsequently established himself in the newspaper business. He was publisher of the *Royalton Banner* and the *Foley Independent*; later he became the associate editor of the

St. Cloud Daily Journal-Press. He served as secretary of the finance committee of the Northern Minnesota Editorial Association and as president of the state editorial association in 1910–11. Eight years after entering Congress, Knutson purchased the *Wadena Pioneer Journal*, which he published until his death in 1953.

For a young man of thirty-six, Harold Knutson was highly visible in central Minnesota when he made his first political bid in 1916 for the congressional seat of the sixth district. He won an easy victory in the Republican primary over C. B. Buckman (Lindbergh's predecessor) and E. L. Rogers. The general election was an equally simple task as he polled 20,889 votes to William F. Donohue's 13,107.[3] Knutson had the unwritten qualifications for election: he was a Scandinavian, a Republican from a farming region. His vocal stand against American involvement in the European war fitted both the temper of the electorate and the posture of his popular predecessor.

The first plank in his personal platform was elimination of profit in war by nationalizing the manufacture of all war materials. Other points included protecting the American farmer, laborer, and businessman by enacting a tariff law that would ensure their prosperity as well as other legislation that would contribute to the social and economic welfare of those who toiled. The *Long Prairie Leader* of June 29, 1916, reported that Knutson had gained the primary victory largely as a result of his own efforts and that he typified what "a farm boy can do who has courage and energy." The *Wadena Pioneer Journal* pointed out prophetically on October 26, 1916, the eve of the general election, that Knutson "has lived and worked in the Sixth congressional district so many years that he knows just about what the people of the district want and will be satisfied with."[4]

Knutson's first vote in Congress was on President Wilson's request for a declaration of war against Germany. True to the congressional tradition that freshmen representatives should be seen and not heard, Knutson said nothing but was one of fifty congressmen who voted against the declaration on April 6, 1917. Subsequently he inserted in the appendix of the *Congressional Record* under that date an "extension of remarks" which gave the impression of having been spoken on the House floor to explain his vote. Although he was severely criticized in an article widely reprinted in local newspapers for preparing an undelivered speech five days after the voting, there was no denying his belated eloquence. "I shall vote," he stated, "against a declaration of war because I feel we have no business meddling in European affairs." He enumerated his other reasons for opposition: entangling alliances which could endanger the Monroe Doctrine and involve the United States in "another holocaust"; endangering the lives of American soldiers; imposing "a burden of taxation that will weigh down generations yet unborn"; and "lastly, I shall vote against war because I feel that a majority of the common people, who live by the sweat of their brow, do not want it." [5]

Knutson's position was consistent with the isolationist precepts of agrarian Minnesota, and he had company in his opposition. Republicans Charles R. Davis of the third district and Ernest Lundeen of the fifth, and Democrat Carl C. Van Dyke of the fourth district were with Knutson the four of Minnesota's ten congressmen who voted against the war. Lundeen of Minneapolis was perhaps the most vehement of the quartet. A referendum of 54,000 voters in his district had resulted in a ten-to-one vote against war. *Vox populi*, he believed, was sufficient justification for his "nay" vote, but echoing sentiments articulated by Lindbergh, Lundeen also fulminated that there was no cause justifying war and that the economic price tag would impose an oppressively heavy burden on the common man. Van Dyke, the only Democrat in the Minnesota delegation, stood against his president and party leader, arguing that this was "not a war for defense of our coast and commerce but a war of aggression in Europe." Davis of St. Peter did not speak to the issue, but he was no doubt influenced by negative straw votes taken in communities in his district, two of them in towns heavily populated by German-Americans. [6]

One historian has noted that the "rather surprising amount of opposition" to World War I "was concentrated in the isolationist and German-inhabited states of the Middle West." Of the fifty congressmen who voted against United States participation, thirty five were from the Midwest. Thirty-three were known to have "progressive" ideas, fifteen were influenced by the ethnic composition of their constituencies, and two were themselves pro-German. Knutson, whose progressivism was then still operative, was well aware of the ethnic composition of his district, which was heavily populated by northern Europeans. The foreign born in the eleven counties averaged almost 17 per cent, or just a bit under the average for the entire state. But of that 17 per cent, Scandinavians totaled 66 per cent and Germans 31 per cent, distinctly higher than the average for the state. For Minnesota as a whole, the five-nation Scandinavian-German total was 67 per cent; for the sixth congressional district it was a telling 97 per cent. [7]

An accomplished politician, the new congressman justified his vote with impassioned rhetoric. He covered the eventuality of American participation in the war by saying, "it will be my fight as it is yours,

and we must leave no stone unturned to bring victory to our arms."
His constituents, he anticipated, would be moved by the emotion
of involvement, and his vote against the war would fade from memory
with his support of the boys "over there." He was prepared for an
adverse public reaction; he knew, as he put it, that he would be
"crucified by the press." [8]

He might have expected the criticism to flow from the metropolitan
papers rather than from those in his own rural district. The former,
however, were more gentle with Knutson than they were with their
own representatives, whose very virility they questioned. The *Minneapolis Tribune* of April 9, 1917, predicted that the four Minnesota
congressmen who voted against the war would find that a war existed
between them and the Minnesota public. The *Minneapolis Journal*
of April 10, 1917, called Knutson "delinquent" and said that he was
guilty of the "sheerest evasion," stating that his action "will serve
only to increase the disgust and indignation of right-thinking people."
Rural papers in Knutson's district largely excused his vote on the
grounds of his inexperience, but the *Sauk Centre Herald* of April 12,
1917, suggested that Knutson had "been led astray by basking in the
company of 'Ernie' Lundeen." The *St. Cloud Daily Times*, a Democratic paper, commented with disdain that Knutson "had voted against
the President's policy, against the government, against battle for
humanity . . . and for the country's enemy." Knutson admitted,
"They have been giving me hell." [9]

As the fighting progressed, the new congressman supported
measures to ensure total victory and voted to delegate extraordinary
powers to the president for the prosecution of the war. He gave no
cause for his patriotism to be questioned. Knute Nelson, Minnesota's
senior senator, assured a St. Cloud constituent that Knutson had faith-
fully supported every war measure, adding "I have no doubt of his
loyalty." [10]

While it appeared that the congressman had deftly climbed from
one side of the fence to the other, he was in fact straddling it. Speaking
against the espionage bill of 1917, which was later often interpreted
to equate dissent with disloyalty, Knutson asked if "the greatest
democracy" feared "to go into this war with a free press and a free
people . . . ? Will Congress dare to assume before the people the
position of favoring a measure that will stifle American liberties?"
Using a commonplace in the arsenal of progressive isolationist thought
and sounding remarkably like his predecessor, Lindbergh, Knutson
urged the conscription of wealth for the war effort, advocated government control of armaments and munitions to minimize the profit

motive, and proposed that the war be put on a pay-as-you-go basis to avoid burdening future generations with a "huge bonded indebtedness." Knutson's fancy dancing on the war issues kept his constituents who opposed the war gratified and those who supported the war pacified. He won re-election in 1918 and 1920, fending off a challenge in the latter year by Lindbergh by a vote of 47,954 to 21,587.[11]

For America, fighting the war took less time than concluding the peace. The war lasted for one year and five months; the settlement, prolonged by controversy over the League of Nations, consumed two years and eight months. Knutson chafed at the delay. He held no brief for the League of Nations, regarding it as an interruptive intrusion in the need to come to terms with Germany. He spoke disparagingly of Woodrow Wilson, calling him "that cold and stubborn man" who "would have no peace save his kind of peace." The election of 1920, which brought Republican Warren Harding to the White House, was eloquent testimony to the American aversion to "foreign entanglements and alien intrigue," said Knutson. The failure to enact a formal treaty had cost the United States a "tremendous loss in trade," and America's depressed economic condition demanded, in Knutson's view, a settlement with the Central Powers so that surplus products from the United States could find their way into overseas markets.[12]

Another postwar issue gave Knutson further popularity with voters of German descent. Faced with huge debts and runaway inflation, Germany in 1923 defaulted on reparations payments, and an angry France, rejecting the caution of Great Britain, seized the Ruhr Valley, the industrial nerve center of Germany. Irate at the French action which significantly diminished any opportunity for German economic recovery, Knutson argued that the reparations demands were unjustifiably severe and that the German market, which had been the nation's best customer before the war, could not possibly be replaced by that of France. He insisted in 1923 that the United States could not permit Germany to be destroyed, because in "the inevitable hour" of "a death grapple for supremacy" between the white and yellow races, "a strong and virile Germany will be of inestimable assistance — yea, she will be indispensable." This expression of support for Germany required Knutson to concede that the United States, if it were to remain prosperous, could not be totally indifferent to Europe. But he also invoked the classic Jeffersonian contrast between the rapacious Old World and the virtuous New World, while conceding that indifference to Europe was not consistent with the requirements for American prosperity. These sentiments were not well received beyond his district. The *New York Times* reported that the speech was "apparently intended chiefly for consumption in his district," and that "the hisses became very strong as he proceeded." [13]

Quite a different attitude is revealed in Knutson's reversal on the question of independence for the Philippine Islands. In 1925 the congressman, now serving his fifth term, opposed independence on the grounds that the Filipinos were not yet ready for self-government, that one would not "confer the power to vote upon a babe the moment it is born." Less than five years later he introduced a bill which would have granted freedom to the Philippines and spent several years working toward that end. It was not, however, Philippine political readiness but the issue of economic competition that caused him to change his mind. The *St. Paul Pioneer Press* criticized Knutson for demanding independence on such grounds, saying that Minnesota dairymen would simply have to endure the squeeze until "America's mission" in the Philippines was completed. Knutson's reply, in a letter to the editor reprinted in the *Congressional Record*, dismissed the argument about America's mission by saying that the United States had played "wet nurse" long enough. He added: "We have relieved distress where there was hunger and established orderly government where there was none. . . . It is generally agreed that the Philippine Islands to-day constitute the greatest single menace to our dairy industry because of their huge exports to our country." It was his contention that the current low prices of butter and lard were due to the "enormous importation of vegetable oils." The congressman's stock could not help but rise with the dairy farmers in his district when he asserted that the dairy business was all that "stood between the agricultural Northwest and bankruptcy from 1925 to 1927." The American farmer was doomed, he argued, as long as the existing United States-Philippine relationship permitted duty-free exports of vegetable oil and sugar to the United States. A further consideration, he noted, was job competition between Filipinos and Americans on the West Coast which in May, 1930, had precipitated race riots. [14]

Knutson's interest in the Philippine independence bill was generated by his membership on the committee on insular affairs through which such measures had to pass. By 1932 he had become so passionately involved that memory failed him, and he asserted, "I have been for independence for over 12 years." While he initially saw merit in maintaining United States bases and interests on the islands — "It is not my thought that we should retire entirely from the Orient" — he soon moved toward a more absolute stance of withdrawing "lock, stock, and barrel." In a time of economic stress the interests of agriculture and labor prevailed over those of investors, imperialists, and militarists, and the Philippines and the United States were separated in 1934; the "divorce" became final in 1946.[15]

Knutson's protectionism, inspired by the depressed state of mid-western agriculture and articulated in the recurring debate on Philippine independence, took on a larger dimension as the contagion spread from farm to city and infected the whole economy. On Thursday morning, October 24, 1929, rumblings on Wall Street of the economic distress that had been felt by Minnesota farmers since 1920 became a roar and the reality of American prosperity a myth. In the course of a few brief weeks $30 billion dollars in paper wealth vanished into thin air. The aftermath of Black Friday was the Great Depression, which persisted with varying severity for ten years. A world-wide collapse of terrifying proportions and duration, it marked millions of people, who lost friends to suicide, jobs to unemployment, and hope to despair; it removed Wall Street from the personal command of financiers and placed it under some supervision from Washington; it lowered the prestige of businessmen, especially bankers and brokers; and it brought Hitler to power in Germany. John Kenneth Galbraith outlined its dimensions when he wrote: "In 1933, Gross National Product (total production of the economy) was nearly a third less than in 1929. . . . In 1933 nearly thirteen million were out of work, or about one in every four in the labor force. In 1938 one person in five was still out of work." [16]

Despite the importunings of 38 nations and 1,028 American economists, the Republican Congress persisted in its belief that a higher tariff would help repair the damage of depression at home. The highest tariff measure in American history, the Smoot Hawley Act of 1930, fostered ill will, stimulated retaliation, and gave the *coup de grâce* to any hope of moderating world depression. Knutson supported the Smoot-Hawley Act because he believed that without the protective tariff, "we must reconcile ourselves to descending to the levels that are to be found in foreign and competing lands" and that the farmer and the worker were the prime beneficiaries. His argument that big business wanted low tariffs fitted neatly into the pattern of his agrarian mistrust of the increasing concentration of industrial ownership. He warned against "the long tentacles of the octopus reaching out to crush individuality and stifle competition" and predicted socialism or worse if the brakes were not applied. This was the kind of Lindbergh talk and imagery that made sense to central Minnesotans, and they remained content with Harold Knutson as their representative.[17]

When the economic decline intensified, Knutson in 1932 blamed not the tariff but the "campaign of propaganda against the tariff which has been financed by foreign manufacturers, by international bankers, and by importers." By 1933 Knutson's economic isolationism had solidified. Speaking to the House, he lauded the independent, virtually autonomous pioneers (many of his constituents were proud that they or their fathers had grown up in pioneer households) and suggested that their self-sufficiency should be national policy. "We can produce nearly everything we consume," he proclaimed, "and everything which is consumed in the United States which can be produced in the United States ought to be produced here." Turning a cold shoulder on foreign trade, Knutson asserted that the protective tariff which he championed was "not a policy of isolation" but rather "a policy of common sense." [18]

By 1934 the Democratic administration of President Franklin D. Roosevelt was persuaded that a de-escalation of the Smoot-Hawley tariff would be beneficial. The new Reciprocal Trade Agreements Act left the Smoot-Hawley tariff on the books but gave the president power to lower rates by as much as 50 per cent with nations willing to reciprocate. Significantly the new trade legislation passed rate-setting prerogatives from the Congress to the president. Knutson, who was horrified by both developments, invoked the eighth verse of the fifth chapter of I Timothy, one of his favorite Biblical references, "But if any provide not for his own, and especially for those of his own house, he hath denied the faith, and is worse than an infidel." Through the years, Knutson authored legislation to deprive the president of the power to negotiate trade agreements and orated against bills extending that authority. Again and again he argued that trade would only drag the United States down to the economic level of the less-favored trading nations, and he took a pot shot at the college professors who held opposite views, calling them "intellectual oddities." In one of his final speeches on the subject in 1945, Knutson tried to puncture the arguments of liberal trade advocates by insisting tongue in cheek that their promised prosperity had already materialized. [19]

Though the issue of trade became critical, the question of war debts and reparations dominated the foreign economic scene between the two wars. During and after World War I, the United States loaned the Allies just over $10 billion with a 5 per cent interest charge. In the 1920s the hard-pressed Europeans, suffering from the debilitation of war, agitated for a reduction or cancellation of the debts. They advanced the argument that since most of the money had never left the United States, it had served as a powerful stimulant to the American economy, and it should be regarded as a contribution to the common cause of defeating the Central Powers. [20]

The French offered to reduce their large share of the reparations bill of nearly $32 billion to Germany to a more reasonable level. But the Americans argued that a loan was a loan; unless the Europeans repaid it, the American taxpayer would have to foot the bill since the sums had been largely raised through the sale of Liberty bonds. Furthermore the debtors had fared far better than the United States at the peace table and had reaped the spoils of war. The United States kept the pressure on, but failure of the European states to pay forced a moderation of the American position. Between 1923 and 1926 decreases in the interest rate charges were negotiated, reducing total debt payments from Britain by 30 per cent, from Italy by 80 per cent, and from France by 60 per cent. Efforts were made to soften the economic burden on Germany with loans from the United States to help provide the wherewithal for reparations payments. This was essential, as the French made it clear that they would pay only as they were paid.

In the seven-year period from 1924 to 1931, an economic revival in Germany caused American private investors to lend that country over $2 billion; in the same period the European debtors paid the United States some $2 billion of their war debts. Thus it was that American investors lent money to Germany, which paid a portion of its reparations to the major Allied powers who in turn paid a share of their debts to the American treasury. But the world-wide depression exacerbated the dilemma, and President Herbert Hoover finally declared a one-year moratorium on war debts in 1931. When Roosevelt came to office, a multipower economic conference convened in London in June, 1933, full of high hopes. It eventually collapsed without conclusions or recommendations. By 1934 all the debtors except Finland had defaulted on their payments, and for all practical purposes the war debts were defunct.

In retrospect one can say, as most expert observers did, that a wiser course of action for the United States would have been to cancel the debts and reap the rewards of a more prosperous Europe. But the American taxpayer took a simplistic attitude toward debt, and the more isolationist the country became, the more anticancellationist it was. Harold Knutson fervently espoused this view, venting his ire on Great Britain and France in particular for their refusal to abandon imperialist ambitions and for their guilt in drawing an innocent America into world conflict. He showed no mercy toward efforts to ease the pain of their payments.[21]

Knutson's attitude was clearly revealed in a satirical sketch presented on the House floor, featuring such thinly disguised countries as Andrussia (Russia), Bergentina (Argentina), Zneezokia (Czecho-slovakia), Evadeland (France), and Utopia with a give-away New Deal administrator as the star. In this Knutson playlet the administrator said to the ambassador from Evadeland: "We are always happy to see the representative of the country that dragged us into the war, borrowed our money, and had the courage to tell us to go and jump in the ocean when we asked for payment."[22]

As late as 1937 Knutson insisted that the debts be paid so that these resources could be applied to the needs of the American people. At a time of continuing depression Knutson pointed out that the money owed to the United States could be used to pay off every house and farm mortgage in the country, leaving enough funds to build 48,000 community hospitals. If the money were loaned at 5 per cent interest, that interest would give every old-age pensioner nearly an extra thousand dollars a year. In Knutson's opinion, the nations of Europe were dead beats. The fact that the Europeans could not earn the coin of repayment unless they were permitted to sell their goods in the United States apparently never occurred to the sixth district congressman.[23]

In the mid-1930s Knutson was riding the crest of a revisionist wave regarding the causes the World War I. Public acceptance of revisionism was reinforced by the work of scholars, the writings of poets, and the conclusions of a Senate committee chaired by Gerald Nye that the munitions manufacturers and international bankers had stampeded the United States into war. Scholarly works questioned German provocation, suggested that America could not solve Europe's problems, and deplored the interruption to reform and the infringements of civil liberties caused by the war. A wider audience was reached by writers like Ezra Pound and John Dos Passos who bespoke the widespread disillusionment with America's loss of virtue on behalf of the "decadent and depraved" Old World. Even an expatriate like Ernest Hemingway was moved to say: "But of the hell broth that is brewing in Europe we have no need to drink. Europe has always fought: the intervals of peace are only armistices. We were fools to be sucked in once in a European war, and we should never be sucked in again."[24]

As Knutson came to regard Europe more spitefully and many people in the nation came to view World War I as a disastrous mistake, he found it politic to resurrect and expand his original arguments against United States participation in that war. Sounding more and more like the Charles Lindbergh of two decades earlier, he deplored the abandonment of neutrality as greed for gold had enticed the nation to sell war materials to the belligerents. The culprits, of course, were the "New York international banking crowd" and the insidious propaganda campaign launched against the people and the Congress by the British foreign office. This skillful campaign of falsehood and misrepresentation was reflected in the metropolitan dailies; the rural press, Knutson always held, was more truly representative of American opinion. Congress might not have capitulated had there been a secret ballot on the declaration of war, but Knutson blamed Wilson more than Congress, charging him with a breach of faith regarding his 1916 campaign promise to keep us out of war. The arming of merchant vessels by the president, said Knutson, "gave the administration the incident it needed to get us into the war." [25]

According to the congressman, even more grievous than the bankers, the British, and the big city press in getting the nation into war was the aftermath of that conflict. The United States had not made the world safe for democracy: "The Czar and the Kaiser had been driven from their thrones," but Hitler, Mussolini, and Stalin had taken their places. Democracy had been diminished as dictatorships flourished. Not only had the nation failed to achieve its foreign policy objectives but, said Knutson in 1945, "Anyone with as much brains as God gave geese knows the depression was a sequence of [World] War I." Americans had lost their individuality and their sense of self-reliance; regimentation, spoon-feeding, and dependence on Washington were the undesirable replacements. In a very real sense for Knutson World War I represented America's loss of innocence and the fall of Eden. [26]

The impact of revisionist thought was felt in Minnesota. In 1936, for example, the Minnesota Department of Education issued a three-part correspondence course called "War or Peace." The prime reason for the war, it stated, was economic — the need to continue shipping and trade. Since most of America's trade and loans were with the Allies, pressure from American bankers, manufacturers, and merchants was brought to bear on the government to get into war on the side of the allied countries. The economic benefits stemming from United States entry were manifested in "tremendous" sales, high prices, and "enormous" profits. Unfortunately, the course literature continued, the causes of war had not disappeared with the coming of peace. Trade wars, struggles for colonies, and the need for armies and navies to protect trade and investment still went on. The existence of military establishments serving competing commercial interests could again lead to war. The course material concluded that "until the economic roots of war are eliminated . . . trade rivalries and the rivalry for colonies will be a constant danger to the peace of the world." [27]

Knutson's thinking, which did not have to undergo revision on many of these issues, made him a supporter in 1937 of the narrowly defeated Ludlow amendment which would have reserved the power to declare war to a people's referendum. Writing to a constituent, Knutson said that if "the American people had had that power in 1917 we would not have had this depression which is a direct outgrowth of that war." The prevalence of the revisionist view was also shown in a 1937 Gallup Poll that asked "Do you think it was a mistake for the United States to enter the World War?" No less than 70 per cent answered "yes," it had been a mistake. In Congress reunions were held of those members who had voted against the 1917 war resolution, and Knutson, who for a time was the only House incumbent in the group, enjoyed a kind of patriarchal status. [28]

When Italy invaded Ethiopia in 1935, Congress, haunted by the specter of another impending war in Europe and bolstered by the revisionist fervor permeating the country, hurried to pass legislation ensuring neutrality by placing an embargo on arms shipments to belligerent countries. Surprisingly, Knutson opposed the first Neutrality Act of 1935 on the grounds that an embargo would prevent the United States from helping small countries and other democracies defend their freedom and independence. Harking back to America's revolution, he wondered "where we would be today if France had had such a law upon her statute books in 1776." And he added, "I would not do anything, knowingly, to bring on a war, but I would do everything in my power to help another country retain its independence." [29]

This position was a temporary aberration. By 1937, when the neutrality legislation was extended, Knutson was back on his usual side of the fence. Perhaps the Italian adventure in Africa did not give him cause for concern (except in the aggressive treatment of a weak nation by a strong one), but with the outbreak of Spain's civil war in 1936 and Japanese aggression against China in 1937, he feared the United States would once again be caught in the conflagration apparently sweeping the world. As tensions worsened early in 1939, Knutson called for even more exacting prohibitions against the export of munitions to belligerents. [30]

Shortly after the outbreak of World War II in September, 1939, Roosevelt called Congress into special session to revamp the Neutrality Act of 1937 by repealing the arms embargo. The congressional debate proved to be one of the most significant in American history to that time. Noninterventionists like Knutson argued against repeal because it was a rejection of neutrality obviously designed to help only one side (the Allies), and because it would aid the self-seeking interests of the munitions industries which wanted to get America into the conflict. Applauded when he was introduced as "the only Member of the present Congress who voted against the declaration of war back in 1917," Knutson warned that Wilson had wanted to be neutral but had been deceived by diplomats, munitions makers, and international bankers. Roosevelt, he claimed, was "openly and avowedly pro-Ally. Therefore, I maintain that the danger of being dragged into war under Roosevelt is infinitely greater than it was under Wilson." The supporters of repeal argued that the existing legislation was essentially unneutral in that it served to help the aggressors. Some went so far as to suggest that America's self-interest would be served by a victory for the democracies.[31]

The outcome of the debate was a compromise in which the embargo was lifted, but American ships and citizens were forbidden to enter defined "danger zones." Allied purchasers of war materials would have to operate on a "come-and-get-it" or "cash-on-the-barrelhead" basis. Knutson, who was less than satisfied with these results, offered a substitute resolution on neutrality to stop what he regarded as the unerring course toward war being charted by the president and his secretary of state, Cordell Hull. The congressman was convinced that the United States, no longer neutral by law, was now committed, and he predicted in November, 1939, without too wide a margin of error that America would be at war within six months.[32]

His increasingly rigid stance can be measured by his changed attitude on naval disarmament. In 1922 Knutson had believed that the American people wanted a navy second to none, that it was the best possible guarantee of national security, and cheap insurance at the price. In 1937 the congressman introduced a resolution asking the president to call a conference to consider naval disarmament. As he did so he remarked, "I feel it is incumbent upon America to take the lead in stopping this mad race of armaments." He repeated his plea for disarmament in the 1938 debate on a stepped-up naval building program, which he vigorously opposed. While he was for an adequate navy, he said, he questioned the propriety of America filling the role of "policeman for . . . humanity," and he refused to "become hysterical over imaginary dangers that only exist in the minds of munitions makers." Knutson further asserted that any increase of naval power would play into the hands of other nations — namely, Britain and France — who would have the United States "pull their chestnuts out of the fire." The cost of the program was, in Knutson's opinion, astronomical, and echoing Lindbergh, he claimed, "You are selling our young men and women into tax bondage that will enslave the next three generations." Once again in 1939 he introduced to no avail his naval disarmament conference resolution. [33]

Later in the same year Knutson took a new tack in his efforts to minimize the military impulses toward war by introducing a bill that would have substituted a department of military defense for the existing system and limited its activities to defensive purposes only. Typically and traditionally he inveighed against the distortion in America's priorities: "We sit here and fiddle with airplanes while ten or twelve million men and women are walking the streets looking for work and over 3,000,000 families are on relief. We are fiddling while Rome is burning. My God, have you lost your sense of perspective?" [34]

By 1940 with war raging in Europe, the pressures for preparedness mounted in the United States. Although Knutson criticized the rearmament policy, he voted for many defense measures. He had previously acquiesced in the necessity for a defense apparatus, but he still refused to acknowledge any real danger to the United States, scoffing at the possibility of totalitarian governments invading America. Even after Hitler had secured the continent and the fate of Britain hung in the balance, Knutson attacked all efforts to aid the British. [35]

In September, 1940, Roosevelt, unable to move Congress to action, gave Britain fifty destroyers in exchange for leases on naval bases in the West Indies, Canada, and Bermuda. Knutson was infuriated, not only by the upset in the congressional-executive balance of power, but also because of his certainty that the deal was tantamount to a declaration of war. The destroyer-base exchange was followed in 1941 by an administration proposal to lend arms and other assistance to "any country whose defense the President deems vital to the defense of the United States." The bill, intended primarily for the relief of Britain, was coincidentally numbered HR 1776, and there was much debate as to whether this symbolism was just or ironic. Knutson thought the lend-lease legislation not only ironic but heretical. In his view, there was no cause to aid an imperial monarchy that had welshed on its debts to the United States and on its commitments to guarantee Poland, Norway, the Netherlands, and Greece against nazi attack. [36]

Knutson continued to deny that the United States was in any danger and rejected out of hand the contention that America in the past had been secured by the British navy. On February 5, 1941, he said that the first line of defense was "132,000,000 free men, women, and children, and so long as we remain free and fully protected there will be no danger of invasion." He did not stipulate then what he meant by "fully protected," but eight months later he would credit the American navy which he had sought to disarm as being "our first line of defense."[37]

In October, 1941, the last major battle for isolation was fought when the Roosevelt administration called for modification of the Neutrality Act of 1939 and the repeal of the ban against arming merchant ships. Knutson feared that such action would "greatly increase" the possibility of American participation in the war. As with the previous issues pairing isolationism against preparedness and aid to the Allies, Knutson's negative vote was in vain.[38]

Paralleling these debates was one development which prompted Knutson to take a stand more in keeping with his 1935 protestation of aiding small countries such as Ethiopia to keep their independence and democracies their freedom. In November, 1939, the Soviet Union invaded Finland to seize territories which Finland had refused to cede as part of Stalin's plan to secure Russian defenses against Hitler, his uncertain ally. With "white-clad Finns on skis" using guerrilla tactics in the north and with the well-fortified Mannerheim line in the south, the Finns managed to inflict initial defeats on the overconfident Russians. American sympathy rallied to the underdog; Finland, which had always been prompt in its payments, was granted a moratorium on World War I debts. In addition, Congress made a loan of $30 million for nonmilitary purposes. "The Finns desperately needed airplanes and tanks, not plows and harvesters," but American public opinion would not then countenance more. Finland was overpowered by the "Russian steam roller" in March, 1940.[39]

A month earlier members of Congress must have been flabbergasted to hear Harold Knutson advocate sending the Finns planes and other tools of war. A further surprise must have been his denial that such an act would constitute any breach of neutrality: "It is maintaining an obsolete and unwarranted rule to pretend that neutrality implies absolute passivity. Even a neutral country must have the right, without resorting to war, to do its part to uphold morality and decency in international relations." Knutson justified his support on the grounds that Finland had remained neutral in the larger European conflict; that it was a democracy; that it was the only nation in the world which had not defaulted on its war debt obligations; and that it stood as a bulwark against Russian control of the Scandinavian peninsula and the spread of totalitarian communism.[40]

The conflict in Knutson's position was more apparent than real. Finland was an innocent abroad; France and England were not. The

Russo-Finnish conflict was viewed as a localized issue, and the likelihood of any contagion spreading to involve other nations, including the United States, was remote. One observer of the Minnesota scene has suggested that isolationist sympathy for Finland was motivated in part by the opportunity it gave to criticize the administration's apathy without any need to alter the isolationist position on the European conflict. And, of course, political profit was to be garnered from Knutson's continuing identification with the Scandinavians in his home district.[41]

The Winter War in Finland not only modified Knutson's strict neutrality but even mitigated — if only momentarily — his Anglophobia. In February, 1940, he confessed that "It would be a tragedy of the first magnitude" if Great Britain were to be destroyed, because the consequence would be "the end of democratic and Christian government" throughout Europe. He admitted that there were times when British behavior so irked him that he "could grab the old squirrel rifle off the wall and go onto a little war of my own." However, he was willing to overlook England's outrageous conduct in the interest of preserving "representative and Christian government."[42]

Whatever the degree of Knutson's neutrality, it was completely shattered by the Japanese attack on Pearl Harbor on December 7, 1941. There was little he could say except the obvious — we must "fight back to the limit of our strength." Since Japan had declared war on the United States, the United States had no choice but to declare war on Japan. The vote on December 8 was anticlimactic. The Senate approved the war resolution 82 to 0; the House vote was 388 to 1, with the sole negative vote coming from Jeannette Rankin, who returned to Congress in 1940 and thus voted twice against American participation in world wars.[43]

Once involved in the war, Knutson sounded the trumpet, but not uncritically. Although the war represented a fight to save representative government, he worried over the increase in presidential powers. In the exigencies of a war crisis, he voted for defense measures that included an increased ceiling on the national debt and an extension of the lend-lease program. But by 1944 he was again voting against lend-lease extensions and American participation in the United Nations Relief and Rehabilitation Administration. Times may have changed, but not Harold Knutson. He looked forward to the end of war so America could be "first" again, so there would be butter for citizens instead of guns for soldiers, and so the nation, relieved of the burden of arms and aid, could be solvent. It should be noted, however, that on one issue Knutson did change. He had no quarrel with Roosevelt's executive order which imprisoned Japanese-Americans on the West Coast. In this instance the congressman supported the exercise of presidential power and manifested far less concern than he had in 1917 for the cause of civil liberties.[44]

As early as February, 1941, Knutson had worried that the United States would fight the worst war in history for peace and freedom only to get Joseph Stalin for Adolf Hitler. He saw little difference between communism and naziism except that a nazi could not get a job in the New Deal. In the fall of 1944 Knutson was confident that Marshal Stalin would write his own ticket and that it would be tragic if the states of Eastern Europe were to become "satellites in the Russian regime." Writing at the war's end, he accurately predicted that Germany would be divided between the United States, Russia, and Britain. Like Alexis de Tocqueville a hundred years earlier, Knutson foresaw the day when there would be only two great powers, the United States and Russia. "This may come in about in ten years, and it possibly may take 25, but it is inevitable," he said in 1944.[45]

Knutson hated communism, yet he had a grudging admiration for Stalin as an artful diplomat and a patriot who looked after his own country first. "It is too bad that we do not have at the head of this government a man with equal foresight and force," he observed in 1945. The congressman had no confidence that Roosevelt (or later Harry S Truman) would stand firm before the onrush of Russian imperialism. With the benefit of hindsight, Knutson argued that the United States should have demanded concessions from the Soviet Union when Hitler's troops were at the gates of Leningrad and Moscow. The threat of discontinuing the lend-lease program, he said, could have acted as a mechanism for control. Even in October, 1945, he felt that it was possible to take action: "The plain fact of the matter is that Russia needs us much more than we need her and the time has come to stand up and tell her where to head in." But Knutson had no firm plan for the containment of communism. He rejected war as a solution; while he would have disliked to see Russia take over Asia, Africa, and much of Europe, "I wouldn't give the life of one American boy to save any of them."[46]

With the war at an end in late 1945, Knutson made a lonely effort to rescue the term "isolationist" from disrepute: "An isolationist is one who believes in looking after his own country and his own people first. Churchill is one [of] the biggest isolationists of the day, and so is Stalin, and I hope to God I am, because I believe in looking after the American people." Departing from the new international outlook of his constituents and congressional colleagues, he called for a foreign policy involving the "least possible interference in the affairs of other peoples." Knutson's vision of an inward-turning postwar America was not to be. The war's aftermath generated the most outward-looking diplomatic posture in America's history. The Minnesotan was a man out of step and out of time.[47]

The termination of lend-lease in 1945 jarred the troubled British economy, and America was asked to repair it with a loan of several million dollars. Knutson exploded, "Just what kind of saps do they think we are?" He invoked his old war debt argument and combined a new one — "we shouldn't finance socialism" — with his perennial hatred of Britain to protest the loan. "Millions for relief but not one cent for Socialist or Communist experimentation," he told Congress. He thought the continuing British demands on the United States so ludicrous that they surely could not be serious. "They are clever those English, and they seldom overlook an opportunity to pull our leg," he said. In one sense, however, he felt that the American people deserved it: "Barnum never said a truer thing in his life than when he said that the American people love to be humbugged."[48]

In 1946, a year of transition, it was becoming increasingly clear that expectations of postwar co-operation were diminished by Russia's unwillingness to permit free elections in the nations of Eastern Europe, and that the United States had no effective diplomatic muscle to counter Russian expansionism. These factors gave Knutson an excuse to score the Democratic administration for appeasement and for "allowing a reign of terror." He remained critical in 1947 when a wholesale shift in the tone of United States foreign policy occurred. After the overburdened British told Washington that they could no longer provide support to the Greek government which was contending with communist guerrillas, the United States was shocked into action. Russian interest in Greece, its control of Eastern Europe, and its threats directed at Turkey seemed to verify that Soviet intentions were in truth hostile. President Truman went before a joint session of Congress on March 12, 1947, and asked for an appropriation of $400 million to supply economic and military aid to Greece. The resulting policy, which came to be known as the Truman Doctrine, was based on the premise that totalitarian regimes imposed by either direct or indirect aggression were a threat to international security and thereby also to the security of the United States.[49]

The British withdrawal dramatized the economic plight of Western Europe, and it became increasingly apparent that some sort of drastic effort would be needed to effect recovery. On June 5, speaking at the Harvard University commencement, Secretary of State George

C. Marshall proposed that the nations of Europe come together, devise plans for recovery, and present to Washington a specific statement of their needs. The result was the Marshall Plan, which committed the United States to provide dollars for the economic rehabilitation of Europe. Implicit in both the doctrine and the plan was the containment of Russian aggression and subversion and the assumption of long-term responsibilities by the United States beyond the limits of the western hemisphere.

Knutson opposed the Truman Doctrine on the grounds that it could lead to another war and that the financial arrangements would threaten America's solvency. It was foolish, he maintained, to spend money on containment far from home when communism was making serious inroads in Cuba, Haiti, and other countries of the western hemisphere. If money were to be spent for United States interests abroad, better that it be spent in America's back yard. Knutson regarded the new doctrine as a subterfuge to protect British oil interests in the Middle East. Moreover if communist expansionism were to be stopped, Knutson thought that piecemeal action was an insufficient response. While he dared not say it openly, he hinted in 1947 at a possible nuclear intervention: "We now have the means within our hands to safeguard the future of America for at least a hundred years. . . . If these pools of oil are necessary for our future security let us act, but let us act like men rather than like crawling worms." In arguing against the Greek-Turkish loan, Knutson maintained that "communism is brought on by maladministration, poverty, inequality, and all the other evils that mankind has been affected with since the beginning of time." Believing also that it could not be stopped with guns and bullets, he still found no solace in the Marshall Plan which was designed to remedy some of those same "evils." In 1948, his last year in Congress, he voted against the plan.[50]

Knutson was a lukewarm supporter of the United Nations. He said little about it in its infancy but regarded it as an uncertain experiment. On the one hand, he said in 1948, "All hope and pray that the United Nations may continue to function, gain in power, and to preserve peace"; on the other hand, he said, "if the United Nations should unfortunately blow up, the buildings could be converted to housing purposes." Knutson was one of only eighteen representatives who voted against the Bretton Woods Agreements Act which laid the ground rules for postwar international finance and established the World Bank and International Monetary Fund. His opposition stemmed from a conviction that the United States would provide the money but be denied control.[51]

In 1947 Knutson once again took up the cause of disarmament, but he was moved less perhaps by foreign policy or military considerations than he was by the economic benefits to be gained from international disarmament. If the world disarmed, he thought, the huge portion of the federal budget devoted to defense could be reduced, thus bringing government spending within reasonable bounds.[52]

As he neared the end of his congressional career, his comments reflected his concern for recapturing the values of self-reliance that had sustained America. Knutson, who never doubted that "the danger to the Republic lies within rather than without," ended his political career as an unreconstructed isolationist. First elected on the promise to keep the nation out of war, he stuck by his isolationist guns with only occasional deviations. To Knutson, America was the center of the universe and the sixth congressional district was the heart of America. Until World War II his ideas so fitted the temper of his constituency that he was the only member of the House of Representatives to serve continuously from before World War I to after World War II.[53]

Knutson's ethnic emphases were positive factors in his political success. He took every opportunity to praise the Scandinavians and Germans who populated his district and bragged that Norway, where he had been born, was the birthplace of "democracy, as we understand the term." He was happy to praise the Finns for their superior culture and "their contribution to the development of the great Northwest." As late as 1937, when Hitler's Germany was on the brink of international outlawry, Knutson remarked that the Germans were "as kindly and high-minded as any other people, and in some instances more so."[54]

Knutson was also a virtuoso performer in politics. His political fences were well tended. He got along well with people, he did favors for his constituents, he remembered names, he was friendly and informal. A national magazine once said that he had "a grip on his district that other legislators regard with awe and envy." Obviously he enjoyed being a congressman; his impressive political popularity enabled him to chart an independent course in Washington, an independence that endeared him to the like-minded voters of his district.[55]

Knutson did not achieve national recognition or influence while he was in Congress. He seemed content with the sixth district and the freedom it permitted him. He did serve as vice-chairman of the National Committee to Keep America Out of War and this prominence made him a target of the 1942 drive to purge Congress of the bitter-end isolationists. As early as 1932 — only halfway through his long period of service — the National Progressive League released a three-page indictment of Minnesota's "outstanding reactionary." Ten years later an article in the *Nation* entitled "Keep Them Out: Our Worst Congressmen," placed Knutson first on the list.[56]

Knutson's most important influence on the national scene came late in his career with his rise to the chairmanship of the powerful House ways and means committee, when the Republicans gained control of the Eightieth Congress in 1946. He received the assignment by virtue of seniority, and his colleagues were less than ecstatic about having him fill the choice post. *Life* magazine, calling him "narrow-minded" and "provincial," stated that his isolationism had embarrassed the party and many Republicans would have liked to "ditch him." *Business Week* termed him "volcanic" and reported that Republican leaders regarded the "wild man" as the "biggest obstacle to party harmony."[57]

What Harold Knutson did with this impressive seat of power contributed in no small measure to his subsequent defeat in the next election. He forced through a tax cut which in turn necessitated reduced appropriations and gave Truman grist for his campaign mill as he toured the country castigating the "do-nothing" Eightieth Congress. On November 2, 1948, the incumbent president, doomed by every prior expectation to defeat, was victorious, and Harold Knutson lost his congressional seat to Fred Marshall, the candidate of the Democratic-Farmer-Labor party, by 4,407 votes. Four years after he left Congress, Knutson died of a heart attack in Wadena. The *New York Times* obituary quoted him as saying that the tax reduction he had championed "helped lick me."[58]

Unlike Lindbergh, whose radical isolationism embraced the progressive thinking on domestic reform issues, Knutson "became one of the most solid reactionaries, isolationists and high tariff advocates there was in Congress."[59] "Isolationism," the *St. Cloud Daily Times* of Knutson's home district pointed out on October 28, 1948, shortly before the election, "has been a dead duck since our experiment with it back in the twenties. There is no safety in burying our head in the sand and pretending that we have no responsibility for the rest of the world." As the United States moved from a reluctant to a more enthusiastic participation in the world community, Harold Knutson neither had the wish nor did he see the need to revise his beliefs. His isolationism became increasingly conservative and, in the end, unacceptable to the voters of the sixth congressional district of Minnesota.

Chapter 4

THE POLITICAL ENIGMA
OF HENRIK SHIPSTEAD

*"I believe the best way to save democracy abroad is to
save it first at home."*   HENRIK SHIPSTEAD, 1939.

ON THE SENATE SIDE of the congressional aisle during many of the
years Knutson served in the House sat Henrik Shipstead, who represented Minnesota for the twenty-four years from 1923 to 1947. Like
Knutson, Shipstead became increasingly conservative in his economic
and political views, but like Lindbergh, he was a loner. When he
found Republican programs and policies inadequate to the cause of
domestic justice, he joined the Farmer-Labor party which magnetized
men of protest and reform. When the latter suffered disgrace and
disrepute in the late 1930s, Shipstead returned to the Republican
fold. Although he spent eighteen of his twenty-four senatorial years
under the Farmer-Labor banner, it was his 1945 vote as a Republican
against the ratification of the United Nations Charter that precipitated
his defeat in the 1946 GOP primary.

Shipstead was born in 1881 in Burbank Township, Kandiyohi
County, Minnesota, to Norwegian immigrant parents. He grew up
on a farm with eleven brothers and sisters and early showed an intellectual bent, carrying books while he plowed and reading while the horses
rested. After completing his early education in New London, Minnesota, he attended St. Cloud State Normal School where he prepared
to become a teacher. "Some of my pupils," he once observed, "were
bigger than I was, and some of them actually knew more than I did.
But I taught them and they taught me. By and large, we both
benefitted." His interest in dentistry as a career was aroused by a
dental student he met on a farm where they were both working one
summer, and he entered the dental school of Northwestern University
in Chicago in 1900. After receiving his degree in 1903, Shipstead
returned to Minnesota, established a practice in Glenwood, and married in 1906.[1]

Henrik Shipstead's political career began in 1912 when he served
as president of the village council of Glenwood, presided over the

charter commission, and later became the newly incorporated city's mayor. In the same year Shipstead, then a Republican, announced his candidacy for the state legislature, but he failed to win the nomination. After serving two terms as mayor, he was elected in 1916 to the state House of Representatives, where he caucused with the liberal faction. The dentist from Glenwood had apparently settled into the comfortable life of professional man and responsible citizen.

The outbreak of World War I changed the pace of Shipstead's sedate career. As controversy swirled around the organization and program of the Nonpartisan League, Shipstead was among its defenders. In the 1918 primary he received the league's endorsement for the United States House of Representatives, running against Andrew J. Volstead for the Republican nomination in the seventh district in the same violent campaign which saw Lindbergh lose his league-backed race for the governorship. Though Shipstead's house was painted yellow by league detractors, he like Lindbergh refused to arm himself. "I move too slowly," he said. "By the time I could get my gun out, it would be too late. I go armed with philosophy." Shipstead lost the election, polling 16,775 votes to Volstead's 19,552.[2]

Both the state Nonpartisan League and the Working People's Non-partisan League gave him a second try in 1920 by choosing him as their candidate for governor. Years later J. A. O. Preus, Shipstead's opponent, said that Nonpartisan League founder A. C. Townley was primarily responsible for securing Shipstead's endorsement. Historian William W. Folwell, who was a Shipstead contemporary, thought that "the Nonpartisan leaders picked Shipstead because he was good-looking, affable, an entertaining speaker, and a good vote getter rather than because of his knowledge of and experience in agriculture." A later scholar suggested that Shipstead "had captivated the League leaders with his simplicity in manner and speech and with his air of humility." The 1920 primary campaign was even more bitter than that of 1918. Shipstead was charged with advocating free love and Bolshevism; his opponents claimed that if he were elected, he would confiscate all the property he could lay his hands on.[3]

The hostility of the established political order to Shipstead's candidacy was exemplified by an editorial in the *Minneapolis Journal* of June 7, 1920, which protested that it did not have anything against Shipstead personally, but that as the endorsee of the Nonpartisan League, he represented "a vicious and dangerous scheme of government." The simple question confronting the voters of Minnesota, the editorial went on, was whether they wanted the government of the state turned "over to the Nonpartisan League, to the Socialist schemers who dominate it, to the projects of exploitation and heavy taxation."

Despite such campaign innovations as painting his name on an airplane and dropping league leaflets from it, Shipstead lost the primary to Preus by 133,832 to 125,861 votes, a narrow margin that was quite a blow to Shipstead who thought he would win. One friendly observer asserted that the defeat was partially due to a million-dollar slush fund raised by Shipstead's opponents and to the use of private police hired by big business to intimidate voters. Depressed but undaunted, the handsome dentist broke with the Republican party and filed in the general election as an independent. In spite of the continued backing of the Nonpartisan League, he was decisively defeated by Preus 415,805 to 281,402 votes.[4]

The Republicans, entrenched for years in Minnesota with no serious opposition, passed a new primary law in 1921 to stem the tide of Nonpartisan League challenges within their party. Under its provisions a potential office seeker could not file for a primary election if he had opposed the regularly nominated candidate of his party in the last election. This, of course, was aimed at preventing Shipstead from running in the 1922 Republican primary because of his 1920 campaign against Governor Preus. The new law also demanded that each voter in the primary declare his intention to support whichever candidate was nominated. There was nothing in the legislation, however, to prevent Shipstead from running under another label, and by this time the Farmer-Labor coalition had in effect become the state's second party.[5]

After the 1920 election, discouraged by defeat, scorned and boycotted in Glenwood because of his association with the Nonpartisan League, Shipstead moved to Minneapolis to set up a new practice. It was there in 1922 that his luck changed. Senator Frank B. Kellogg was renominated by the Republicans. The farmers (Nonpartisan League) and the workers (Working People's Nonpartisan Political League), again meeting separately, found common cause in their nomination of Shipstead. The 1922 senatorial contest in Minnesota attracted national attention because of the Farmer-Labor party's entry into American politics and because of the Democrats' distaff nomination of Anna Dickey Olesen as Kellogg's opponent.[6]

Although incumbent Senator Kellogg believed himself to be sympathetic to agrarian interests, he could not escape the fact that as an exceptionally successful corporation lawyer he was a vivid symbol of the privileged class. There was surface symbolism, too. Kellogg rode in a chauffeur-driven Pierce-Arrow; Shipstead drove an old Ford into a town, addressed the people on economics, took up a money collection for tires and gasoline, and moved on to the next community. Though his campaign oratory centered on the depression in farm prices which had struck in 1922, Shipstead also sounded a warning about war and peace reminiscent of Lindbergh and Knutson. "The conditions that led up to and got us in the world war still exist," he said. "We are economically and politically entangled in foreign alliances and intrigues of foreign nations. American diplomacy and foreign policy must be divorced from Wall Street influences."[7]

Shipstead's cause was assisted by the hostility between Kellogg and Governor Preus, who had wanted the senatorial nomination but was chosen again for the gubernatorial post. In his campaign Preus usurped some of the Farmer-Labor party platform in an effort to undercut the movement. The Republican party, composed of both conservative and liberal elements, did not present an unbroken front against Shipstead. Some prominent Republicans, like Representative Thomas D. Schall of the tenth district, supported him. Kellogg lacked the personal magnetism either to draw his party together or to campaign effectively.

As a result, Shipstead trounced both Kellogg and Mrs. Olesen on whose behalf William Jennings Bryan had come to Minnesota. The vote was 325,372 to 241,833 to 123,624, respectively. It was Preus's view that Minnesota's Germans were important in Kellogg's defeat as they expressed their antagonism to the wartime repression of Burnquist's public safety commission by voting for Shipstead. Although Magnus Johnson, the Farmer-Labor choice for governor, was beaten by the incumbent Preus, 1922 marked a rise in the fortunes of the third party. In addition to Shipstead, the state's voters sent three Farmer Labor backed legislators to Congress, twenty-four men to the state senate, and forty-six members to the lower house of the legislature. Arthur Naftalin asserted that Minnesotans were showing their political independence in this period by supporting a third party.[8]

Whatever the reason, Minnesota had elected its first Farmer-Labor senator — the only non-Republican to hold that office since 1863. Surprisingly, Shipstead was at once placed on the prestigious foreign relations committee, a seat he was to retain throughout his Senate career. There is some speculation that the powerful, conservative chairman, Henry Cabot Lodge, put him on the committee so he could not make radical mischief on the committees concerned with domestic issues. Shipstead informed Lodge that he was proud to have the appointment, but that he would not "let up on being hostile and disagreeable and mean and nasty to the Republican and Democratic parties. I will *not*. I am a Farmer-Laborite and I am against both old parties, and I want it understood that I am." Lodge was reported to have laughed and remarked, "tell the Senator that he is put on the Committee not for himself, but in recognition of the great party which he represents." Some observers of the Washington scene enjoyed Shipstead's personal declaration of independence, and Will Rogers quipped, "Shipstead is the only Senator in Washington who can hold a caucus in a telephone booth."[9]

Although he had been billed as a wide-eyed radical, Washington soon learned that Shipstead's radicalism was not explosive. His sallies into political rhetoric were frequently interspersed with homely references to his father's enthusiasm for William Jennings Bryan and to his own admiration for John Peter Altgeld, the radical turn-of-the-century governor of Illinois. The senator's personal habits were reserved and courtly; his conservative and correct deportment greatly disappointed Washington society which had expected him to storm the capital sporting overalls and shouting slogans. Referring to the discrepancy between his actions and the labels applied to him, Shipstead said, "It doesn't necessarily follow that a radical has to be a damned fool."[10]

Shipstead's radicalism was essentially confined to agrarian interests and foreign affairs. In both areas his philosophy flowed from Thomas Jefferson's principles which he regarded as "the definitions and axioms of free society," believing with Jefferson that democracy was contingent upon a free and prosperous agriculture. The freedom of the worker to organize was, in Shipstead's view, dependent on the freedom of the farmer. The ills of agriculture stemmed from dependence on the railroads, an excess of industrialization, and a failure to give farm products equal tariff protection under the law. The forty-two-year-old freshman senator's conception of foreign policy was also rooted in his belief that freedom was the essential ingredient of rational and moral action, that Europe was the antithesis of the United States and could not be expected, therefore, to pursue foreign policies in the interests of mankind. Like Jefferson, Shipstead's distrust of Europe — a continuing thread in the warp and woof of his isolationism — stemmed from a firm conviction that Europeans were circumscribed by their history, their diplomacy, and their greed. These were apparent, he felt, in World War I and its aftermath.[11]

As Shipstead saw it, the real tragedy of the war was that the Allies had broken faith with the United States by their actions in forcing the Treaty of Versailles upon Germany, thus making the victory one of conquest rather than one of "peace without victory," which was the professed intention of Woodrow Wilson. "Peace on any other basis than that of justice is slavery," said Shipstead, as he argued that the settlement had sown the seeds of the next war. The European victors, he pointed out, could scarcely wait to acquire their winnings from the vanquished Germany as they "took the German colonies of Africa and Asia, the oil fields of Mesopotamia, and other possessions." When France sent troops into the Ruhr region in 1923, Shipstead's reaction was similar to that of Knutson. France had showed its determination to destroy Germany and revealed to the world "the armor of imperialism and conquest. As such she is a menace to all humanity, endangering the peace of the world," said the senator in 1924.[12]

Like Lindbergh, Shipstead distrusted the banking and financial circles of the United States, castigating them for putting their money on the Allies to win. When it appeared that they had backed a loser, he said, "they had to rush $40,000,000,000 of the American people's money, and sacrifice 150,000 of the 'flower of American youth,' to fix the horse race so that the horse upon whom they had placed their money could win."[13]

The senator from Minnesota held no brief for the League of Nations, viewing it as a "superdictatorship" which established the newly aligned victorious countries in the guise of a peace organization to sanctify and guarantee the "loot" of war. He insisted that "it is an organization for carrying on war against any state that refuses to bow to the will of this superdictatorship of the world."[14]

One reason why Shipstead so vented his wrath on the League of Nations was his great objection to Article 231 of the Treaty of Versailles, which justified the crushing war payments demanded of Germany by finding that nation guilty as charged with starting World War I. This article was a particularly bitter pill for Germany to swallow, and the hostile feelings it aroused were slow to ebb. Beginning in 1928 Shipstead, whose sympathies had been revealed in his protest over France's occupation of the Ruhr in 1923, introduced a series of resolutions calling for revision of Article 231. They were justified, he asserted, by evidence "showing that the said article 231 was based on hysteria, hypocrisy, and falsifications 'forged in the fires of war.'" This resolution and its annual successors came to naught. In 1931 he took a different tack with a resolution absolving the United States of any responsibility for Article 231. When that was defeated in a Senate floor vote by 64 to 10, he introduced another to refute Senate acquiescence "even by implication" in the charge of German war guilt. This, too, failed to pass.[15]

Shipstead's antipathy to the League of Nations extended to the question of American participation in the Permanent Court of International

Henrik Shipstead,
about 1930.

Justice. Commonly called the World Court, the body was established under the Covenant of the League of Nations, although its membership was not restricted to that of the league. One diplomatic historian has noted that "Unlike the Hague Court of 1901, which provided panels of judges for special tribunals, the World Court was a permanent body for the settlement of international disputes. Its creation owed something to the example of the United States Supreme Court and much to the inspiration and leadership of American legalists." [16] There had been public agitation for membership since the court's inception, and there were political figures who, although against United States membership in the League of Nations, were for its adherence to the court. The Senate finally took up the treaty early in 1926.

Shipstead opposed the court because he considered it out of harmony with American constitutional traditions. On the crucial issue of compulsory or optional jurisdiction, Shipstead believed that if the court came to be dominated by optional jurisdiction, it would simply "fade away"; if it were to be dominated by compulsory jurisdiction, "we shall be surrendering a larger and larger proportion of our American independent sovereignty." The senator shared the fear that the court issue was part of a larger scheme "suggestive of ignominious furtiveness" to sneak the United States into the league through a back door "marked 'Entrance of mandates and money lenders.'" Despite the ferocious opposition of Shipstead, who offered several reservations, and the thinning ranks of the "irreconcilables," the Senate voted 76 to 17 to adhere to the World Court. In the end, however, the isolationists succeeded in attaching five reservations to the treaty; the fifth one so severely limited the court's jurisdiction that it was forced to reject the terms of United States membership. Between 1926 and 1935 efforts were made to moderate the obstructing reservation and to reopen the issue. Shipstead never veered from his original opposition. He referred to the court pejoratively as a "gold brick," as a "poisonous fungus," and as part of a "system antidemocratic in character and which aims at a system of imperialistic superdictatorship . . . extending its autocracy over the world."[17]

As Shipstead stood solidly against the League of Nations, the World Court, and German war guilt, so, too, did he align himself with other midwestern progressive isolationist thinking. He opposed conscription, for example, and regarded universal military service as "the foremost weakness of all our modern political development." Concerned that conscription was the most powerful weapon in the arsenal of the modern state, he introduced a measure which would have authorized the president to propose an international treaty abolishing all military duty. Nothing came of this effort, however.[18]

Shipstead was also skeptical about disarmament conferences. While applauding the idea, he feared that the conferences themselves were not honest efforts to prevent war, but were held only to set the rules of the game so that in future wars killing would be conducted "in a nice, humane, and orderly manner." Still he was sufficiently optimistic to introduce resolutions in 1925 and 1926 calling on the president to initiate negotiations. None of them passed. In 1930 representatives of Britain, France, Italy, Japan, and the United States met in London and agreed on a treaty presumably limiting naval expansion, although the upper permissible limits were beyond what Japan and the United States presently possessed. The five-power naval pact ran into trouble in the Senate as its members, including Shipstead, tried without success to get President Herbert C. Hoover to submit the background papers on the conference. Hoover's refusal was regarded as an infringement on Senate authority to ratify treaties, but the agreement was finally approved by a vote of 58 to 9. Although Shipstead could not register his vote by virtue of a general pair with two absent senators who would have voted affirmatively, he announced that had he been free to do so, he would have voted against the treaty.[19]

Senator Shipstead voted in 1929 for the ratification of the Kellogg-Briand Pact which purported to outlaw war, but he later became dubious about its effectiveness. "Under the guise of self defense, wars of conquest can still be carried on," the *New York Times* of February 7, 1932, quoted him as saying. Believing that the people as a whole were pacific in nature, he placed much higher hopes on insulating America from future wars by the requirement of a public referendum before Congress could declare war. Like Harold Knutson who supported the Ludlow amendment in the House, Shipstead was one of several coauthors of comparable resolutions introduced in 1939 by Senators Robert La Follette of Wisconsin and Gerald Nye of North Dakota. Following in the Lindbergh tradition, he was also one of the cosponsors of another 1939 resolution initiated by Homer T. Bone of Washington which would have imposed a severely high tax rate on munitions industries to take the profit out of war.[20]

But Shipstead placed his prime hope for peace on the economic power of the United States. For more than a decade beginning in 1925, he argued that by organizing this power into a coherent program, America could "dictate peace to the world for the next one hundred years." Instead of assuming "an abject, creeping, crawling, cringing, dollar complex by salaaming to the opinions of the diplomats, the bankers, and the imperialists of Europe," the United States should offer dollars for disarmament. He suggested that loans to the nations of Europe to finance productive industries, to build homes, and to buy food should be provided in exchange for the dismantling of the European military establishment.[21]

Except for this innovative deviation, the senator from Minnesota was one of the anticancellationist isolationists on the war debt issue. In the matter of German reparations which were so intimately tied to the war debt quandary of the Allies, Shipstead protested in the *New York Times* of July 11, 1932, that they were a "dishonest claim" involving the erroneous assumption that "Germany was solely guilty of starting the war" — a position consistent with his unsuccessful quest to rescind or revise Article 231 of the Versailles treaty. Yet he opposed the proposed American loans to Germany to help in their payments, because he believed they were engineered "by the Morgan syndicate of American bankers," and would only draw the United States more tightly into the meshes of the imperial governments of Europe. More particularly he was against any program that would be of even indirect benefit to France. Shipstead regarded Hoover's 1931 call for a moratorium on war debts as another in a long series of shams which would do nothing to alleviate the reparations burden on Germany or to reduce its arms build-up. In that economically depressed year, the senator echoed the recurrent theme of the domestic reformer: "I think economic salvation, like charity, should begin at home." [22]

In order to counter a proposed extension of the moratorium in 1932, Shipstead, harking back to his dollars-for-disarmament scheme, introduced a resolution that would have canceled all outstanding debts owed the United States if each European nation reduced military expenditures by 5 per cent a year for ten years and signed a treaty abolishing conscription and ending Germany's reparation obligations. Shipstead was incensed that the debtor nations chose to arm and not to pay, pointing out that the payments of debtor countries to the United States amounted to less than 3 per cent of their budgets and only 13 per cent of the money they spent on armaments. In his opinion, the United States, while paying lip service to disarmament, was actually financing the rebuilding of Europe's armies by refusing to insist on payment. [23]

In the mid-1930s when the reparations issue was essentially moribund, Shipstead proposed legislation and made speeches urging that the debts be converted into engraved bonds of small denomination as permitted in the treaties. These bonds could then be used by American tourists in Europe and by international merchants. The result would be a balancing of the financial accounts and a stimulation of international trade. If Europe still refused to pay in money, the United States would accept European-held islands in the western hemisphere such as Jamaica, Trinidad, and the Bahamas, "in payment for all or part of the debt." [24]

Though this might have appeared to be an imperialist bent for the acquisition of territory, it most assuredly was not. Shipstead was especially critical of United States interventions in Latin-American affairs, dissenting from the foreign policies that prevailed during his time in office and vehemently defending the rights and liberties of the states south of the Rio Grande. During the first quarter of the twentieth century, the Caribbean had become virtually an American pond. Following the acquisition of Puerto Rico in the Spanish-American War and the establishment of a protectorate over Cuba in 1901, United States interests were firmly established with the perpetual leasing of the Panama Canal Zone in 1903. In the first years after the turn of the century, there was almost continuous unrest in Central and South America. Revolutionary situations in certain of these countries appeared to threaten American interests and security and provided foreign powers with a possible excuse to intervene. Under the Roosevelt Corollary to the Monroe Doctrine, established by Theodore Roosevelt in his 1904 message to Congress, intervention by the United States as an international police power was justified to maintain order. In 1912 United States marines occupied Nicaragua and retained command there until 1933; in 1915 naval intervention in Haiti put that country under United States supervision until 1934; and a year later the marines were sent into the Dominican Republic, where they remained until 1924.[25]

Shipstead challenged Theodore Roosevelt's policy of making the United States the "policeman of the western continent." He considered it a manifest perversion of the Monroe Doctrine, saying in 1927: "Today the Monroe Doctrine remains only as a diplomatic subterfuge. Its ideals are being used as a cloak to cover acts subversive of human liberty and contrary to the institutions and tradition of our nation." He accused the state department of acting as a "commercial agency and diplomatic referee" for North American business interests in Latin America. He had no use for such "dollar diplomacy." While he admitted that certain material advantages did accrue to Latin America, he was more concerned about the morality of the United States. "The country that denies freedom abroad has lost freedom at home," he declared.[26]

Shipstead questioned the rationale of each United States intervention. In the Dominican Republic, the official justification was to put down bandits, but, as the senator mused in 1928, "It is a strange coincidence that we did not hear anything about bandits in the Dominican Republic until sugar went from 3 or 4 cents a pound to 26 or 27 cents a pound, and sugar lands became very valuable." The same year he said of Haiti: "In the constitution we wrote for them we incorporated a provision that foreigners could own land, and it was necessary to have marines at the polling places to keep the people quiet." American intervention in Nicaragua in 1926 was on the pretense of a communist conspiracy. In 1932 Shipstead pointed out that "We then changed the policy and decided we were not there to drive out communists and to stop this conspiracy, but we decided we were there to control an election." [27]

The senator believed that the use of American troops for intervention or small wars without congressional approval constituted a dire threat to congressional authority as provided in the Constitution — an issue which was again to surface with greater urgency in the late 1960s and 1970s. He also questioned the propriety under international law of intervening in order to protect American life and property in the event of civil strife. After returning from a Caribbean tour in April, 1927, he observed that the United States would be suspect in the area as long as the marines were there; he hoped American policy would move in the direction of good neighborliness, pointing out that "the time is coming when we will need friends." [28]

Two appropriate initiatives, in Shipstead's view, would be restoration of the integrity of the Monroe Doctrine, and building on the existing treaty of amity to encourage a federation of Costa Rica, El Salvador, Honduras, Nicaragua, and Guatemala, which would help stabilize the area. In 1960, thirty-three years after this Shipstead proposal, these republics with the encouragement and assistance of the United States took a first step by organizing the Common Market of Central America. Shipstead did not know that his fellow Minnesotan, Secretary of State Frank Kellogg, would soon go a long way toward the senator's first objective by implicitly disavowing the Roosevelt Corollary in a 1929 statement that was not to become public knowledge until 1943. [29]

As Shipstead aired his suspicions of the League of Nations and the World Court, insisted that the Europeans pay their debts, called for disarmament and other devices to prevent war, and objected to United States intervention in Latin America, his popularity in Minnesota was undiminished. Though ostensibly a Farmer-Labor senator, he was never closely associated with the party or its policies. He clung tenaciously to his political independence, and although he earned the ire of his party, the independent-minded Minnesota electorate cheered him on. The veteran political reporter, Charles D. Cheney, observed in the 1940s that "Henrik Shipstead is a visible proof that Minnesota is an unbossed state. In his long senate career he never had support from the would-be bosses in his own party. He has gone it alone." Though there was some agitation in Farmer-Labor circles to replace him with a man more responsive to party dictates, no levelheaded politician chose to cross him. A *New York Times* article speculated that if Shipstead had run as a Republican in 1928, he would have drawn so much voting strength from the Farmer-Labor party that it would have been destroyed. [30]

The senator's partisan intentions kept both friends and opponents on edge. From 1928 until 1940 he followed a tactic of delay and confuse; he would file for election at the last moment and rumors would abound — would he file as a Republican, would he retire. Some political reporters intimated that this encouraged many aspirants to file for office, thereby dividing Shipstead's opposition. But he never had primary opponents worth fearing until the 1946 election, which he lost.[31]

In 1928 he was an easy primary victor (86,093 votes to 9,529) over William Watkins, whose basic support came from the extreme leftists in the Farmer-Labor party. In the general election that followed, Shipstead trounced Arthur E. Nelson, a Republican and a former mayor of St. Paul, by 655,169 to 342,992 votes. Despite charges of a deal with George F. Cashman — the Democratic candidate who withdrew in favor of Shipstead late in September (probably to gain Farmer-Labor support for Alfred E. Smith, the Democratic presidential candidate) — the total is particularly impressive in light of the fact that every other Farmer-Labor candidate but one was defeated in the 1928 election. Furthermore Shipstead carried every county in the state, every ward in Nelson's city, and all but one in his own city of Minneapolis. His power base was firmly rooted in both rural and urban Minnesota. As early as 1930 the *Minneapolis Tribune*, which had crusaded against Shipstead when he first sought national office, gave him a reluctant compliment even as it denounced the Farmer-Labor party. "True, we don't recall any more loyal or efficient representative of Minnesota than Senator Shipstead," the paper said editorially on June 27, 1930.[32]

Henrik Shipstead again won his party's endorsement in 1934, though by a close margin, probably because he pursued his independence to the point of greatly embarrassing Floyd B. Olson by giving him a tardy and halfhearted endorsement for his gubernatorial re-election bid in 1932. Francis H. Shoemaker, former Minnesota congressman and former resident of Leavenworth penitentiary, opposed Shipstead unsuccessfully in the primary. Shipstead ignored both his party and its platform in the general election contest against Einar Hoidale, a Democrat, and N. J. Holmberg, a Republican. The Farmer-Labor platform repudiated capitalism and called for its abolition, a radical sentiment not shared by Shipstead. His stance had little effect on the outcome, for, as former Governor Preus pointed out, Shipstead apparently began ignoring platforms as early as 1920. The senator's political appeal was so widespread that Franklin Roosevelt, who was expected to endorse Hoidale on a visit to Minnesota, withheld any endorsement and included both candidates on the presidential train. Holmberg garnered 200,083 votes, Hoidale 294,757, and Shipstead was returned to office with 503,379, the largest vote received by any candidate in the 1934 Minnesota election.[33]

Shipstead won these elections by using the same tactics. He campaigned on a program of domestic reform and improvement (a field beyond the scope of this book to which he devoted most of his energy in Congress) and a foreign policy which was tailor-made for Minnesota. He drove an old car through the country and into the small towns, speaking informally everywhere he went. The farmers, many of them of Scandinavian descent, flocked to him, attracted by his ideas, his isolationism, and his individuality. With an acute sense of public relations, he took great care to cultivate his image as the staid and wise statesman. Even before television made an attractive physical appearance more important in political campaigns, Shipstead saw to it that his pictures made him "look like a matinee idol of the Greek god type," as the *New York Times* of October 11, 1928, put it. Judging from the campaign photographs, one would be inclined to agree that the senator had indeed found the fountain of youth.

In 1940 Shipstead filed for re-election as a Republican; the prodigal son had returned. In 1936 Governor Olson had died of cancer and without his energetic leadership and firm hand on party dissidents, the Farmer-Labor organization had collapsed and was virtually dead by 1940. Under Elmer A. Benson, who succeeded Olson as governor, "forces of internal confusion, disorganization and collapse" plus left-wing infiltration caused the party to disintegrate as an effective political force. A communist attempt to take over the party caused many rank-and-file Farmer-Laborites to flee to the Republican camp.[34]

In a 1940 newspaper announcement of his filing, Shipstead hinted that he had contemplated defection as early as 1934 because he regarded the Farmer-Labor platform as "communistic and un-American." In 1936, he continued, he had demanded a house cleaning of "subversive influences, communistic leaders and racketeers," but "This promise was made to me but never kept." He regretted that "the leadership of the party of the farmers, the workers and the small business and professional men which I helped to form has been taken over by a small group of selfish, greedy, and subversive men who are neither workers nor farmers and seem to owe little responsibility to either group." Although his first stand in twelve years on a presidential race was for Franklin Roosevelt in 1936 (which may have been a tit for tat thank-you to FDR for refraining from endorsing his Democratic opponent in the 1934 senatorial contest), Shipstead asserted that he had voted for the GOP ticket in 1938. He also reminded the voters of his earlier affiliation with the Republican party — "the party to which I belonged for many years."[35]

Even though the *New York Times* had carried on October 8, 1939, a Shipstead announcement that he would run as an independent in 1940, people were not prepared for the shift. According to a front-page story in the *Minneapolis Star* of August 1, 1940, his decision to run as a Republican "stunned men and women in Republican, Farmer-Labor and Democratic parties alike as he set off the bomb and the reverberations went thundering over the state." Shipstead's popularity followed him into the Republican camp, and he devastated the opposition. In the primary election with eight candidates, Shipstead polled 168,876 votes and his closest rival, Martin A. Nelson, polled 97,812. In the general election, Shipstead's 641,049 votes led Farmer-Labor Elmer Benson's 310,875, Democrat John E. Regan's 248,658, and the Trotskyist Anti-War party Grace H. Carlson's 5,743. His total was more than the other three combined.[36]

The turmoil of Minnesota politics in the 1930s was matched by the turbulence in the world. Japan invaded Manchuria in 1931, Italy attacked Ethiopia in 1935, and Hitler entered the Rhineland in 1936. The Spanish civil war became international with Hitler and Mussolini aiding the rebels led by General Francisco Franco and the Soviet Union assisting the "Loyalists." Emboldened by success, Italy, Germany, and Japan expanded their conquests until, pressed to the limits of compromise and accommodation, Britain and France declared war on Germany on September 3, 1939.[37]

In this period the United States was in a generally isolationist mood, attempting to insulate itself from involvement through the nostrums of neutrality. A number of components were present in the isolationism of the 1930s: ethnic isolationists among German-Americans who remembered the hysteria of World War I and among Irish-Americans who never forgot the "English excesses on the Ould Sod"; radical agrarian isolationists who still feared involvement might result from the machinations of bankers and munitions makers; intellectual isolationists who protested militarism and war as corrosive of civil liberties and domestic reform; and conservative isolationists who believed war would be accompanied by more spending, heavier taxes, bigger government, and greater exercise of presidential power.[38]

Spokesmen in the Minnesota congressional delegation reflected these national sentiments. Republican William Pittenger, a Harvard Law School graduate who represented the eighth congressional district for fourteen years between 1929 and 1947, asserted in 1931 that "We have been led into the mire and the quicksand of European problems" and "We had better begin to look at world affairs from the standpoint of what is good or what is bad for America and not from the standpoint of the international financiers." Republican August H. Andresen, who served the first district for thirty-three years in Congress, castigated the international bankers in 1932, terming them "parasites on society" and calling the foreign policy experience of the United States "disastrous." In 1935 Senator Thomas Schall said that before 1917 the United States was "the Hercules of the nations of the world," but "because we tangled ourselves up in a European war," we were now suffering the consequences of poverty and hard times. Senator Ernest Lundeen, one of Schall's successors, commented approvingly of the idea of a "fortress America." "Here, standing on our own soil, we are invincible. Here we are unconquerable. Beyond the oceans, no man knoweth what the issue will be," warned Lundeen in 1938. And from Senator Shipstead came the question as late as February, 1941, "Can we inspire and inject into the human soul the principles of democracy, and eliminate the pagan philosophy of nazi-ism and communism and fascism by going all over the world with bombs and sticking people with bayonets?" Disillusionment and economic depression reinforced tradition, and the *Minneapolis Journal* of November 12, 1936, expressed the widespread sentiment: "We are determined that never again shall American boys shed blood in the cockpits of Europe." [39]

What one writer has termed the "storm-cellar" decision for neutrality came as close to being unanimous as any major policy in United States history. Despite the national and nonpartisan votes for neutrality in the acts of 1935, 1936, and 1937, there is evidence that, as in 1917, the strongest holdout for isolationism remained the Middle West, where it was reflected in public opinion polls and congressional voting. One study of votes in Congress between 1933 and 1950 located the preponderance of isolationist sentiment in the region consisting of Ohio, Michigan, Wisconsin, Minnesota, Iowa, North and South Dakota, Nebraska, Kansas, Wyoming, and Idaho. In the two-year period immediately preceding Pearl Harbor in 1941, votes to strengthen United States preparedness and to assist the Allies reinforced the conclusion that no other section of the country could match the isolationism of the Middle West. Of the Minnesota delegation in Congress only Farmer-Laborite John T. Bernard, representing the eighth district from 1937 to 1939, voted against neutrality legislation. He did so in a dramatic solo protest against the Spanish Embargo in 1937, and later that same year he was one of thirteen congressmen who voted against the third Neutrality Act. From 1939 through 1941 the nine Minnesota representatives (eight Republicans and one Farmer-Laborite) voted with rare exceptions in accord with isolationist doctrine. On a dozen relevant bills before the House only Pittenger, Richard T. Buckler, by then the lone Farmer-Laborite, and Melvin J. Maas occasionally veered from the line. [40]

On twelve roughly comparable bills in the Senate, Shipstead was consistent in his opposition to measures strengthening United States defenses and aiding the allied nations fighting Hitler in Europe. Although his newly appointed fellow senator from Minnesota, Joseph H. Ball, was charting a very different course after 1940, there was still validity in Henry L. Stimson's 1938 criticism of midwestern sentiment. "We have a little ring of fresh-water statesmen," he said, "who have tried to exclude the fact there was a world outside the salt water." [41]

Like many of his isolationist brethren, Shipstead viewed World War II as a rerun of 1914–18. When Britain and France censured Italy for the invasion of Ethiopia in 1935, Shipstead charged that the whole business was nothing but a plot to get Italy some spoils and still save face in the League of Nations. He worried that the United States was again being wooed into a war "which is none of our business." In his opinion, the Japanese invasion of Manchuria in 1931 had similarly been none of our business, and if the Chinese failed to use their resources in their own defense, "they can not expect us to squander ours in their behalf." Harking back to his long-held contention, he blamed Hitler's rise to power in Germany on the failure to revise Article 231 of the Treaty of Versailles. [42]

Shipstead and his like-minded colleagues worked vainly to avoid American participation in the war. In 1939 he voted against the fourth Neutrality Act which repealed the arms embargo; in 1940 he voted against the bill establishing conscription and supported a measure that would have limited the size of the army; and in 1941 he was back on his old track of supporting the Nye Resolution which would have required a public referendum on foreign wars. In the same year House Resolution 1776, the lend-lease bill, empowering the president to give all aid deemed necessary to any country whose defense was vital to the United States, was at issue. Shipstead's chief objection lay in the extraordinary discretionary powers it conferred on the president. The senator compared lend-lease to an act which gave Hitler the emergency powers that allowed him to impose a dictatorship over Germany. He called the proposal "A bill to surrender all that has made 1776 the most glorious year in American history." Despite Shipstead's objections to "the most monstrous legislative formula ever proposed in the Congress," lend-lease — to the salvation of Great Britain — became the law of the land in 1941. [43]

In many of his pre-World War II protestations, Shipstead reiterated his fears of bankruptcy, depression, dictatorship, and the death of democracy. In early January, 1941, a group of prominent Minnesotans who favored aid to Great Britain sent the senator a telegram asking for a clear statement of his views about the role of the United States in the war. Shipstead replied in part: "You are deeply troubled about what may happen to Britain and certain other European countries. May I suggest that the time is here when we should all be deeply troubled about what may happen to the United States and its democratic institutions. . . . I apologize to no one for thinking of my country first." He resented and rejected the allegation that Britain was America's first line of defense, saying "I do not like to see Uncle Sam skulking between the hind legs of the British lion." As long as the nation possessed a strong navy and air force, it was invulnerable, and "The defense of the United States and the Western Hemisphere, in my opinion, is all we can undertake." Shipstead never pretended to understand the rationale of American intervention in the war, including the position taken by many fellow Norwegian-Americans. He countered those opponents of his position with the question: "Do you believe that it is our duty to rearrange the boundaries and the economic and political systems of the various countries of Europe and Asia?" [44]

Shipstead's intransigence raised a storm in Minnesota, which was caught up in a great isolationist-internationalist debate. Under the new Republican leadership of Governor Harold E. Stassen and Senator Joseph H. Ball, party support for isolationism was waning. Other protests against isolationism were emanating from the urban press, especially the Cowles newspapers of Minneapolis, and from the Committee to Defend America by Aiding the Allies. That organization, a rallying point for Minnesotans who refused to accept the isolationist prescription, had as its members a small but influential group recruited from the business, professional, and academic sectors of Minnesota, mostly in the Minneapolis community. Evolving in the late 1930s and early 1940s was a new coalition of liberal Republicans and Democratic intellectuals who lived in an urban, industrialized society and who rejected, because it was not part of their experience, the agrarian precepts that had previously characterized the state's Republican and Farmer-Labor parties. [45]

After Pearl Harbor, Shipstead, like other isolationists, felt compelled to vote in favor of the resolutions declaring war, as well as measures increasing the country's defense capability and mobilizing small business facilities for a war economy. He could not, however, bring himself to support conscription, and in October, 1942, he again voted against selective service as he had in 1940. [46]

As the possibility of peace emerged in 1944, Shipstead worried that history would repeat itself and that the postwar settlement would be vindictive. He expected Europe to continue to play the game of power politics. He could see no evidence to suggest that economic exploitation, which he, like Lindbergh, regarded as the cause of struggle and war, would cease; by the end of 1945, as the war settlements were being worked out at allied conferences in Tehran and Yalta, Shipstead saw his worst fears coming to pass. Like Knutson, he warned that the peoples of Europe and Asia would be transferred "from the hands of one dictator into the bloody and tyrannical hands of another. . . . Our 'justice' has become a masterpiece of mockery. . . . The 'interim agreements' . . . have become brutal, immoral, and uneconomic absurdities." [47]

If history remembers Shipstead for any single act, it will probably be his vote — along with that of North Dakota's William Langer — against ratification of the United Nations Charter on July 28, 1945. Unlike the League of Nations, the new organization was not tied to the peace settlements, but Shipstead argued that since it was to enforce the peace, one had to know first what these settlements would be. "The final agreements are still in the womb of the secret conclaves of power politics of the three great powers," he said in 1945. He thought the Charter so vague that it was virtually devoid of meaning: "Who among us here can honestly say . . . that he knows what it means, what it guarantees, against whom its sanctions are directed, or how it will prevent war?" He held the classic isolationist fear of a superstate. "Have we, through our diplomacy and our participation in international politics," he asked, "become so enmeshed that it is now impossible for us to maintain our political independence on a basis of justice and peace, or are we now at the end of the rope as an independent nation?" [48]

In a long and rambling critique in 1945, the senator from Minnesota proposed three conditions for American participation: first, that the right of withdrawal which was not provided for in the Charter be regarded as "inherent in the very concept of sovereignty"; second, that the Monroe Doctrine be held inviolate; and finally, that any armed forces furnished the security council "shall at all times and under all circumstances be completely under the control of the United States Government." In sum, the senator from Minnesota opposed the United Nations as a superstate, as a perpetuator of the inevitable evils of the coming peace treaties under a five-power alliance, and as an unlawful entity under the Constitution. [49]

Senator Shipstead noted that the debate between isolationists and internationalists had ended in 1941. He believed that since the United States had devastated Europe by liberating it and had created a vacuum by annihilating Germany, it had a responsibility to help the peoples of Europe recover and to make sure that the power vacuum was filled not by totalitarian concepts but by democratic ones. As early as 1943, when the Allies were hopeful of continued co-operation with the U.S.S.R., Shipstead anticipated that the Soviet Union might be coy with those who had invaded Russia in 1918. A year later he expressed concern over Russian influence and intentions in Eastern Europe.[50]

By 1946 Roosevelt's dreams for continuing harmony among the "Big Three" — Britain, the Soviet Union, and the United States — were shattered; Russia was pursuing a course of seemingly unabashed expansionism. Shipstead's worst fears were being realized. He noted that instead of saving democracy in World War I, communism had been established in Russia, fascism rose in Italy, and naziism had come to Germany; now through a repeat performance of war and secret agreements, the world had simply substituted Russian tyranny for German totalitarianism. Furthermore, according to Shipstead, the United States, by agreeing to the Moscow Declaration and by ratifying the United Nations Charter, had signed "a blank check," which had been filled in at Yalta when Franklin Roosevelt agreed to Russian protection of Outer Mongolia, Russian control of Manchuria, and Russian ownership of the Kurile Islands in exchange for Stalin's promise to enter the Pacific war. The Soviet Union won at the bargaining table what Japan had hoped to achieve by war. Shipstead concluded that "these betrayals have made possible Russian conquests that outrank the greatest conquests in history." Any incipient internationalist leanings he had collapsed with the rising fortunes of the Soviet Union. His hopes for a peace conference that would see all armies withdrawn from all nations, that would begin disarmament and end conscription, were colored by a persistent conviction that civilization had already been destroyed.[51]

His pessimism was out of tune with the optimism and ebullient character of the new Republican party fashioned and dominated in Minnesota by Harold Stassen, governor from 1939 to 1943, war veteran, delegate to the United Nations Charter conference in 1945, and confirmed internationalist. Shocked out of its isolationist posture by war, Minnesota was no longer a bastion of isolationism. Edward J. Thye, Stassen's successor in the governorship, was hand-picked by Stassen to challenge Henrik Shipstead in the Republican primary of 1946. So changed was the atmosphere in the state that Thye was thought to be a sure winner over Shipstead.

The veteran senator concentrated his efforts in the rural areas where isolationism still had pockets of strength, and the battle was on. National attention was riveted on the campaign because it represented what seemed at the time to be the last-ditch fight of isolationism against internationalism in Minnesota, and because it was regarded as a test of Stassen's political strength. Contradictory but valid reports said that "Minnesota is by no means as isolationist as many misinformed Easterners might suppose," and that Shipstead's "intransigent isolationism was no handicap in the German and Scandinavian areas of Minnesota, where isolationism is still a potent force." The *Nation*, once an admirer of the Minnesotan, lamented, "The sad truth is that of the old Shipstead only the passionate isolationism remains." [52]

Not enough passionate isolationists remained in Minnesota to offset the new internationalism or to resist the efficiency of the Stassen-Thye organization, and the Honorable Dr. Henrik Shipstead, United States senator since 1923, suffered the ignominy of being thrown out of office in a primary election by a vote of 238,210 to 160,619. The man who had carried every county in the 1928 general election won only twelve counties in the 1946 Republican primary. Years later Shipstead explained his defeat largely in terms of his vote against the United Nations Charter. Yet he continued to justify his position, saying in 1953, "After serving for 24 years on the Foreign Relations Committee of the Senate, I could not do otherwise than oppose it." In the 1946 campaign, he did not merely defend his vote against the United Nations Charter, he proclaimed it. The veteran political reporter, M. W. Halloran, observed, "It was sometimes difficult to tell whether the United Nations or Stassen, accused as a dictator, was the principal issue in the campaign." [53]

Henrik Shipstead was an enigma in Minnesota politics. His early radicalism was never fulfilled; indeed, as Malcolm Moos and E. W. Kenworthy said, it "grew fat and lazy." Yet he endeared himself to dairy farmers of the state with his successful fight for a tax of ten cents a pound on colored oleomargarine and by his long-time support of the rural electrification program. Merchants applauded his persistent efforts to get approval for dredging a nine-foot channel in the Mississippi River from St. Louis to Minneapolis, thereby greatly enhancing the development of inland waterways for commercial purposes. He also advocated the construction of the St. Lawrence Seaway. In the field of conservation, he foreshadowed the wilderness concept by successfully cosponsoring with William I. Nolan of the fifth district the Shipstead-Nolan bill in 1930 to protect and conserve land and water resources in the Rainy Lake area on the Minnesota-Ontario border. However, no important foreign policy legislation bore his name. He opposed United States participation in the League of Nations and the World Court; he opposed America's entry into World War II; and he opposed the United Nations. Interestingly, he had insisted in 1926 that he was "not an isolationist in the proper use of the term."[54]

Shipstead distinguished between political isolationism which he admitted and economic isolationism which he denied. But he was not entirely consistent in his views on trade, and his switch was based on his reading of agrarian interests. Even though his campaign literature of 1922 asserted that high tariff walls "raise prices to consumers" and "make monopolies richer and people poorer," his last campaign piece in 1946 bragged that his demands for higher tariffs on farm products had been among his distinguished services to the farmers of Minnesota. On the other hand, in 1930 he argued that the Smoot-Hawley high tariff bill was "one of the greatest and most vicious isolationist policies this Government ever enacted." He called the act "a form of isolationism to which I never subscribed," and opposed it because it would shut farmers out of needed overseas markets.[55]

The essence of his ideas on foreign relations encompassed an intense fear of war, an aversion to the corrupt diplomacy and governments of Europe, a hatred of the powers of financiers, and a desire for America to stand perfected as an ideal for the world. His hatred of war was rooted in its wasting of life and in its destruction of democracy. His compassion was real and so was his conviction that war would give the coup de grâce to the freedoms essential for a democratic society. From the shambles of two wars, he saw totalitarianism arise, and he concluded that battle did not serve the cause of democracy.[56]

The Minnesotan held to the historic American view that the conniving of European nations condemned them to continual warfare. United States intervention in their wars and in their dealings could not redeem Europe but would simply sully America. Shipstead's suspicions of the manipulators of wealth came out of his experience that midwestern values and those of the East were contradictory. He clung to the belief that America could remain safe in its continental fortress until after World War II, when the image of Russia stretching from the Pacific to the Baltic upset his conception. Even then he felt that American economic power should be used as a quid pro quo for disarmament, that the United States could rectify the continuing disarray among nations if it stood alone and perfect as an example to others, using its resources and persuasions to bring justice and peace to the world. But this admission of limited international commitment was never backed by legislative action. He did not perceive that any other nations shared the same values nor that co-operation or alliance might serve the cause of peace that he espoused. He resisted change. In his fourth term his rhetoric was no different from that of his first term, nor was his vote.

A 1946 article in *Harper's* attributed Shipstead's "political longevity . . . to his unexampled ability 'to walk from Carlos to Washington and back on sucked-out egg shells without cracking a shell.'" Less sardonic but more explicit was the judgment of Floyd Olson's biographer, George H. Mayer, who wrote that Shipstead's appearance and manner "helped to nourish the myth that he was an elder statesman who decided every question on its merits. His carefully cultivated candor on small matters concealed a disposition to equivocate on large issues, which was all the more effective because it was done with an olympian disdain that the voters mistook for independence." His personal attention to the needs of his constituents, as with all effective politicians, was an important ingredient of his success.[57]

Shipstead returned to Minnesota, where he lived out his last years and where he died on June 26, 1960 — the fifteenth anniversary of the signing of the United Nations Charter. The state's newspapers paid him cautious tribute. The *St. Paul Pioneer Press* recalled that he was "once among the senate's most powerful members." The *Minneapolis Star* said that "Mr. Shipstead was a towering figure in the state's political history." The *New York Times* remembered his independence: "Politicians attempting to assess his popularity with the voters as a lone wolf circulated the story that when he prayed, he always began, 'Lord, this is Shipstead speaking.'" Changing times diminished the eulogies. The *Minneapolis Tribune's* epitaph seems most fitting: "Even those who opposed Mr. Shipstead most vigorously found much to respect in him. There was a rugged sincerity about him that attracted many persons. Yet the voice of isolationism which he raised belonged to another era. And it seems, at his death, a distant one indeed."[58]

Chapter 5

THE IMPASSIONATE DIPLOMACY OF FRANK B. KELLOGG

"I have confidence in mankind and I am happy that I have been privileged to participate in the conclusion of a treaty which should make it easier for men and women to realize their long cherished ideal of peace on earth." FRANK B. KELLOGG, 1928.

THE SEEMINGLY UNBROKEN LINE of Minnesota's isolationist representation — however diverse — was interrupted by the public career of Frank B. Kellogg. He was a Republican and a traditionalist. He did not share Charles Lindbergh's radicalism, and he commented that his onetime political foe represented "nothing except all the follies and absurdities of every 'ism' imaginable." Although he won his public reputation as a trust-buster, he earned his private wealth as a highly successful corporation lawyer. While he had supported Theodore Roosevelt in his 1912 quest for the presidency, he maintained a surface neutrality and did not join the Progressive party. Kellogg was far less parochial in his views than Harold Knutson and far more the party loyalist than Henrik Shipstead.[1]

Since his entry into elected office coincided with the beginning of World War I and since he served subsequently as ambassador to Great Britain and as secretary of state, it is not surprising that he supported a measure of involvement with the world that went beyond that of Lindbergh, Knutson, and Shipstead. It was not an involvement that he wished to impose as had his predecessor, Cushman Davis, or one that he wanted to see institutionalized as did his successors Joseph Ball, Harold Stassen, and Walter Judd. Though he was not an imperialist, the young Kellogg (doubtless influenced by Davis, who was his older cousin and senior law partner) had not been immune to the expansionist fever of America's war with Spain. Public sentiment, he was confident, supported America's acquisitions of Hawaii, the Philippine Islands, Puerto Rico, and Cuba.[2]

If his internationalism in the interwar period was not as fully developed as that of his Republican successors in Minnesota, it was also less exuberant than that of Davis. In a very real sense, Kellogg was a steppingstone between the imperialism of the 1890s and the internationalism of the 1940s and beyond. He tried to moderate some of the more blatant forms of American imperialism; he tried to secure amity among nations even though his perceptions of the causes of tension were superficial; and he tried to substitute judicial and legal instruments for war even though his proposals were timid and ineffective. Kellogg's foreign policies were often simplistic, less sophisticated and complex than those that would be developed by internationalists of another generation. Yet they represented an outreach as extended as the prevailing temper of Republican politics and mood of national isolation probably would have tolerated in his day.

Frank Kellogg was born on December 22, 1856, at Potsdam, New York. When he was nine years old, he and his family moved to Olmsted County, Minnesota. After finishing common school, he worked on the family farm until he was nineteen. He then found the opportunity to study law in Rochester, and after two years of preparation, passed the bar examinations, set up practice in partnership with Burt W. Eaton in 1880, and was successively elected Rochester city attorney and Olmsted County attorney. After he had successfully prosecuted his first big case (dealing with a railway bond issue) in which he had consulted with Cushman Davis, Kellogg was invited in 1887 by Davis' partner, Cordenio A. Severance, to become the third partner in their St. Paul law firm. At the age of thirty-one, Kellogg and his bride of a year, Clara M. Cook, moved to the state's capital city. There he and Severance handled much of the business of the new partnership, while Davis was fulfilling his responsibilities as the newly elected United States senator from Minnesota.[3]

After Davis' death in 1900, Kellogg, following in his partner's footsteps, became active in Republican politics. He served as Republican national committeeman from 1904 to 1912, but it was the practice of law which propelled him to national prominence. A St. Paul newspaper, believing that its paper supplier was violating the provisions of the Sherman Antitrust Act, asked Kellogg's help. He confirmed its suspicions and advised the newspaper to ask the United States government to prosecute. Kellogg was designated a special assistant attorney general to try the case in 1906, thus earning his first spurs as a trust-buster. His subsequent successful prosecutions of the Harriman railroad interests and Standard Oil gave rise to rumors that he was being considered for high appointive office. But none of these materialized. Widespread word that Kellogg, a friend and supporter of Theodore Roosevelt, would ascend to the United States Supreme

Court was unfounded, and Roosevelt's intention to make him attorney general could not be implemented after Roosevelt's defeat in his third-party bid for the presidency in 1912.[4]

Nevertheless, Kellogg could take considerable solace from the recognition of his peers in his election to the presidency of the American Bar Association that same year. With the upcoming election of 1916 in which Minnesotans for the first time would vote directly for their senators and with disaffection in certain circles for the incumbent, Moses E. Clapp, Kellogg was subjected to considerable pressure to announce his candidacy. Finally late in 1915 he issued a statement of declination which prompted words of regret from Republican Senator William E. Borah of Idaho, who wrote, "you have a host of friends who recognize your great ability and would have been glad to have your services for the country." Nor was the controversial westerner the only one who regretted the decision. Over seventy editors of Minnesota newspapers banded together and signed a petition asking Kellogg to reconsider. Upon this expression of support, he succumbed. From California where he was vacationing, Kellogg sent a telegram to Robert C. Dunn, one of the editorial petitioners, authorizing the announcement of his candidacy. He wrote his friend, Dr. William J. Mayo of Rochester, that he had misgivings about this decision "but everyone must do his share." Throughout the remainder of his life, it was this sense of duty coupled with a faintly disguised ambition which made him a captive of public service against his often-expressed desire to return to private life.[5]

During the entire course of his career, Kellogg was sensitive to the nuances of public opinion, and he was not above trying to influence newspapers to his side. Early in 1916, worried about the possible impact of the *New York Times* on his electoral chances, he wrote a friend asking that the editors be apprised of his positions on preparedness and the Philippines in the hope that they would not oppose him because they knew him only as a "trust-buster." On the other hand, he fretted that he did not want a lot of New York papers supporting him lest it appear that "Wall Street was trying to put me over in Minnesota." He felt that his strong card was the backing of many country papers. Kellogg also benefited from the political acumen of his skillful campaign manager, Charles J. Moos, whom he later rewarded with the postmastership of St. Paul. Among the volunteers in the campaign was Henrik Shipstead, who succeeded Kellogg in the Senate six years later.[6]

As the clouds of World War I rolled ever closer, Frank Kellogg carried out his promise to campaign on issues, not personalities. He was a sound, if not stimulating, advocate of preparedness. "I talked preparedness in nearly every speech," he wrote to Charles Evans Hughes, the Republican candidate opposing Woodrow Wilson for the presidency — preparedness, economy in government, antitrust prosecutions, and a reasonable reduction of tariffs. In a draft of a letter to Lindbergh, who was one of his primary opponents, refusing an invitation to public debate, Kellogg protested that Lindbergh misunderstood his positions: "On careful reading of my statements on preparedness any fairminded person will be convinced that I am anything but a militarist, that in fact, I propose the rich carry the financial burden of preparedness in order that the blood of the poor will not be spilled later on. . . . I advocated a tariff board consisting of experts in order that our economic conditions would be bettered. My speeches during the past ten years in favor of government regulation of trusts are an open book." On the other hand, his friend Theodore Roosevelt wired that it was a "good omen that you should have won on preparedness." [7]

Win he did, in surprisingly easy victories in both the primary and general elections. But Kellogg was out of the pattern of Minnesota politics at the time he won his Senate seat. His primary victory was partly the result of a four-way race that included incumbent Senator Clapp, Lindbergh, and former governor, Adolph O. Eberhart. Similarly in the general election, he won over Democrat Daniel W. Lawler and Prohibitionist Willis G. Calderwood, whose combined votes exceeded Kellogg's by about 10,000. [8]

In the Senate, Frank Kellogg set about fulfilling his promises. The preparedness issue did not confront him. By the time he took office the issue was war and he voted to go to war. He also supported war revenue taxes on business and wealth rather than "upon the great toiling masses of the Nation" and he favored expanded trade. Like Davis, he was overly sensitive to the importance of foreign commerce on the economic health of the United States, although like Lindbergh, his attitude toward the tariff was protectionist for the farmer. [9]

Kellogg failed in his initial ambition to become a member of the Senate foreign relations committee, although his senior colleague, Knute Nelson, had assured him that there would be "no trouble" in his obtaining the post and although Roosevelt intervened on his behalf. Later he refused to promise committee chairman Henry Cabot Lodge that he would support his decisions and carry out his policies in exchange for a seat on the committee in 1918. It was not until early in 1921, long after the Senate had rejected the Versailles treaty, that he achieved the coveted membership. [10]

In his famous fourteen-point enumeration of war and peace aims on January 8, 1918, President Wilson had given the Congress and the country his vision of the world after the war. The fourteenth point called for "A general association of nations" to secure "mutual guarantees of political independence and territorial integrity to great and small states alike." It was apparent then, and more so as the negotiations at Versailles proceeded, that Wilson was willing to compromise other issues to gain the establishment of the "association of nations." In the interim, however, the president had weakened his support at home by a series of impolitic moves. For one, even though he had declared politics off limits for the war's duration, he urged the people to elect a Democratic Congress in the fall election of 1918. He got a Republican majority in both Houses. For another, he neither consulted congressional leaders nor invited them to be represented in the delegation to Versailles. (Many noted that President McKinley had appointed two Republican senators — Cushman K. Davis was one — and one Democratic senator to the five-man delegation to the Paris peace negotiations in 1898.) Finally, Wilson himself went to Europe when many thought he should be tending to the nation's business at home.[11]

After more than two months abroad, the president returned to the United States and invited the members of the Senate foreign relations and the House foreign affairs committees to meet with him at the White House to hear a progress report. Six days later, as Congress adjourned, a Republican round robin signed by thirty-seven senators and senators-elect insisted that the Covenant of the League of Nations be considered separately after the treaty of peace. The Senate divisions on this issue were not simple: a protreaty group, all Democrats but one, supported ratification without qualification; the "mild reservationists" favored ratification with slight changes; the strong reservationists, all of whom were Republicans, approved ratification but with many revisions; and the "irreconcilable" senators, led by Borah, opposed ratification under any circumstances. Nevertheless, when a special congressional session was convened in May, it was the opinion of many that the Versailles treaty with the Covenant of the league would be approved.[12]

But the opponents had time on their side, and they made the most of it. Lodge consumed two weeks of Senate foreign relations committee time by reading the treaty aloud. Extensive hearings ate up an additional six weeks. As it became clear that these delays were eroding support, Wilson decided in September to stump the country, but his collapse and subsequent illness destroyed his capacity for leadership.

When the foreign relations committee finally brought the treaty to the Senate floor, forty-five amendments and four reservations were attached. The amendments were rejected because their implementation would have required the treaty negotiators to reconvene. The Senate then appended fourteen so-called "Lodge reservations." Wilson was a stubborn holdout. Although he had indicated that he would be willing to accept mild reservations, he would not permit any weakening of Article X, which bound the United States (and all signatories) to defend the territorial integrity and existing political independence of league members. Even the mild reservationists wanted to modify this article which Wilson considered the heart of the treaty. The impasse was total.

On November 19, 1919, the treaty with the fourteen reservations was defeated by a Senate vote of 55 to 39. Four Democrats joined the Republicans who were willing to accept the reservations, but thirteen "irreconcilable" Republicans, who were against any league in any form voted with the forty-two Democrats who were loyal to their president and opposed to the reservations. Public pressures forced a reconsideration on March 19, 1920, but the outcome was similar. In May Congress passed a joint resolution declaring World War I at an end, but it was vetoed by President Wilson. Finally in the summer of 1921 with Warren G. Harding in the White House, Congress successfully and unilaterally put an official end to the war. In the next month the United States signed separate peace treaties with Germany, Austria, and Hungary. In the years that followed the United States vacillated between ignoring the League of Nations and cooperating with it on selected nonpolitical issues, but the question of American membership was never again seriously pushed.[13]

Senator Kellogg had not been among the 37 who signed the Republican round robin, nor as we have seen was he willing to compromise his independence and follow Lodge as the price of membership on the foreign relations committee. He appeared willing to give the League of Nations a fair trial and he was one of the mild reservationists. In his first Senate speech on the subject on December 4, 1918, when Wilson was on his way to Paris, Kellogg argued that while he did not favor a supergovernment, he felt that a closer relation in a concert of nations would go far to end the "terrible struggles" of war. He believed that public opinion within the United States and around the world supported the general principles of the League of Nations to prevent war. He was not unmindful of the teaching of the founding fathers, but he thought it possible to join an association of nations without jeopardizing national institutions, privileges, and rights. Arguing that some measure of self-defense was necessary and that the growing arms competition must be halted, he could not accept the idea of a world police force. He thought the concept of collective security "impracticable and unthinkable."[14]

Noted Republicans whom he numbered among his friends sought to influence his views on the League of Nations, but they were not of one mind. Elihu Root, secretary of state from 1905 to 1909, was ambivalent; Theodore Roosevelt was wedded to an anti-Wilson peace plan campaign; and William Howard Taft, then president of the League to Enforce Peace, was for a time in almost constant communication with the senator from Minnesota. He urged Kellogg as a Republican lawyer to lead the fight for ratification. Taft argued that it would be an opportunity for Kellogg to take this great progressive step for the country and the party. "Seize it, my dear fellow, and nothing is beyond you," Taft wrote in 1919. It must be said that Kellogg tried, although he made it clear to Taft that reservations were necessary in order to get votes.[15]

During the second week of June, 1919, Kellogg invited Nicholas Murray Butler, president of Columbia University, to a dinner meeting in Washington with Republican senators who presumably favored some sort of league. According to Butler's autobiography, the discussion resulted in an outline prepared by Butler of certain reservations which were then shown to Ambassador Jean Jules Jusserand of France. He, in time, received the assent of the British and French foreign offices to the reservations. Jusserand then went to Wilson and suggested that if the president would allow his supporters to accept those reservations, there would be enough Republican votes to ensure ratification. Wilson refused. In August, Kellogg, again working with Republican colleagues, proposed four minimal reservations to be considered as a basis of compromise with Democratic senators. In a Senate speech Kellogg made it clear that these four reservations were not to be construed as opposition to the League of Nations but as protection of United States traditions, rights, and privileges. The four points were: the United States would be the sole judge of its obligations in the event of its withdrawal from the league after the requisite two years' notice; recommendations of the league council under Article X were to be advisory only, and the employment of American military, naval, or economic forces or sanctions could be authorized only by act of Congress; the United States would reserve the right to determine questions of domestic jurisdiction and neither the league nor any member could make recommendations concerning these domestic questions; and league arbitration or inquiry could not extend to the domain of the Monroe Doctrine.[16]

In January, 1920, the senator from Minnesota was appointed by Lodge to an informal, bipartisan committee which collapsed in disagreement over Article X. In March Kellogg led another vain compromise effort to persuade the Democrats to accept reservations to that article. It was with some reason the senator could write, as he did earlier to Taft, "I have done everything I could to bring about harmony and get the treaty ratified." In the end, although he opposed or supported reservations in one form or another in the days of debate, Kellogg voted for the treaty with the fourteen Lodge reservations. He was clearly impatient with Wilson's intransigence, asserting that reservations were necessary. "I am otherwise willing to go as far as anyone in establishing an effective league of nations and a treaty of peace," he said in 1919.[17]

It seems apparent that Kellogg's enthusiasm for the league might have reached a higher pitch if the traditional executive-legislative jealousy over prerogatives which so often characterizes great issues had been absent, and if a Republican had occupied the White House. After Harding's election in November, 1920, Kellogg wrote Taft that he thought the treaty should be taken up again when Harding took office. "With a foreign commerce which exceeds that of any nation in the world, how is it possible for us to be indifferent to the conditions of Europe? . . . I am not in favor of shouldering all the burdens of Europe or mixing in all their quarrels," wrote Kellogg, "but we ought to belong to a league or association of nations . . . not only to maintain peace, but to restore conditions of stability and credit." Later when he discovered that the new president had "no intention of sending the Versailles Treaty or the League of Nations to the Senate in any form," he expressed his regret that the United States would not be a partner in some sort of world association. Since he was then a member of the Senate foreign relations committee, he would have been in a better position to exert influence on the issue. He accepted the inevitable, opting instead for disarmament conferences and negotiations which might lead to a more or less permanent international forum.[18]

In 1922 Kellogg was confronted with the reality of a campaign for re-election. In his preoccupation with the business of the Senate, he neglected politics. Admitting that he was not paying much attention to the campaign, he concluded that he might be out of the Senate when the returns were in. He was irritated by the prospect of a primary campaign against Ernest Lundeen and Richard E. Titus because of "that fool law of ours." Kellogg did not go back to Minnesota for the primary campaign, which he won easily. He seemed pleased that there would be a three-way general election race against Anna Dickey Olesen, the Democratic candidate, and Shipstead, the Farmer-Labor candidate. "This is much better for me than it would be if they had combined," he told Herschel V. Jones, publisher of the *Minneapolis Journal.* However, a number of factors conspired to make the campaign for the general election more difficult. Especially at issue was the depression in farm prices, and despite Kellogg's declared devotion to the agrarian ideal, he was, in the minds of the voting public, the perfect image of the corporate lawyer. He did not unbend easily, he possessed the surface manifestations of wealth, and his theories about remedial farm legislation did not conveniently coincide with those of either rural or urban voters. Some of his urban supporters believed that he had, as he described it, "joined the farm bloc and supported the bills which were passed simply as a political expediency to placate farmers and that it was a shift from my former attitude. As a matter of fact, from the time I came to the Senate I supported in every way possible all legitimate legislation to aid the farm industry." He insisted that he had prevented more drastic legislation from being passed, a position which increased the enmity of the radical-minded farmers in the Farmer-Labor party.[19]

The hard-fought campaign was intensified in its closing days when Senator Robert La Follette, the controversial leader from Wisconsin, came to Minnesota to stump for Shipstead. La Follette had good reason to campaign against Kellogg, who had presented the Minnesota Commission of Public Safety's resolution to expel the Wisconsinite from the Senate in 1917. Furthermore, the two men had had serious differences over issues of war and peace. La Follette's radicalism, his flamboyant manner, and his stunning rhetoric were in clear contrast to Kellogg's stiffness. And his attack on Kellogg was merciless and personal: "he is by nature a subservient, cringing creature. God Almighty has given him a hump on his back, crouching, cringing, un-American, unmanly," said La Follette. The major Twin Cities journals reacted loyally. The *Minneapolis Tribune* of November 2, 1922, accused La Follette of seeking personal revenge. The real issue, said the *Tribune* three days later, was "between constitutional representative government — real Americanism — and extreme radicalism." The *St. Paul Pioneer Press* of November 2, 1922, maintained that La Follette had "no understanding of those fundamentals upon which American freedom rests."[20]

Kellogg's indifference to the minutiae of politics and his aversion to campaigning were among the debits which must be figured in the nearly 85,000 vote margin of his defeat by Shipstead. To these must be added his voting record on farm legislation which did not convince farmers that he had their best interests at heart, his vote for war which earned him the enmity of Minnesota's Germans, his public support of prohibition which did not endear him to the brewers of his home city, and his moderate internationalism which did not strike a sympathetic note with Minnesotans who were reasserting their suspicions of Europe. On more than one occasion, Kellogg said that he was not disappointed by the result of the election. "My only serious regret is that I think Minnesota is turning to radicalism," he wrote an admirer in 1922.[21]

When Kellogg ended his Senate term in March, 1923, he was sent by President Harding as a delegate to an international conference in Chile. He took the occasion to travel to other South American countries and to visit with their leaders. Both the experience and the exposure later stood him in good stead as secretary of state. Even before he assumed that high office, he was sensitive to the concerns of the Latin Americans, saying "It behooves our people to pay as much attention to the South American countries as possible." He believed that "principal officials like the secretary of state" should travel frequently to those countries because "they appreciate such attention."[22]

Kellogg returned to St. Paul, rejoined his law firm, and anticipated the pleasures of private practice and leisure time for his two recreational interests, horseback riding and golf. The interlude was unexpectedly short-lived. Calvin Coolidge, who succeeded to the presidency upon the death of Warren Harding on August 2, 1923, asked Frank Kellogg to serve as ambassador to the Court of St. James in London. The appointment was a puzzlement. It was not generally well received in the United States, except by Minnesotans who took pride in the recognition of a leading citizen. The accepted explanation was that the president was grateful to Kellogg for his kindness when Coolidge was locked in the obscurity of the vice-presidency, that their views generally coincided, and that Kellogg had the necessary private means to man an important ambassadorial post. Although there were strong protests from insurgent Republicans and some Democrats, Kellogg's appointment was confirmed by a lopsided vote of 75 to 9, despite the fact that both Minnesota Senators Shipstead and Johnson voted against him.[23]

The British press took kindly to the appointment. The *London Daily Graphic* of October 27, 1923, said that Kellogg "comes from a State which hasn't the best reputation for culture or impressiveness. It is full of Swedes . . . Germans, corn belts, small towns, main streets, and uplift societies. But, like Sinclair Lewis, the novelist, Kellogg has managed to live all these things down." Kellogg's ambassadorial career was largely uneventful. The one issue which commanded his attention was the implementation of the proposal formulated by a Chicago banker, Charles G. Dawes, to revise the schedule of reparations payments by Germany to the Allies. Some sort of plan was necessary to get Germany back on its financial feet, and Dawes's report became the basis of an eventual agreement. At a formal conference convened in London to accept the report, Kellogg played a useful behind-the-scenes role in bringing the French and the Germans together. The final act took place in Paris, where the actual divisions of reparations payments were agreed upon according to the protocol of the conference held earlier in London.[24]

Otherwise, Ambassador Kellogg's time was taken up with the day-to-day business of the embassy and a demanding social schedule. He was cordially received by the British, and Mrs. Kellogg's graciousness and charm were helpful in cementing relations on a personal basis. Kellogg's correspondence during this period reveals a continuing commitment to a moderate internationalism. While he still opposed political alliances ("none of them for me"), he was firm in his belief that "we can't ignore the rest of the world in view of our great commercial interests." Though he insisted that "the prosperity of the world is bound to be our prosperity," he failed to turn the prescription around and advise, as some were doing, that the United States cancel the war debts of Europe. His legal predilections made him lean to "the extension of arbitration, and the judicial settlement of disputes between nations." He continued to be concerned about Minnesota politics, and he worried that the organizational energy of the "radicals" might push Minnesota into the La Follette camp in the 1924 election.[25]

After that election in which Minnesota went strongly for Coolidge, rumors began to fly about changes in the cabinet. Kellogg, in a letter to a friend, wrote that he did not want any more public positions. He seemed not tempted in the slightest by the office of attorney general, but "As to the Secretary of State, it is, of course, a very great honor." He ruled out any such possibility, believing that Charles Evans Hughes would stay on and protesting that he had experienced his share of the "glamor and tinsel" of public office. Two weeks later Kellogg received a letter from Hughes saying that he was resigning. "Now the President desires you to take my place," wrote Hughes. "It is my earnest wish that you should do so as you are the best

**Secretary of State Frank B.
Kellogg in 1925**

qualified man in the country by reason of your legal training and broad
experience and your close acquaintance with the developments incident to the formulation and carrying out of the Dawes plan." Hughes
concluded by saying that Kellogg's acceptance of the secretaryship
would be "the fitting crown of your distinguished career."[26]

Evidently Kellogg agreed, although his manner was diffident. Writing to a friend, he said that "much as I desired to retire to private
life, I thought I ought to try it on. I realized the great burdens of
the position, especially following Mr. Hughes, and I did not expect
the newspapers to go into ecstasies over my appointment, as I understand they have not, but I am getting rather callous in my old age
and I will do my best and let it go at that." Another friend, in a
congratulatory letter, probably came closer to explaining Kellogg's
motivation. "I am reminded," he wrote, "of the days when I was
in Washington and you were a Senator, that you told me your dearest
wish was to become a member of the Senate Committee on Foreign
Affairs. Since then your ambition has been gratified in ways unfor[e]-
seen at that time."[27]

The years of Kellogg's stewardship as secretary of state from 1925
to 1929 were marked by "domestic tranquility and international calm,"
although he would not have shared this appraisal.[28] He considered
himself beleaguered and besieged by the issues which dominated the

period: disputes and difficulties in Latin America; uncertainties emanating from the new nationalism in China; continuing controversies over war debts payments by the nations of Europe; modest efforts to enlarge the dimension of disarmament; arbitration and conciliation agreements; the World Court; and the Kellogg-Briand Pact.

Coolidge and Kellogg did not hesitate to call on men of prestige and competence to assist in solving foreign policy dilemmas. It was a practice which served them well, especially in the western hemisphere. Since 1879 Chile and Peru had been embroiled in a dispute over the ownership of the provinces of Tacna and Arica. The United States had attempted to resolve their differences by extending its good offices — to no avail. Feeling that he needed a fresh viewpoint on the situation, Kellogg summoned Henry L. Stimson in April, 1926, to provide a new analysis. Stimson's conclusion that the issue could not be resolved by the preconceived notion of a plebiscite was verified by the failure of the Plebiscitary Commission initially headed by General John J. Pershing. Kellogg expended considerable energy on this issue in his four years as secretary of state, consulting frequently with his predecessors Hughes and Root. He once confessed in a letter to Mrs. Kellogg, "It is the first big job I have ever undertaken and made a failure of." Partition was finally agreed upon shortly after Kellogg left office and Stimson, who succeeded him, praised his persistence in achieving a settlement.[29]

Another knotty problem was Nicaragua. By 1925 when Kellogg took office, the United States had been intervening in Nicaraguan politics for fifteen years. In 1923 the economically and politically immature nations of Central America had signed a treaty of amity, by which they pledged themselves to refrain from interfering in each other's affairs and to withhold recognition from Central American governments established by revolution or *coup d'état*. With help from the United States, Nicaragua adopted new procedures to ensure honest popular elections by ballot rather than by bullet. American marines, who had first arrived at the request of Nicaragua in 1912, departed in August, 1925, following the election of a new administration in 1924. With their departure, fighting broke out, the United States once again interceded, and revolution followed. The United States had two interests in the area: to keep intact the Central America treaty structure, and to preserve the exclusive and perpetual rights, under the Bryan-Chamorro treaty of 1916, for an alternative canal route to the one in Panama through Nicaragua. President Coolidge called on Stimson, whose mission succeeded in stopping the revolution which had engaged the whole country. Sporadic outbursts of guerrilla warfare continued, however, for years to come. Even though orderly elections were held under American supervision in 1928 and 1932 and an efficient nonpartisan constabulary was trained by the marines who were ultimately withdrawn in 1933, resentment against United States intervention was the order of the day.[30]

The situation in Mexico was a mishmash of inept diplomacy coupled with revolutionary nationalism, and land, oil, and religious issues. In the early days of Kellogg's stewardship, American policy, following the lead of an unperceptive American ambassador, James R. Sheffield, was generally aggressive and unsympathetic to Mexican aspirations. Following the appointment of Dwight W. Morrow as ambassador in the summer of 1927, tensions eased, differences were resolved, and American policy became more moderate in tone. Morrow, an unorthodox diplomat, was sensitive to Mexican concerns; his appointment was clearly a credit to the Coolidge-Kellogg talent for recruiting men of private means with a highly developed sense of public service.[31]

One Kellogg biographer asserts that he presided over a "retreat from imperialism in Latin America." Kellogg himself insisted that the United States had no desire for domination in the Latin states, but that it was "hard to make these countries realize that we are not imperialistic and ambitious." In one of his last statements as secretary, he issued a commentary on the Monroe Doctrine which was evidently not communicated; when he asked Stimson to have it released, President Hoover stepped in and demurred, saying that "it might cause embarrassment in other matters." In this document, Kellogg disavowed by implication the 1904 Roosevelt Corollary, which had claimed the right to use the Monroe Doctrine to enforce "good behavior" in Latin America. Kellogg stated that the Monroe Doctrine was not to be understood or interpreted "as inhibiting any form of government which any American Republic might desire to establish for itself." [32]

Finally released in 1943, the Kellogg commentary might be regarded as a fitting if unintentional postscript to the Sixth International Conference of American States held early in 1928. As a gesture of good will, President Coolidge had opened the conference in Havana. But resentment against United States imperialism was intense, and an anti-intervention motion was withdrawn only after Hughes, who headed the distinguished delegation from the United States, had marshaled all his powers of persuasive eloquence. It has been suggested with some justification that the very discussion of the issue "was a step in understanding, if not in accomplishment." Kellogg, who was never impervious to the power of public opinion, can be credited, by virtue of compulsion and choice, with a growing intelligence in dealing with North America's southern neighbors.[33]

Although relations with America's northern neighbor, Canada, were uncomplicated, Kellogg took a great personal interest in that dominion of the British empire. He once said, "I was born near that invisible line which divides (or I should say more properly unites) Canada and the United States and have lived all my life near the Canadian border. . . . we have a treaty engraved upon the hearts of the peoples of both countries which is stronger than any written obligation and the most powerful incentive to peace, that is, the treaty of mutual understanding, mutual respect and admiration." He took considerable pride in the fact that the first degree he ever received was an honorary doctor of laws from McGill University, that the first meeting of the American Bar Association ever held in a foreign country took place in Montreal during his presidency, and that the first exchange of ministers between the two countries occurred during his time in office.[34]

He was eager to initiate the development of the St. Lawrence Seaway project for the mutual benefit of both nations, but he understood Canadian sensitivities, observing "I do not think that too much agitation helps us in Canada." He urged the American minister to Canada to drop a hint to Prime Minister William Lyon Mackenzie King that it would be to Canada's advantage to conclude some sort of agreement with respect to the St. Lawrence "while I am Secretary of State." His only travel outside the United States during his time in office, except to Havana for the Conference of American States and to Paris to sign the Kellogg-Briand Pact (with a stop in Ireland on his return voyage), was to Ottawa — another expression of his personal "touch of sentiment as to Canada."[35]

In the Far East the main object of American diplomacy was to assist in providing stability for China. Kellogg rejected past panaceas of parceling out China "in concessions or by spheres of commercial influence by armed force." No one, he wrote his friend Silas Strawn "was more sympathetic than myself in the movement to restore to China all her sovereign powers and to do everything possible for her prosperity and stability."[36]

Factional strife in China in April, 1926, had interrupted negotiations to revise existing tariff treaties and to consider reforms in extraterritoriality privileges, which exempted American citizens doing business there from Chinese law and taxation. Extraterritoriality cursed America's relations with China from 1844, when it was first imposed, until 1943, when the United States finally and formally agreed to China's judicial independence.[37]

Throughout the Chinese civil unrest of 1925–28, Kellogg exercised great restraint. Although 5,000 American marines were dispatched to China in 1926, their mission was not to influence the course of events, "but only to safeguard American nationals directly threatened." It was Kellogg's view that "leadership inheres in moderation as well as forceful action." Consequently he rejected the importunings of his ambassador (among others) for retribution against the Nationalists because of their attacks on foreigners, including Americans.[38] Ultimately the Nationalist forces under Chiang Kai-shek established, in Kellogg's words, "something of a civil government." Negotiations were resumed, and with American co-operation, China was able to free itself from tariff restrictions which had hamstrung the country economically for generations. The matter of extraterritoriality was thereafter played down. Kellogg's attitude was essentially one of good will, and his policies were consistent with his attitude.[39]

One of the most consuming concerns of diplomacy in the interwar period was to wind down the arms build-up stimulated by World War I. It soon became apparent that the agreements of the 1921–22 Washington conference were incomplete; naval competition had been transferred from capital ships to other fleet categories — destroyers, submarines, and especially cruisers. The Geneva conference was called in 1927 at the instigation of Coolidge and Kellogg to complete the task of naval disarmament. It was attended only by Great Britain, Japan, and the United States, and there was immediate disagreement between the two English-speaking powers over the matter of cruiser tonnages. The issue could not be resolved, and the meeting broke up in bitterness. In the aftermath Kellogg, writing to Coolidge, blamed the British navy which "has gone mad" or British compulsion to continue shipbuilding "to furnish employment. Perhaps both." He especially resented charges that the United States had not done its homework in necessary advance preparations; when Vice-President Charles Dawes seemed to admit as much in a speech, Kellogg called him "an unmitigated ass."[40]

Although the secretary of state had advocated United States membership in the World Court in his first public address after taking office (Harding had submitted the protocol to the Senate in 1923), he moved cautiously out of deference to senatorial sensitivities. The Senate approved the preliminary memorandum on January 27, 1926, by a vote of 76 to 17, but attached five reservations. The most important of these provided that no advisory opinions affecting the United States could be entertained without its consent. Since this would have required the acquiescence of the forty-seven member nations, it served to prevent American membership. In 1929, at Kellogg's urging, Elihu Root worked out an acceptable compromise which was submitted to the Senate by President Hoover. Final action on the issue had to wait until 1935, when the Senate fell seven votes short of the requisite two-thirds majority for ratification.[41]

In his last days as secretary, Kellogg wished that he "could have done something in the way of getting into the World Court, getting additional treaties of arbitration ratified by the Senate but I have the treaties made with all South America and most of the countries of Europe and it is doubtful if I could do much more along the lines of peace." In fact he had presided over the negotiation of eighty treaties embracing a wide range of issues. None seemed so important, however, as the one properly termed the Pact of Paris, but usually referred to as the Kellogg-Briand Pact.[42]

The history of the Kellogg-Briand Pact is a remarkable story of private pressures operating on public men. On the one hand, Nicholas Butler and James T. Shotwell of the Carnegie Endowment for International Peace were interested in the concept of the renunciation of war as an instrument of national policy. In Chicago a wealthy businessman by the name of Salmon O. Levinson was espousing the outlawing of war — an approach endorsed by Senator Borah who had introduced a Senate resolution to that effect as early as 1923. In 1926 and 1927 Butler and Shotwell had separate opportunities in conversations with French Foreign Minister M. Aristide Briand to suggest that he make some sort of proposal renouncing war as a policy instrument. Franco-American relations were at a low ebb; France resented America's insistence on war debt payments, and the United States interpreted France's refusal to attend the ill-fated naval disarmament conference in Geneva as hostility to American antimilitary initiatives. On April 6, 1927, the tenth anniversary of America's entry into World War I, Briand in a public address directed at the American people announced France's willingness to join the United States in "any mutual engagement . . . to 'outlaw war.'"[43]

There was no official response. The Briand offer had not been, after all, a communication between governments but rather an address by an official of one nation to the people of another nation. On April 25, 1927, Butler wrote a letter to the *New York Times* asking for a reply to Briand; the state department maintained a studied silence. There was some evidence to suggest that experienced American diplomats regarded the proposal as a negative alliance. The attitude of Secretary Kellogg on this point was quite clear: "we will not under any circumstance commit ourselves to the European system of alliances and counter-alliances to maintain the balance of power upon that Continent." [44]

In the early days of June the American government finally capitulated to the pressures of the French foreign office. There is irony in the fact that the airplane diplomacy of the son of Kellogg's old political enemy should have contributed markedly to the creation of a treaty which Kellogg finally came to regard as his crowning achievement. When Charles A. Lindbergh, Jr., landed at Le Bourget field near Paris on May 21, 1927, it was clear that the cause of aviation had been advanced. It was less clear that diplomacy had been similarly served. Suddenly the world was smaller and the tensions between the United States and France were dissipated in mutual acclaim and pride. The American ambassador to France, Myron T. Herrick, wrote Kellogg that "Lindbergh's coming was just the spark that was needed to light the flame of goodwill which has spread all over the country." [45]

A luncheon given by Briand in honor of the young flier was also the occasion of the first comment by the French foreign minister to an American diplomat about his six-week-old proposal for a Franco-American pact to outlaw war. An editorial in the *Cleveland Plain Dealer* noted that "If Lindbergh's flight to Paris were to bring about a permanent, binding agreement on this point [*outlawing war*], it would have accomplished as much for world peace . . . as it already has for the development of aviation." [46] The rising tide of favorable opinion compelled an American response.

On June 20, 1927, Briand submitted to Kellogg through the American ambassador in France the simple draft of a three-article pact renouncing war, providing for pacific settlement of disputes, and ratification of the pact by each country. A memorandum to Kellogg, prepared by the state department's chief for Western European affairs, essentially opposed the pact, and Kellogg wrote Coolidge that he concurred and planned "no answer to France at this time." On the other hand, he endorsed the suggestion of a universal agreement not to resort to war; "no reason why the United States should not agree with Great Britain or Japan and any other country not to make war," he wrote. The idea of a multilateral agreement had been implanted and was confirmed when Kellogg was led to believe that Senator Borah and the Senate foreign relations committee would approve such a treaty. [47]

Thus on December 28, 1927, Secretary Kellogg proposed to Briand that the two governments "might make a more signal contribution to world peace by joining in an effort to obtain the adherence of all of the principal powers of the world to a declaration renouncing war

as an instrument of national policy." The French counterthrust in
January, 1928, was a proposal for a bilateral pact outlawing "all war
of aggression." After several diplomatic exchanges, the French agreed
to the Kellogg proposition on March 30, 1928, and wheels were put
in motion to solicit Germany, Great Britain, Italy, and Japan as original
signatories along with France and the United States.[48]

Everyone wanted to get on the band wagon. The American ambassador to Great Britain, Alanson B. Houghton, put the matter percep-
tively: "The Secretary has started something going which will be hard
to stop. His proposal may be mere sentimentalism, but it happens
to be the kind of sentiment most human beings share." In a communication to President Coolidge, Kellogg noted that "There seems to be
a very strong desire all over the world to join this treaty. . . . There
is almost universal endorsement in this country and, in fact, I might
say, abroad, as indicated by various parliamentary debates and the
public press."[49]

Nevertheless, Kellogg was confronted with questions of interpretation and threats of reservations from other nations and from segments
of opinion within the United States. The six major issues with which
he had to deal were: self-defense — Kellogg insisted the right was
inherent and there was nothing in the treaty restricting or impairing
that right; the League of Nations Covenant — in Kellogg's opinion,
the Covenant could be construed as authorizing war in response to
aggression but not requiring it; the treaties of Locarno — treaties of
neutrality that Kellogg presumed to be of a similarly defensive nature;
relations with a treaty breaking state — Kellogg made it clear that
abrogation of the treaty would automatically release the other parties
from obligations to the violator; and universality — the secretary of
state, although wishing the treaty to be world-wide in commitment,
did not want to delay its coming into force. Therefore, he proposed
limiting the original signatories to what were then construed as the
six big powers, while leaving the door open to the Locarno treaty
countries. As it turned out, they chose to become original signatories,
as did India and certain dominions of the British empire.[50]

In the United States, Kellogg had to cope with arguments about
self-defense and the Monroe Doctrine. In a letter to Walter Lippmann,
then editor of the New York World, Kellogg devoted three pages to
taking issue with Lippmann's assertion that the antiwar treaty
expressly justified wars of self-defense. "What the new Treaty does,"
Kellogg wrote, "is to throw the burden of proof upon a belligerent
State to show that its resort to war was necessary as an act of self-
defense, and the difficulty of establishing that fact in certain circum-

Kellogg signing the Pact of Paris, August 27, 1928

stances should be an effective deterrent." In correspondence with
Senator Borah and Colonel Robert R. McCormick of the *Chicago Tribune*, he dealt with such objections as the treaty's alleged conflict
with the Monroe Doctrine. He argued that the Monroe Doctrine as
an expression of self-defense was not limited to the United States
itself but could properly be interpreted to extend to "any interests
or rights the United States may have."[51]

On July 13, 1928, the secretary of state wrote to Coolidge, endorsing
the idea that the signing of the treaty be "a solemn and impressive
occasion" penned by the ministers of foreign affairs and that he be
authorized to go to Paris for the event. The authorization was later
retracted by the president who was irate over a recent naval agreement
between the French and the British, but by this time Kellogg was
committed. Coolidge instructed him to avoid comment on any subject
other than the signing of the treaty and not to make his planned stop
in London, a snub made more expressive by his brief visit to Ireland.
The Pact of Paris was signed with appropriate ceremony on August
27, 1928.[52]

The next step confronting Kellogg was the process of Senate
ratification. Though he had been initially optimistic, believing that

"sentiment is so strong in this country" that the Senate could not fail to ratify, there were a few ticklish moments. In general the senators were not hostile, though many considered the treaty of questionable value. Some may have shared the views of New York's governor, Franklin D. Roosevelt, who wrote that "Secretary Kellogg's plan . . . fails in two points. It leads to a false belief in America that we have taken a great step forward. It does not contribute in any way to settling matters of international controversy." Kellogg had to deal with the concerns of conservatives who feared it might constitute recognition of the Soviet Union, who continued to fret about its implications for the Monroe Doctrine, and who worried that it might oblige the United States to use sanctions against violators.[53]

In the end ratification was achieved by a vote of 85 to 1 on January 15, 1929. (The lone dissenter was Senator John J. Blaine of Wisconsin who feared the pact was tantamount to approval of British imperialism.) Ratification prompted this bit of eloquence from Senator Smith Weldman Brookhart of Iowa: "I desire to call attention to the fact that the Union of Soviet Socialist Republics and the United States of America are the only two nations that have ratified the treaty . . . and I hope these two great revolutionary countries will now proceed to outlaw war throughout the world." The following day the president sent a letter to Kellogg congratulating and commending him for his "statesmanlike ability" in negotiating and securing approval of the pact.[54]

In the matter of the treaty, Kellogg had been converted from skeptic to proselyte. In a letter to his wife, he wrote that the pact "will be [the] greatest accomplishment of my administration or any administration lately." He became increasingly assertive in its defense, saying typically that while the treaty did not "constitute an absolute guarantee against war," it brought "every war of the signatories before the bar of public opinion." Like many statesmen of his day, he had a naïve faith in the power of public opinion. Throughout the rest of his life, his speeches were peppered with such statements as "A mighty tide of public opinion has set in which is sweeping through the world toward the goal of peace. . . . The moral influence of an idea is greater than the power of armaments in maintaining peace." Or the elimination of war "will be accomplished when the conscience of mankind is stirred and public opinion revolts against war."[55]

As the storm clouds again gathered in the mid-1930s with Japan's aggression on the Asian mainland, a civil war in Spain, and Italy's invasion of Ethiopia, Kellogg could say of the treaty — in what was probably his last public statement — "Its effectiveness must depend upon a nation-wide, indeed a world-wide public opinion which will demand that the treaty be observed. But the very existence of the Pact, the open acknowledgment by governments of the principle it embodies, — these alone afford a rallying point and a strong foundation for that world opinion." The flaw in Kellogg's optimistic outlook was that world opinion was not then sufficiently cohesive to make its restraints felt. Without organization or power, opinion is amorphous. The Kellogg-Briand Pact represented "the high-water mark of American endeavors for world peace," combining "political and military isolation with that of moral and material involvement." It all too soon became apparent that the pact's pretensions and its weaknesses outweighed its ability to keep the peace. As Kellogg had admitted in June, 1927 — before his conversion to the cause — "What use is there for an agreement that you will not resort to war for the settlement of disputes unless there is some machinery for settling them?" [56]

But before the world caught fire in the conflagration of World War II, Kellogg would receive honors and acclaim for his work in bringing the pact to pass. Foremost among these was the Nobel Peace Prize for 1929, awarded in 1930. As early as May, 1928, rumors were circulating that he might get the prize. In the next year, he conducted a vigorous campaign, explaining "If it were not for the fact that this matter had been advertised all over the world last year, I should not care anything about it now, but to be endorsed last year and not this year would be rather embarrassing." When he journeyed to Oslo, Norway, to receive the prize on December 11, 1930, he traveled not from St. Paul, Minnesota, but from The Hague in the Netherlands, where he had been elected three months earlier to serve as a judge of the World Court. Another Minnesotan receiving a Nobel Prize that same year was Sinclair Lewis, the first American to gain the award in literature. Kellogg was the fifth American to win the peace prize, following Theodore Roosevelt, Elihu Root, Woodrow Wilson, and Charles Dawes. In his acceptance speech, Kellogg warned that "in the end, abolition of war, the maintenance of world peace, the adjustment of international questions by pacific means will come through the force of public opinion which controls nations and peoples — that public opinion, which . . . shapes our destinies and guides the progress of human affairs." [57]

Kellogg spent the rest of his years in unexacting tasks with his law firm in St. Paul and with the international tribunal in The Hague. Ill health forced his resignation from the World Court in the fall of 1935. After Kellogg's death on December 21, 1937, he was buried from the National Cathedral in Washington, D.C., where visitors may see a stained glass window depicting the ideal of universal peace. The accompanying list of Kellogg's accomplishments — senator, ambassador, secretary of state, judge of the World Court, and joint author of the Kellogg-Briand Pact — is the more remarkable for having all been achieved after he had reached the age of sixty. When he became secretary of state, he was the second oldest man to hold the office.[58]

It is the custom of historians to look lightly at the Kellogg years and to term them devoid of accomplishment. But the temper of the times would scarcely have permitted a more aggressive policy. The American people were generally prosperous and content that peace made possible a placid foreign policy. It would have been a rare president and secretary of state who could have engendered a greater international commitment. Kellogg served his laconic president well, and his diplomacy eased international tensions and did not add to them.

Kellogg once confessed to William Hard, "I am willing to admit that I am sometimes wrong and that the Administration is sometimes wrong but in the natural course of events, it is impossible for the Administration or for me to be always wrong. . . . I do not object to a reasonable amount of criticism." Several years later he wrote a letter of appreciation to journalist Henry Suydam who had prepared an article on his stewardship for the *Brooklyn Daily Eagle*. It, too, seemed to indicate that Kellogg was fully cognizant of his own shortcomings. The article pointed out that Kellogg had "few fresh ideas to contribute to the conduct of American foreign relations," that he was "not a picturesque or commanding figure," and that he possessed "shortcomings of temperament and imagination." He was criticized for going into Nicaragua, but he was admired for his agility in getting out. His policies in China were wise, it was said, and he had improved relations with Latin America. While Kellogg allowed Ambassador Sheffield "a free hand to antagonize Mexicans," he gave an equally free hand to Ambassador Morrow to conciliate them. Kellogg's chief fame, the article continued, was in the consummation of the antiwar treaty, even though he was initially unenthusiastic and disinterested. While Kellogg's performance could not be termed brilliant in conception and method, he "re-established the principle of American responsibility in world affairs" at a time when his former constituents in Minnesota were still predominantly isolationist in sentiment. In retrospect, except for the last point, this contemporary assessment had lasting qualities; America's responsibility proved ephemeral at best.[59]

Kellogg was a man of transition. Although he came from the farm, he became urban and urbane. Although he had to work for his livelihood in his childhood, he acquired wealth. His energy and his conscience never permitted contentment only with material things. Perhaps because he never had a high school or college education, he put a high premium on his honorary degrees; in his later years he served as a trustee of Carleton College in Northfield, Minnesota, and made generous contributions to that institution. He associated with the political and industrial giants of his day and moved easily in their milieu. Though he had enthusiastically supported the Progressive party of Theodore Roosevelt, he could not countenance the Progressive party of Robert La Follette.[60]

"History is principally made up of the deeds of men at arms," Kellogg once remarked. He tried to make history of the deeds of men at perpetual peace — and failed. But in that failure the company is a large one indeed. No Minnesotans — and few Americans — have occupied such high positions of public trust in advancing, as Kellogg sought to do, the ideals of an educated and enlightened public opinion, the utilization of arbitration and conciliation for the pacific settlement of disputes, and the implementation of disarmament and arms limitation agreements. If he did not go far enough, he went as far as his pragmatic and cautious temperament would permit. In the 1930s when isolationism still held sway in Minnesota, he would say to his fellow citizens that the United States could not "avoid war by reducing contact with other nations and by maintaining isolation." But the mild internationalism of Frank Kellogg was destined to lie dormant in Minnesota until it was revived and strengthened under the Republican leadership of Joseph Ball, Harold Stassen, and Walter Judd.[61]

Chapter 6

SENATOR JOSEPH H. BALL:
PIONEERING INTERNATIONALIST

*"I am squarely opposed to an isolationist policy. The
facts of the world today convince me that it is untenable
and impractical."* JOSEPH H. BALL, 1941.

IF THE 1920s were marked by isolationism, affluence, and an uncertain
peace, the 1930s were notable for isolationism, poverty, and un-
checked aggressions in Asia, Africa, and Europe. The depression
which could not be confined within the borders of the United States
laid the foundation for a war that similarly could not be contained on
a single continent. The failure of men to deal wisely with economics
and politics propelled the nations of the world into the most pervasive
conflict in man's history. A crisis of this magnitude obviously called
for a reassessment of relations among nations. No longer, so it
appeared, could peace be secured by a *Pax Britannica* or by a balance
of power arrangement.

Determined to be only a spectator to the distasteful events going
on about it, the United States during the 1930s erected a wall of
neutrality, which crumbled with the failing fortunes of the countries
aligned against Hitler's Germany. As America moved toward participation in World War II, the attitude of the people began to change.
The old diplomacy, it was agreed, had been inappropriate and ineffective; a new diplomacy initiated by the United States would attempt
to institutionalize the peaceful settlement of disputes. American
leadership was essential because its refusal to join the League of
Nations had undermined that organization's capacity to deal with
national aggressions and because its great power status was by then
an established fact. The climate of public opinion was growing receptive to a vision of a postwar world heretofore held only by a small
band of American internationalists.

Throughout the interwar decades there had been persistent efforts,
public and private, to turn the nation outward. Andrew Carnegie,
for example, had given away $311 million, much of it to activities
and projects reflecting his belief in arbitration and conciliation as sub-

stitutes for war; organizations like the Council on Foreign Relations and the Foreign Policy Association pricked the conscience of isolationist America; and the study of international relations was accepted as a respected curriculum in the halls of academe. As war came to the world in 1939, other groups like the Committee to Defend America by Aiding the Allies were formed. Well-known newspapers also played an important part in changing the mood of the country.[1]

Minnesota was not impervious to these influences, though it remained one of the strongholds of isolationism. What might have endured of Frank Kellogg's gentle internationalism could not effectively compete with the overwhelming isolationist presence of Henrik Shipstead and Ernest Lundeen in the Senate and Harold Knutson and like-minded colleagues in the House. Minnesota's ultimate shift to internationalism was achieved by the dramatic coalition of events leading to war and new political leadership in the state. That leadership emerged not from parties challenging Republican dominance but from young Turks rebelling within the GOP.

The prime movers for the new direction were Governor Harold E. Stassen, Senator Joseph H. Ball, and Congressman Walter H. Judd, all of whom were "ahead of their party and ahead of the people."[2] This triumvirate changed the fabric of Republican foreign policy thought not only in Minnesota but in the nation. As one scholar remarked, "it is significant that those who took the lead in converting the Republican party to a party favoring international cooperation were public men of the Middle West — Burton of Ohio, Ball of Minnesota, Stassen of Minnesota, and Wendell Willkie [of Indiana]."[3]

In his autobiography, Eric Sevareid recalled his despair in 1941 that the tradition of isolation was maintained in the face of nazi conquest and devastation in Europe. "From my northwest country had come only one leader who had renounced our native tradition and seen that it was too late — Senator Ball, whom I remembered as a shaggy, fierce-eyed reporter around the state house in Minnesota. Two — with Governor Stassen, whom as students we had glibly written off as a simple 'power politician' and who was doing more for the intelligent cause now than the rest of us put together."[4]

From Senator Ball in 1944 came a similar assessment of the climate of Minnesota opinion in the prewar years: "for twenty years all candidates of all three parties talked straight isolationist doctrine whenever they touched on foreign policy. They repeated over and over again the old arguments: that in 1917 we were inveighed by 'sinister influences' into a war in which we had no stake, that America could not settle the ancient quarrels of Europe and Asia, and that our welfare was unaffected by them." [5]

Joseph Hurst Ball was born in Crookston, Minnesota, on November 3, 1905. He attended Antioch College in Ohio and the University of Minnesota. He was variously a newspaperman and a free-lance writer until he joined the *St. Paul Pioneer Press* as a general reporter and rose to the post of political writer in 1934. Through this assignment Ball came to know Harold Stassen, becoming his friend, adviser, and publicist; indeed, he was called Stassen's "Boswell." [6]

Ball's immediate predecessor in the Senate was Ernest Lundeen; his senatorial colleague during most of his eight years in office was Henrik Shipstead. When Lundeen died in an airplane crash in 1940, Governor Stassen, after keeping the party and the people on tenterhooks for nearly six speculative weeks, appointed Ball to fill the vacant seat. He was the youngest Minnesotan ever to serve in the Senate. The new senator's views on foreign affairs were largely unknown to the public, but Stassen made it clear that he had taken them into account. Years later Stassen recalled that "views on foreign policy did have a very important bearing upon my appointment of Joseph Ball as United States Senator. . . . I knew of his views and we had discussed them before he was appointed." [7]

Ball's appointment came as a shock to Republican regulars who expected one of the party faithful to get the post or at least warm the chair until Stassen himself succeeded to that office in 1942. One Republican editor exploded, "Joe Ball, United States Senator! Good God!" Nat S. Finney, a Minneapolis newspaperman, gave this colorful portrayal of party reaction: "The county chairmen from the Lake of the Woods to the Iowa border went around for weeks with bloodshot eyes and apoplectic faces. Some grumbled incoherently. . . . Had they known what line Ball was going to take when he got down to Washington the arteries of the old-guardsmen would have popped like so many carnival balloons." Despite the railing of party officialdom, the appointment was generally well received. [8]

From the outset of his senatorial career, Ball made it clear that he would neither follow in Lundeen's footsteps nor join forces with Senator Shipstead; he was both vocal and vigorous in his opposition to isolationism. In Ball's initial statement after his appointment, he said, "I certainly believe the world would be a much better place if Britain were not conquered by Hitler. On that basis I am in favor of all aid possible to Britain without crippling our own defenses." [9]

When the administration of Franklin Roosevelt moved in 1939–40

Newly appointed Senator Ball and his wife being greeted by Congressman Melvin J. Maas (left) and Senator Shipstead, October, 1940

to modify the neutrality laws by initiating lend-lease, "there was practically no group in Minnesota from whom the President could expect complete support," concluded political scientist George W. Garlid. "The Democrats were too weak"; the Farmer-Labor party was "wedded to a policy of non-involvement"; and most Republicans were in the isolationist camp. In the presidential contest of 1940, despite Stassen's close association with the Wendell L. Willkie campaign, not "a single political leader in Minnesota was willing to launch a frontal attack upon the isolationist position." Garlid explained the reluctance in these terms: "The tradition was too strong, the sentiment ran too deep, the isolationist rhetoric had been too long advanced, and finally the startling events abroad which presaged the bankruptcy of the isolationist position had come too rapidly, to render such an assault politically appealing." The political scientist also observed that "during the summer and fall of 1940 more Minnesotans agreed with those who intensely and outspokenly voiced their isolationist convictions than with those whose attitudes had altered." [10]

Ball took his Senate seat on October 14, 1940, a little more than a year before Pearl Harbor. It was his impression then that the people of Minnesota were deeply divided with the majority probably opposed to involvement. In the spring of 1941, Charles A. Lindbergh, Jr., then a leader of the America First organization, returned to his native state to extol the virtues of isolationism. Senator Shipstead shared the platform and Lindbergh's sentiments. A week later on May 17, Ball answered Lindbergh. Addressing 4,500 persons at a Norwegian Independence Day celebration in Minneapolis, he said, "I welcome the opportunity . . . to refute the defeatism and confusion which the America First leaders have preached in this city and are spreading throughout the nation." The point at issue, he claimed, was whether we "sit back and try to stop Hitler at New York, Baltimore and Charleston . . . or shall we help stop him at the cliffs of Dover?" The Norwegian-Americans, whose home country had fallen to Hitler in April, 1940, gave Ball a standing ovation.[11]

The *St. Paul Pioneer Press* commented that with "Minnesota listed among the ten strongest anti-war states," Ball's talk certainly was not designed to curry votes. A *Minneapolis Tribune* editorial suggested that "the response must have been gratifying and encouraging to a man who is willing and even eager to stake his political future on convictions from which a great many, and perhaps the majority, of his constituents dissent. Never was the case for all aid to Britain more convincingly made in Minneapolis." A few days later the executive secretary of the Minneapolis unit of the Committee to Defend America by Aiding the Allies wrote that "several of our best newspaper men" felt that Ball's speech had changed opinion, while Lindbergh's efforts had "made no converts to his cause."[12]

In Washington Ball's unequivocal stand was interpreted as a turning point in shifting the Republican party away from extreme isolationism, and he was acknowledged as the first midwestern senator to take so staunch a position against the majority of his party. He was one of a new Republican breed beginning to emerge on the national scene and was the first Minnesotan occupying national elective office to break decisively with the prevailing Republican view of the world.[13]

Ball's convictions and consistency were marks of political courage. While he was praised in some circles, he was also subjected to threats of political reprisal unless he opposed the Roosevelt administration's foreign policy. "Some have called me unprintable names, and a few have even told me I would be tarred and feathered if I did not change my position," he said. His advocacy of intervention led to early talk of potential opposition to Ball in his first election in 1942. Representatives Harold Knutson, August H. Andresen, and Melvin J. Maas were mentioned. So was Charles Lindbergh, Jr., who, rumor had it, would move back to Minnesota and establish residence in order to run against Ball.[14]

While Ball was calling for all-out aid to Britain to stop "the onward march of Nazi barbarism," Shipstead was calling for the removal of the interventionists from the cabinet, especially Secretaries Frank Knox of the navy and Henry Stimson of the war department, both of whom were Republicans. The senior senator claimed that with 85 per cent of the people against foreign war, the United States should "mind its own business" and rid itself of the idea that the fates of Britain and America were intertwined.[15]

Throughout 1941 a series of key internationalist-isolationist votes were taken in the Senate. One of the most important debates was on lend-lease. In early December, 1940, the British prime minister, Winston Churchill, had made a personal appeal to Roosevelt for greatly increased military supplies. Roosevelt's response was a proposal to Congress that the United States simply lend or lease war equipment as one would lend his garden hose if his neighbor's house caught on fire. The bill was passed out of the Senate foreign relations committee with eight negative votes. The Republicans opposed were Shipstead of Minnesota, Gerald P. Nye of North Dakota, Arthur H. Vandenberg of Michigan, Arthur Capper of Kansas, and Hiram Johnson of California; the Democrats opposed were Bennett "Champ" Clark of Missouri and Guy M. Gillette of Iowa; the Progressive opposed was Robert La Follette of Wisconsin. The only geographical outsider among this isolationist midwestern coterie was Hiram Johnson. Over the long haul the lend-lease program was an essential life line in the war. Within a year and a half of its inception, thirty-five countries were receiving aid. Even after the United States entered the war, the program continued; by 1944 American efforts under lend-lease totaled $11 billion.[16]

Although Ball was concerned about the amount of power the lend-lease act delegated to the president, he was "the first Midwest Republican to swing for the bill." The basic issue, as the senator told his constituents in a radio address on February 13, 1941, was to determine the future direction of American foreign policy. The United States could return to a rigid policy of isolation, or it could "abandon that policy for good, and take our place as a top-ranking world power prepared to play our full part in world affairs." By so doing, Ball continued, the United States could "use the full force of its economic and political influence to bring about, first, the kind of world in which this Nation will have maximum security and opportunity for economic and social progress for its people; and, second, the kind of world in which all nations and all peoples can live together in peace."[17]

The vote on lend-lease was a preview of things to come; Ball sided with the majority of sixty, Shipstead with the minority of thirty-one.

(For his support of the lend-lease bill, Ball earned the sobriquet of "Cannonball" from Minnesota isolationists.) In the House the measure had previously passed by 260 to 165; of the eight-man Minnesota delegation, only Representative Pittenger voted approval. Another crucial issue was a further modification of the neutrality laws. The harassment of American destroyers by German submarines prompted Roosevelt to ask Congress early in 1941 for repeal of the prohibition against arming merchantmen to uphold the policy of protecting the freedom of the seas. Ball voted in favor of this revision.[18]

Opinion in Minnesota was beginning to turn from the rigid isolationism of the past. The daily papers for the most part supported the directions of FDR's policies. The Committee to Defend America by Aiding the Allies, although by no means a mass movement, was well organized. The plight of the occupied countries in Europe, especially Norway, had awakened the conscience of Scandinavian Minnesota to American responsibilities abroad.[19]

The beginning of the war for the United States in 1941 found Senator Ball contemplating its end and the need to "establish a workable pattern for world peace and stability — a pattern that will stop and punish any future would-be Hitlers long before they gain such strength as to throw the whole world into war." In the 1942 election campaign the senator, calling the isolationists "tragically wrong," commented, "The foreign policy of the United States is the overshadowing issue in this campaign as the nation faces the desperate task of winning this war." Reconstructing the impact of World War II on the mood of the American people the year after the war ended, Ball noted that "The sneak attack on Pearl Harbor on December 7 [1941] ended our public debate and united the nation. . . . Pearl Harbor . . . cut the ground from under the strongest argument the isolationists had had, namely, that our oceans made us secure from any attack. . . . The atomic bomb was the final clincher, shattering the last vestiges of isolationism."[20]

Ball's reading of the public mind was confirmed by responses to a Gallup Poll in July, 1942, which posed the question: "Would you like to see the U.S. join the League of Nations after the war is over?" In October, 1937, only 33 per cent favored the concept; by July, 1942, the figure had escalated to 73 per cent. The change among Republicans in the same period was even greater — from 23 per cent to 70 per cent. Equally striking was the shift of opinion in the west central section of the nation which rose from 31 per cent to 76 per cent. In the space of five years Republicans had made a significant turnabout in their attitudes toward international organization, and the Midwest, including Minnesota, had moved from the second least to the second most supportive region in the nation.[21]

Republican opinion in Minnesota was emphatic and precise. The preamble of the party platform adopted in St. Paul on September 19, 1942, stated: "We resolve that the mistakes made after the last war must not be repeated. Security for the United States and our way of life cannot be based any more on separation from the world, but only on carefully worked out co-operation. . . . We must stand with other free peoples, each carrying their proper share of the load to secure permanent peace and freedom for all. America must lead in a new world order." After quoting this statement, the *Minneapolis Star-Journal* of September 21, 1942, commented editorially that it constituted "the most straightforward declaration yet made by the Republicans of any middle western state."

Though there had been rumors that Stassen would seek the office, Ball's opponent in the 1942 primary for the senatorial nomination was Walter K. Mickelson, an avowed isolationist. His candidacy, however, was a lost cause. Mickelson was clearly out of step with his own party in which a younger and more liberal element had taken charge. The political magic of Shipstead was fading, too, as evidenced in the fruitless campaign he waged on Mickelson's behalf. Ball's plurality of nearly 87,000 votes was the largest of all major office contenders, and Mickelson's crushing defeat was interpreted by the *Minneapolis Star-Journal* "as a rebuke for Shipstead" and a repudiation of the isolationism he and Mickelson espoused.[22]

The Farmer-Labor party chose former Governor Elmer A. Benson to run in the general election against Ball, but he lost by a margin of 142,000 votes. Against Benson's charge that Ball favored "a more or less imperialistic foreign policy," the senator campaigned on the principle that the United States "should take a hand in 'policing the world' to preserve the peace." Ball's victory prompted local expectations that in this young man of thirty-six, there might emerge another Minnesota star in the senatorial constellation. Raymond Clapper, a nationally syndicated columnist, applauded the courage of Stassen and Ball in meeting the issue of postwar organization head-on in their election campaigns: "They did it in the face of an isolationist tradition, in the face of the heritage of Shipstead and Lundeen, and they won."[23]

It was in his concern for an organizational commitment to prevent future wars that Senator Ball made his most enduring contribution to American foreign policy. Senate Resolution 114 represented a congressional initiative endorsing the establishment of an organization of nations united to preserve the future peace. The resolution was soon nicknamed B2H2 for the sponsors: the "B's" were Ball himself and Harold H. Burton of Ohio (who later served on the United States Supreme Court), both Republicans; the "H's" were Lister Hill of Alabama (who served in the Senate until 1968) and Carl A. Hatch of New Mexico, Democrats. All but Hill had shared records of service on the Truman committee, which was known for its disclosures of corruption in war industries. Hill, in effect, substituted for Truman whose duties as chairman precluded another major task.[24]

The introduction of the resolution was not capricious. The sponsors consulted with Acting Secretary of State Sumner Welles, who was enthusiastic, and with President Roosevelt, who was cautious. The president agreed in principle but was fearful that the action might stir up a hornet's nest of isolationist sentiment. But Ball was adamant, and on March 16, 1943, he introduced Senate Resolution 114. It urged that the United States ask the allied nations to form a permanent organization during the war, included a provision for economic rehabilitation after peace came, outlined the need to establish procedures for the peaceful settlement of disputes and disagreements between nations, and called for a co-operative military force to respond to any future aggression. It was this last point — the concept of a world policeman — that was to become the focus of debate in the ensuing months.[25]

In his initial statement Ball pointed out that the resolution's authors were "spokesmen for a considerably larger group of Senators. . . . In a larger sense, we speak for all the millions of Americans who are longing for constructive and immediate action toward winning peace as well as victory in the war. . . . The resolution represents the ideas and viewpoints of many individuals, and we believe it offers a sound starting point for Senate action." In elaborating his arguments, he stated the authors' conviction that an organization of peace-loving nations offered the best hope for maintaining the stability of the world. He pointed to the dismal record of past devices — balance of power diplomacy, multilateral treaties such as the Kellogg-Briand Pact, and nonaggression agreements. The failure of the League of Nations, in Ball's judgment, was caused by two factors: the nonparticipation of the United States and the fact that member nations did not delegate national sovereignty to the international body. He stated that this time the United States should take the initiative in asking its allies to join in the collective effort and that it was incumbent on the Senate, representing the American people, to take the first step. He concluded his presentation by reminding his listeners that after the last war, the peace had been lost. "History must not repeat itself," said Ball, "that tragedy must not happen again." [26]

An observer of the Washington scene, who was not sanguine about the chances of the B2H2 resolution passing the Senate, applauded it as "a definite focusing point for public discussion of post-war United Nations policy. More important is the possibility that the resolution may foreshadow a genuine revitalization of the Republican party, a real attempt to come to grips with the post-Harding world. Joseph Hurst Ball finds himself in the vanguard of the new movement." [27]

Ball's resolution was intended to be in the forefront of public opinion and to challenge both the legislative and administrative branches of government to meet the issue of international organization. While it was widely heralded in Minnesota and throughout the country, key officials were cool to the idea for reasons best set forth by Senator Arthur H. Vandenberg of Michigan. The resolution, he said, "seeks to particularize prematurely. It could easily redivide America at home. It could easily divide our Allies abroad. . . . It could jeopardize victory itself. It seems to me . . . that we can successfully generalize to accomplish every good purpose and to avoid the pitfalls." [28]

To "generalize" was precisely Secretary of State Cordell Hull's plea. He wanted a resolution couched in broad terms to avoid public controversy over conflicting details of postwar settlement and organization, one which could commandeer an overwhelming Senate majority. A special subcommittee of the Senate foreign relations committee was named by its chairman, Senator Tom Connally of Texas, to consider the B2H2 resolution. The strategy of the subcommittee, according to Connally, was to "sit on the resolution until public opinion rallied strongly, and then . . . report out 'a very broad-guage [sic], generalized resolution.'" In meeting with the subcommittee, the four authors agreed to compromise but not to emasculation. Ball was critical of Hull's caution, and all four argued that America's major allies wanted assurance that the United States would not give a repeat performance of withdrawal into isolationism at the war's conclusion. [29]

As they lobbied the Senate so too "the four horsemen," as Vandenberg dubbed them, lobbied the people. The wives of Senators Ball and Hatch set up a mail-answering service to cope with the enthusiastic public response which was running at a favorable twenty-to-one ratio. Ball was not a flashy speaker but his sincerity was convincing, and he proved to be an especially effective spokesman for the cause. He was deluged with speaking requests. And the senators were not alone. A number of national organizations saw the resolution as a rallying point to educate the public on the need for a postwar organization with sufficient teeth to keep the peace. The Non-Partisan Council to Win the Peace, the Women's Action Committee for Victory and Lasting Peace, and the United Nations Association bent their efforts on behalf of B2H2. The most active United Nations organization in the Middle West was to be found in Minnesota, where there were more than a thousand members who distributed thousands of copies of the resolution throughout the state.[30]

Public enthusiasm for B2H2 proved to be substantial. In May, 1943, a Gallup Poll question asked "Should the countries fighting the Axis set up an international police force after the war is over to try to keep peace throughout the world?" Seventy-four per cent answered affirmatively, 14 per cent were opposed, and 12 per cent had no opinion. But on this most controversial feature of the resolution, the Senate was at odds. An Associated Press poll conducted the month before, asking the ninety-six senators if they were ready now to commit the United States to a postwar international police force, had elicited this response: No 32; Yes 24; Not Responding 40. Vandenberg concluded that "This would seem to end all Senate chance for the Ball Resolution . . . because even its authors agree that it would be fatal to have a sharply divided Senate."[31]

In the House of Representatives, J. William Fulbright of Arkansas looked askance at the procrastination of the Connally subcommittee and the controversy over an international police force and decided to try his hand at a settlement. In April, 1943, he submitted a resolution to create appropriate international machinery with power adequate to prevent future aggression and to maintain lasting peace. Not until June did the House, believing the Senate would not act on the B2H2 resolution, decide to move ahead on its own in a rare foreign policy initiative on the part of representatives. It was agreed to delete any hint of an international police force, and on June 15 Fulbright introduced the new version, which declared the "sense of the Congress with respect to participation by the United States in prevention of future aggression and the maintenance of peace." The administration, however, shied away from even this modest expression of intent, and House leaders decided to postpone action until after the summer recess when congressmen would have a chance to gauge home opinion.[32]

For many congressmen there was to be no rest during the recess. Eight bipartisan teams toured the country to drum up support for the B2H2 and Fulbright resolutions. Senator Ball and Representative (later Senator) Albert A. Gore of Tennessee were the first team to

Joseph H. Ball, 1943

go out traveling through the western states. The most vigorous tour was undertaken by Senator Truman of Missouri and Representative Judd of Minnesota. They went to the Great Plains states and spoke to twenty-seven meetings in nineteen cities. Later Ball made a midsummer tour of the Dakotas and Minnesota and participated in a final swing through Illinois and Missouri. The state department was impressed that the internationalists had apparently reached "the great mass of the American people" for the first time.[33]

Meanwhile Senator Vandenberg was searching for a middle-ground solution. A conference of Republican leaders at Mackinac Island, Michigan, in September issued a foreign policy declaration initially drafted by Vandenberg, which called for "responsible participation by the United States in postwar cooperative organization among sovereign nations to prevent military aggression and to attain permanent peace with organized justice in a free world."[34] The significance of the Mackinac resolution lay in its commitment of the Republican party to the principle of international organization.

In the interim Senator Ball had also turned publicist by writing a pamphlet entitled *Collective Security: The Why and How* emphasizing the message that the principle of international law must be firmly established in the minds and deeds of men and nations. He contended that Americans were prone to overcomplicate the problems of peace.

The senator did not dismiss the knotty difficulties certain to confront the United States, but he felt strongly that they could best be dealt with in the framework of an international mechanism set up for just such purposes. Without a framework of collective security, Ball foresaw still another armament competition among nations. He was suspicious of the balance of power concept, seeing danger in the possible division of the world by great powers into spheres of influence. The basic issue of World War II, in Ball's opinion, was "whether we and the world shall move forward in the paths of democracy and peace, or whether the world slips backs into the old system of tyranny, oppression and war." [35]

When Congress reconvened in mid-September, 1943, pressure for action had intensified. The House passed the Fulbright Resolution on September 21 by the overwhelming margin of 360 to 29. All but three of the opponents were Republicans, and all but five were from the Middle West. The only Minnesota congressman who voted against it was Harold Knutson. (William Pittenger of the eighth district did not vote, and Joseph P. O'Hara of the second answered "present.") During the debate, the resolution had been criticized on the grounds that it was too strong or too weak, prompting Fulbright to comment, "The one thing I gather from this discussion is that it must actually be about halfway between, and therefore about right." Senator Ball did not think it "about right." He thought it ambiguous, and he called for the Senate to speak "clearly and specifically as to the policies or programs which it believes will best safeguard the peace after we shall have won the war." [36]

The Senate reacted jealously to House intervention in what it regarded as its foreign policy domain. Senator Connally, who had followed orders from the administration and procrastinated over the B_2H_2 resolution for twenty-five weeks, was especially angry. "God damn it . . . everybody's running around here like a fellow with a tick on his navel, howling about postwar resolutions," he said. [37] The easy passage of the Fulbright Resolution gave President Roosevelt confidence that the time was now ripe for Senate action.

Connally then drafted his own resolution, which called for cooperation with the other United Nations in waging the war and securing the peace. The key clause, to Vandenberg's delight, included a statement about sovereignty and constitutional process, the basic elements of the Mackinac declaration: "the United States, acting through its constitutional processes, join with free and sovereign nations in the establishment and maintenance of international authority with power to prevent aggression and to preserve the peace of the world."

While the Connally draft was stronger than the Fulbright version, it was weaker than B2H2, and the "four horsemen" were determined to improve it. Senator Claude D. Pepper of Florida, as a member of the foreign relations committee, agreed to serve as their inside man and try to strengthen the resolution. One amendment substituted the words "an international organization" for "international authority," and the other added the words, "including military force." Although the amendments were rejected by a vote of 16 to 5, the Connally version was reported out favorably by the committee, 20 to 2 (the dissidents were isolationists Hiram Johnson and Robert La Follette).[38]

The Senate took up the resolution on October 25, 1943, in what the New York Times of the following day called "the most important Senate debate on international affairs since the rejection of the Versailles Treaty and the League of Nations covenant nearly twenty-four years ago." The B2H2 senators pressed for floor adoption of their amendments. Senator Ball made the opening speech for the internationalists, who were dubbed the "willful fourteen." The debate continued for two weeks. While the Senate discussions went on, the foreign ministers of the United States, Britain, and Russia had been meeting in Moscow. At the close of their sessions on November 1, they issued the Moscow Declaration, the fourth article of which called for creating "at the earliest practicable date a general international organization, based on the principle of the sovereign equality of all peace-loving states . . . for the maintenance of international peace and security." The "willful fourteen," elated at this specific call for an international organization, urged the Senate to be "at least as clear and forthright in its expression as the agreement signed at Moscow."[39]

A compromise was arranged. The fourth article of the Moscow Declaration designating an international security organization was accepted as one amendment, as was a second specifying that any such treaty would require Senate ratification, although the committee text already included a safeguarding reference to "constitutional procedures." Ball, Burton, Hatch, and Hill announced that they would vote for the amended resolution, which passed by the impressive margin of 85 to 5 with the Minnesota senators voting yea and nay — Ball for and Shipstead against. The B2H2 resolution had served as a lightning rod to attract public and congressional attention to the need for some sort of commitment to a postwar organization for collective security.[40]

Now that both houses of Congress had gone on record, Ball called on the president for action. In a Saturday Evening Post article entitled "It's Your Move, Mr. President," Ball put his case for executive-legislative co-operation to plan the peace. Idealistic and probably impractical as it may have been in a wartime setting, he advocated lifting the traditional curtain of diplomatic secrecy separating the president from the Congress and the American people. Ball was clearly obsessed with the wish to avoid a Lodge-Wilson type of confrontation in the peacemaking process after World War II. He was especially concerned that the Senate be represented at all preparatory and consulting conferences, since, according to American constitutional dictates, it would have to ratify any treaty establishing a United Nations organization. The senator disliked what was later called "summitry." The picture of a few heads of state deciding the fate of millions was anathema to him. While many applauded Roosevelt's meetings at Cairo and Tehran, Ball was critical because the legislative partner was unrepresented. As early as March, 1943, when the B2H2 resolution was first introduced, Walter Lippmann caught this concern, remarking that "The fundamental question which has been raised by Senators Hatch, Burton, Ball and Hill is how the Senate can be enabled to play its part in the conduct of American foreign relations. . . . The test is whether the Senate will agree that a way must be found to associate the Senate continuously with the President before and during the momentous negotiations that have to be undertaken." [41]

There was a superficial similarity in the Shipstead-Ball dislike of secret and exclusive diplomacy. Although they shared a common concern for Senate prerogatives in the conduct of foreign policy, Shipstead's emphasis was on substance, Ball's on process. Shipstead, remembering that the League of Nations was tied to the Versailles treaty, could not vote for the United Nations Charter because the peace agreements had not been made known. Ball, recalling the failure of the League of Nations cause in the United States largely because the Senate had been unrepresented and unconsulted, wanted to avoid a duplication of this tactical error.

The junior senator from Minnesota was unstinting of himself in writing and speaking of the new United Nations organization. It should, in his view, be backed by both force and law, and the rule of unanimity of the old League of Nations should be replaced by the rule of the majority. His vision of the immediate postwar world included five fundamentals: fair and impartial machinery for settling disputes; an international police force of ships, planes, and men; the elimination of extreme and unreasonable trade barriers; disarmament, first of the Axis powers, ultimately by all nations; and punishment, as individuals, for the aggressors who started World War II. Ball's efforts and activities did not go unnoticed. He was described in *Time* as "jut-jawed" and "serious" and was generally thought of as one of the ablest young Republican internationalist Senators.[42] It may not be totally idle to suggest that Stassen's appointment as a delegate to the 1945 San Francisco conference, which wrote the United Nations Charter, was in part an indirect reward for the hard work of his fellow Minnesotan to detach the GOP from its isolationist moorings.

Senator Ball worried that, even with a strong UN Charter, the greatest danger to future peace was that the war-weary people of the world would turn their attention to domestic problems. Even after the United Nations had become a *fait accompli* in 1945, Ball was quick to point out ways in which it might be improved. He had six definite suggestions: (1) eliminate the veto and establish a system of majority rule; (2) create a true international police force; (3) insist that the international force should possess the only existing stock pile of atomic bombs; (4) provide for a complete interchange among nations "of all scientific knowledge, including military applications"; (5) authorize the security council to order the international police force to move on any nation guilty of possessing atomic weapons and destroy them; and (6) place under UN trusteeship all the trouble spots — Indochina, Java, Korea, Palestine, Trieste, perhaps even Austria and Bulgaria.[43]

In a speech at Syracuse University in April, 1946, the senator said that the United States should support the United Nations "with all the influence at our command." He maintained that, despite the negativism of the Soviet Union, the organization offered the only hope of establishing international law and justice on a firm foundation of government. Once again he was critical of the veto power in the security council which contravened his original proposal of majority rule. And while Ball advocated international action, he did not, in the absence of arms control or disarmament agreements, eschew the need for national preparedness. He was alarmed about the rapid demobilization of the country's armed forces after the war and suggested that there was no substitute for strength in the defense of our principles if worst came to worst. No doubt he had in mind the apparent adventurousness of the Soviet Union in organizing buffers around its flanks.[44]

Initially the senator championed the Marshall Plan of economic aid to Western Europe, but not without qualification, and ultimately he voted against it. He recognized the danger of a communist take over of a weakened Europe but suggested that dollars were not the only answer. Ball became increasingly skeptical that the European Recovery Program, as the Marshall Plan was formally known, could succeed in making Europe self-supporting. Not only did he challenge the cost figures, making an effort to reduce the annual amount from six to four billion dollars, but he was fearful that controls would be inadequate so that American dollars would be "dissipated by 'unwise' policies on the part of recipient governments." [45]

Ball confessed that on this issue he again found himself in a minority of the Republican party, "as I was in 1941 when I supported Lend-Lease." In the final analysis he opposed the Marshall Plan because he objected to it as "a blank check," and he doubted that Russian aggression could be countered by economic assistance alone. In a letter to a constituent, he admitted that the decision to vote against the Marshall Plan had been a tough one, but since the United States lacked "a coherent political foreign policy" and a "hard-headed" attitude about the allocation of funds, the economic aid would, in his judgment, "be largely wasted." To a friend he confided that the Marshall Plan was like attacking a fire with a brigade of buckets rather than with a fire hose. In short, it was an insufficient weapon unless backed by political and military support to deal with Russian aggression. When the suggestion was made that it was at least a step in the right direction, Ball replied that his vote had to be a testimonial to the inadequacy of the plan. [46]

Early in 1948 before the European Recovery Program was approved by Congress, Ball came forth with the interesting idea — somewhat reminiscent of Shipstead's dollars-for-disarmament plan in 1925 — that the receipt of United States dollars be made contingent on the formation of a union of Western nations to protect the American investment in world peace. This was precisely the direction in which the United States moved, making aid conditional on economic co-operation among the European recipients. Out of this insistence came the Organization of European Economic Cooperation, which has been recognized by most observers as the precursor of the economic alliance popularly termed the Common Market as well as other institutional arrangements reflecting the commonality of Western European concerns. [47]

Politically Ball was either an idealist or a novice or possibly both. In any event he let the political chips fall where they would as he continued the Minnesota tradition of partisan independence. A key to his political attitude and the cornerstone of his belief are suggested in his Syracuse speech of 1946. He argued that the challenge to democracy in the postwar world could be handled effectively if the electorate knew the facts and heard both sides of every issue, and if political leadership were inspired, not by the majority opinion of the moment, but by its dedication to fundamental principles. In a sense it was Ball's devotion to these ideals which led to his defeat. [48]

The beginning of the political end for Joe Ball came in the presidential campaign of 1944. Even though he was not a leader of commanding national stature, the senator was a recognized spokesman of the internationalist, independent wing of the Republican party generally known as "the Willkie vote." As the campaign got under way, Willkie was pushing hard for an advanced stand on international organization. He had not yet committed himself in favor of either Thomas E. Dewey, his successor as the Republican standard-bearer, or the incumbent FDR. When Willkie was stricken with what proved to be his final illness in October, 1944, Ball carried on their mutual fight for a world organization having real authority and power. Though he had pledged the support of the Stassen organization to the Dewey candidacy, Ball apparently had reservations about campaigning for the New York governor. He was not convinced, he said, that Dewey "would fight vigorously for a foreign policy which will offer real hope of preventing World War III." [49]

Years later Ball told Robert Divine that he made the statement because he "feared Dewey had become the captive of isolationists within the party" and he hoped "to force him to disavow their support." Two weeks later on October 12, the senator asked three pointed questions of the presidential contestants, indicating that his support would be contingent upon their responses. His questions were: whether they favored the United States immediately entering a United Nations security organization; whether they favored applying any reservations to a United Nations council which would weaken the power of a security organization to stop aggression; whether they would implement a policy for the United States to give the UN security council the right to commit American military forces to agreed upon actions without prior congressional approval. [50]

The crucial question was the last. Dewey answered the first two affirmatively, but he did not respond to the third in a major foreign policy address on October 18, 1944. Three days later Roosevelt gave his reply in a speech before the Foreign Policy Association of New York. Using one of his typical homey analogies, the president asserted that "The Council of the United Nations must have the power to act quickly and decisively to keep the peace by force, if necessary. A policeman would not be a very effective policeman if, when he saw a felon break into a house, he had to go to the Town Hall and call a town meeting to issue a warrant before the felon could be arrested." [51]

Persuaded that Dewey had evaded the issue which the president "had met squarely and unequivocally" concerning the "vital question on which the isolationists had kept America out of the League of

Nations," Ball announced, "I shall vote for and support President Roosevelt." The reaction was mixed. Some were quick to criticize. State Senator J. V. Weber of Slayton was furious. Ball, he said, is "guilty of the vilest double cross in the political history of Minnesota. Impeachment, if that were possible, would be too good for him." Others were equally quick to hail the senator as a statesman who put his country before his party. Among them was the Minnesotan who had been the first American to win the Nobel Prize for literature. On October 29, 1944, Sinclair Lewis lauded Ball's decision and commented: "I am a friend and admirer of Gov. Thye and of many other Minnesota Republicans, but I believe that President Roosevelt represents far better than Mr. Dewey all that is best in the political ideals of Harold Stassen and Wendell Willkie and of those plain people of Minnesota to whom you and I belong." [52]

While internationalists praised Ball's stand, most Republicans tried to dismiss it as insignificant. However, in Minneapolis on October 24 Dewey belatedly replied to Ball's third question, saying that he "did not insist that the American delegate return to Congress for authority to use force in a crisis." Indeed Dewey placed himself close to Roosevelt's position, asking only that "Congress be allowed to decide how much authority it would surrender to the President in regard to the use of force for collective security." By then Ball was committed. He justified his support of FDR in a speech several days later, pointing out that "the Roosevelt administration has reversed the isolationist foreign policy of the United States . . . through reciprocal trade agreements, the good neighbor policy, the destroyers-bases trade, lend-lease, selective service, repeal of the arms embargo, the United Nations conferences on food, currency stabilization, relief and rehabilitation, and finally the Dumbarton Oaks conference." [53]

Nat Finney, who was an experienced observer of the Minnesota political scene, believed that politics rather than principle caused Ball's defection from the Republican ranks. In his view Ball wanted Willkie to lose the GOP nomination and Dewey to lose the 1944 election to pave the way for Harold Stassen's nomination in 1948. Personal pique may also have been a factor. Ball was suspicious of Dewey's foreign policy beliefs, because he remembered, as a political reporter, that Dewey's presidential aspirations in 1940 had commanded the support of the America First organization. The fact that Dewey never consulted Ball reinforced this suspicion and perhaps offended his pride as a foreign policy spokesman for at least a part of the Republican party. But weight must be given to principle over politics or pique. One person close to Ball emphasized that he simply did not think in those terms; he was not a conniver. This appraisal seems more consistent with the individualism, idealism, and integrity of Joseph Ball.[54]

In any event the junior senator from Minnesota was a politician without a party. Despite his desertion of Dewey in the election of 1944 and despite his voting record (more with Roosevelt than against him), he showed no signs of wanting to join the Democrats. Republicans, including those in Minnesota, agreed that a publicly announced defection "was no way to run a party." After the war Ball was more consistent in supporting Republican party positions. Increasingly he opposed both the domestic and the foreign policies of the Roosevelt administration. His leadership in the field of labor legislation, especially his advocacy of the Taft-Hartley bill, caused his mention as a possible vice-presidential candidate. This was a remote possibility for two reasons: his support of Roosevelt in 1944 was a political mistake which his party associates never would have rewarded by higher office; it was known that Stassen would be a serious contender for the presidency, automatically ruling out consideration of another Minnesotan for the top team.[55]

Joe Ball's campaign for re-election to the Senate in 1948 began inauspiciously. He started with a handicap of hostility from various hues of political thought — from the right because of his internationalism and his endorsement of Roosevelt, from the middle because of his vote against the Marshall Plan, and from the left because of his support of the Taft-Hartley legislation. Furthermore, Stassen's endorsement was regarded by many as lukewarm at worst and ambivalent at best. Stassen denied that he had hedged the endorsement, maintaining that he was being "factual and reasoned," not "extravagant [or] unrealistic." Privately he was not optimistic about the outcome because of Ball's differences with the party, but "notwithstanding these differences he should nevertheless be reelected." It is not generally known that Ball offered to relinquish his Senate seat if Stassen would agree to run. Stassen declined, as he had in 1946 when Thye and others urged him to choose this option for political advancement.[56]

Citizen uncertainty was clearly revealed in a March, 1948, Minnesota Poll which showed 28 per cent for Ball, 11 per cent for Mayor Hubert H. Humphrey of Minneapolis, who was being talked of as the leading nominee of the young Democratic-Farmer-Labor party, and an impressive 50 per cent undecided. By the end of April Humphrey had captured the lead in the Minnesota Poll, a lead he was not to relinquish. "I don't like Ball," and "Ball isn't for labor," were cited as typical comments from poll respondents who backed

Humphrey. A later sampling in July documented the wide margin of Humphrey's support among Republican voters — 20 per cent — while Ball could command only 9 per cent of the DFL voters. Moreover, the independent voters, a key factor in Minnesota elections, were also pro-Humphrey. The mayor won decisively, defeating Ball by 729,494 votes to 485,801.[57]

A postelection, post-mortem in the *Minneapolis Star* of November 3, 1948, analyzed the campaign and offered a potpourri of reasons for Ball's defeat. He was busy in Washington and had failed to campaign actively; Republicans, judging from the past history of the state, had placed too much reliance on their belief that a big-city mayor could never be elected to the Senate from Minnesota; Ball's "championship of the Taft-Hartley bill, which aroused organized labor"; and his "opposition to the Marshall plan for European recovery," which was contrary to widespread state support for the measure. (A Minnesota Poll showed that 73 per cent felt the United States should help Europe resist communism.) A close associate of Ball cited his vote against the Marshall Plan as the probable decisive factor in his defeat, the proverbial straw that broke the camel's back. Finally his desertion of Dewey for Roosevelt in the 1944 campaign could not be discounted. The *Star* article stated that "Probably none if any Republicans voted against Senator Joe because of his 1944 defection, but many of them refused to get enthusiastic about him. They didn't get out and fight to get independents to vote for him. And independents cast a third of Minnesota's votes; they decide its elections."[58]

In the aftermath of his defeat, Ball's career took a turn toward obscurity. Like many former officeholders who relish the infectious stimulation of Washington, D.C., Ball became a lobbyist for the Association of American Shipowners. In 1953 he moved to New York City, where he served as vice-president in charge of terminals and stevedores for the States Marine Lines. Since 1962 Mr. and Mrs. Joseph Ball, private citizens, have lived on a farm in the Blue Ridge country of western Virginia. The former senator from Minnesota became an exile from his home state and from liberal politics. "I would be considered an arch-conservative," he said in 1967, "in the context of today's politics."[59]

Joe Ball's impact on American foreign policy was brilliantly and briefly meteoric. In eight years as a senator he helped reorient the world outlook of Minnesotans and aided in the process of committing Americans to participation in an international organization. The campaign for the B_2H_2 resolution undoubtedly generated the steam that forced the Fulbright and Connally resolutions through the Congress, and it played a major part in winning almost unanimous support for the United Nations Charter. By other actions he lost partisan Republican backing, antagonized labor, and bewildered independents. A new political coalition, the Democratic-Farmer-Labor party, and a new presence, Hubert Humphrey, were elevated to the Senate in the election that surprised all the pundits, returning Harry S Truman to the White House and retiring Joseph H. Ball from the American political scene.

Chapter 7

HAROLD E. STASSEN'S
SEARCH FOR PEACE–
AND THE PRESIDENCY

*"When I left college — the University of Minnesota —
my really No. 1 aim was to do something for world peace,
or something toward nations living together."*
HAROLD E. STASSEN, 1968.

As JOSEPH BALL HELPED to generate the commitment of the United States to a postwar international organization, so Harold Stassen, by virtue of his membership on the American delegation to the San Francisco conference which created the United Nations, helped to fulfill that commitment. This extraordinary coalition was composed of two dedicated young men from Minnesota who were doomed to ultimate political failure — Ball from indifference, Stassen from ambition. Both were Republicans, and both were at home in the Minnesota traditions of independence and of greater concern with public issues than with personalities.

When Harold Edward Stassen was elected governor of Minnesota in 1938, he was at thirty-one the youngest man thus far ever elected a chief executive of one of the United States. He had graduated from the University of Minnesota with a scholastic average previously unexcelled. His early political successes made him a serious contender for the presidency in 1948. By the late 1950s his luster tarnished, and during the 1960s, he acquired the reputation of the "available man" — whether as a candidate for president of the United States, governor of Pennsylvania, or mayor of Philadelphia. Despite Harold Stassen's unquestioned talents and political perception, he was an underachiever by his own terms. A Minnesota political scientist, assessing the former governor in 1960, wrote that while he was "A resourceful and creative leader, with a keen mind and boundless energy, he perhaps carries within him the tragic flaw of the traditional tragic protagonist; at any rate his critics view his overriding ambition for power as too ill concealed and as the primary cause of his reverses." [1]

Sustaining this judgment and adding another dimension to it, John Gunther pointed to Stassen's ambition as his chief defect along with his "enigmatic coldness" and his lack of "human spark." Most revealing is Gunther's report of Stassen's reply to a query. "He believes," Gunther wrote, "in three things: (1) himself; (2) world organization; and (3) the people — if you give them an even break." [2]

Stassen's failures do not lessen the remarkable record he made as governor of Minnesota from 1939 to 1943, and as an administrator and adviser during the Eisenhower regime from 1953 to 1958. As a private citizen, he continued to generate ideas reflecting his originality and concern over issues of public policy. Perhaps his most lasting achievement in Minnesota was his transformation of the state's Republican party. After eight years of Farmer-Labor rule, Stassen was elected governor in 1938 with support he inspired and organized from a new generation of Republicans, young, energetic, and looking toward change and innovation. He left an indelible mark on the character of the Minnesota GOP, which in the years that followed supported party leaders of liberal and internationalist persuasion. As governor Stassen turned his back on isolationism, chose Ball for the United States Senate, and helped to create a climate of opinion which made possible the subsequent elections of men like Walter Judd.

The significance of the Stassen influence on his party must be put into a historical perspective of overwhelming Republican dominance in Minnesota politics. Democrats had not been a significant influence; from 1900 to 1944 they had elected only one senator and five congressmen. In the Stassen era the Democratic party was dormant, if not dead; it would be revived only by its union with the stronger Farmer-Labor party in 1944. After Pearl Harbor all of Minnesota's representation in Washington in 1942 was Republican except for Farmer-Laborite Harold C. Hagen of the ninth congressional district, who would defect and join the Republican ranks in 1945. When President Roosevelt's predilections toward support of the Allied cause became manifest in the 1939–41 period, Republicans, angered by his record and eager for office, were dead set against his foreign policy. This was not entirely an ideological posture — much of the motivation rested on the hard fact of political opposition. In Minnesota, however, Republicans of the Stassen stripe searched out and supported candidates with internationalist views. The endorsement of Roosevelt by Ball in 1944 was perhaps the most unusual expression of that attitude. [3]

The story of Stassen's early life has a Lincolnesque quality. Born on April 13, 1907, to parents of modest means — they were truck farmers in West St. Paul — he worked at odd jobs to finance his education. He graduated from high school at fifteen, from the University of Minnesota at nineteen, and — despite an all-night run as a railroad conductor — concluded his law school training before he was twenty-one.[4]

Stassen joined forces with Elmer J. Ryan, a fellow law school graduate of opposite political persuasion, to start the practice of law in South St. Paul. Within a year he filed for public office and was subsequently elected Dakota County attorney. Stassen set about organizing the Young Republican League and made it an instrument of his 1938 campaign to gain the nomination and win the election against Elmer A. Benson, the incumbent governor. Stassen has stated that his nomination "basically came from the young men and young women in the Republican Party. . . . Then others who were more independent-minded and some of the business people began to also support us." His long-time political ally, Edward J. Thye, had similar recollections about the components of Stassen's support, identifying them largely as both young and new to politics.[5]

Benson, who had succeeded to the governorship upon the death of Floyd Olson, found himself presiding over the dissolution of the Farmer-Labor empire. There was controversy over communism, and there were charges of corruption; Joe Ball, then a young St. Paul newspaperman, was on the scene to report fully the difficulties and dissensions. The time was obviously ripe for change, and the voters gave Stassen the largest electoral majority yet recorded by a Minnesota governor.[6]

His margin of victory drew Stassen a political coattail legislature that responded by enacting nearly all of his reform measures into law. His administration gained wide support from the people. The pollster, George Gallup, expressed astonishment at the degree of favorable opinion — a whopping 81 per cent; only in the one-party South had he encountered comparable enthusiasm for a political figure. Stassen was not, however, without his critics. The conservative old guard in the GOP called him a boy scout, and "Farmer-Laborites scoffed at Stassen's claim to kinship with midwestern liberalism and progressivism." His champions outnumbered his critics, however, and he was re-elected governor by comfortable margins in 1940 and 1942.[7]

Harold Stassen emerged on the national political scene when he gave the keynote address at the Republican National Convention in 1940. He was then thirty-three years old. When he first outlined his speech, he had intended to sustain the generally accepted Republican view that the United States should stay out of European entanglements and war. Further, he would call for the repeal of the Reciprocal

Harold E. Stassen, 1940

Trade Agreements Act of 1934 because he believed, with Lindbergh, Kellogg, Knutson, and Shipstead, that low tariffs hurt the farmers of the Midwest. Wendell Willkie, who came out of political obscurity to become a dark horse contender for the nomination, pleaded with Stassen not to go the isolationist route. Willkie said that if Stassen "put the Republican Party on record as saying what is going on in Europe is none of our business, then we might as well fold up." [8]

Stassen obliged and generalized in his speech, saying that the American people could not bury their heads in the sand, that technology, communications, travel, and trade "increase the impact of what happens in one part of the world upon the rest of the world." He told the convention that "Blackouts of dictators take the place of lighthouses of free men. It is our grave responsibility to keep burning brightly the light of liberty." While Stassen criticized the Democratic administration for a foreign policy that had been "a big noise and a little stick," he also cautioned that unforeseen foreign policy problems would require future decisions which it would be inappropriate either to attempt to anticipate or to "tie our hands before meeting them. As they are reached they must be faced," he continued, "and the people of this nation must be made aware of what they mean so that informed public opinion may find expression in the policies of the government." The address gave little comfort to the isolationists.[9]

As keynoter, Stassen was supposed to stay neutral in the nominating process. But the pressures from all sides to gain his support were very great, and in midweek of the convention, he cast his lot with Willkie and served as his highly efficient floor manager. The decision may have been a serious tactical error, for the Republican establishment did not look lightly on this break with precedent. Nonetheless, as much as any single factor, it shaped Stassen's commitment to internationalism. Willkie became the candidate, Stassen became chairman of his advisory committee, and the two men became of one mind about one world.[10]

With Ball and others, Stassen in the early years of the war began thinking of the peace to follow. Having stated his conviction that "the walls of isolation are gone forever," he turned his attention to the need for postwar international co-operation. He rejected the "devious diplomacy" of the past and argued that "The nations of the world must not merely agree that they wish to live together in peace; they must establish a mechanism of government to achieve this end." In sum, he called for a continuing organization of the United Nations of the world with limited powers to function in seven major fields: "(1) temporary administration of Axis, backward or disputed territories; (2) maintenance of a police force; (3) regulation of international airways; (4) supervision of sea gateways; (5) stimulation of trade; (6) promotion of health and literacy; (7) enforcement through a basic code of justice." In town and city across the nation, Stassen reiterated his prospectus for peace.[11]

When Governor Stassen began his third term in 1943, he addressed a joint meeting of the St. Paul and Minneapolis Foreign Policy associations at the University of Minnesota. His recommendations for a world organization were specific: a one-house parliament should be organized; representation should be based on literacy, national resources, and financial contributions to the world government; the parliament should choose an executive; the executive should be permitted to name a seven-man council or cabinet with the approval of the parliament, and the cabinet should be assigned responsibility for administering major functions.[12]

Stassen was beginning to be recognized as a national leader. He was in demand as a speaker; he received honors and offices; he was a governor whose desk with increasing frequency was an airplane seat. Whispers of the presidency reached a mild crescendo. When Sinclair

Lewis arrived in Minneapolis to star in his play, *Angela Is Twenty-Two*, the two "Reds" met for the first time. Red Lewis, so the story goes, said to Red Stassen, "How about you running for president?" Stassen replied, "We aren't talking about that at all. We've a job to do here." Lewis was later to say of Stassen, "He's the man for 1944. Big, calm, practical, progressive, with the most amazing eyes I ever saw — the eyes of a man who can calm anybody or any situation." Others were similarly struck by this quality of calm deliberation. A journalist commented in 1943, "He has that kind of arresting personality which involves much more than ordinary leadership or administrative ability — the kind of personality which enables him to master opposition by persuasion rather than by beating it down." [13]

Nearly eight months before the elections of 1942, Stassen told his constituents that he would resign during his next term to join the armed forces. With World War II raging, he said, "The drive for victory against the totalitarian forces that threaten the future of free men will be conducted in the main by the young men of my generation. I want to be with them." True to his word, he resigned as governor on April 27, 1943, and was sworn in as a lieutenant commander in the navy attached to Admiral William F. Halsey's staff in the Pacific. Many of Stassen's close political associates considered the decision to be poor strategy. Governor Thye, his successor, believed that had Stassen stayed, he could have wooed and won the delegates needed to secure for him the Republican party's nomination as president. Instead, upon his return from the war, Thye said, "he forced himself too hard and he made moves which raised questions as to his . . . political judgment." [14]

As Stassen set off for war, he put his farewell words into an article in which he tried to allay concern about national sovereignty and repeated his ideas on the establishment and functions of a postwar international organization. His most telling prose could be found in two short statements: "in our kind of world there are no hermit nations . . . a nation which tries to live unto itself will die unto itself" and "A world that is made safe for differences will be a world in which people will believe many diverse things — by no means all of them conforming to the pattern of what we in democratic America believe to be right. Those differences, however, will not involve conflict, provided they are brought within an orderly organized structure of international society." [15]

While Commander Stassen was on active military duty in the Pacific, his backers were on active political duty in the United States. Although Stassen had promised Willkie that he would not be available in 1944 and had instructed his friends to support the Indianan, those friends entered Stassen's name in the Wisconsin primary. As it turned out in the vote on April 4, Governor Thomas Dewey of New York, who became the Republican nominee, was the front runner; the two absentees, General Douglas MacArthur and Commander Harold Stassen, were about even, and Wendell Willkie was at the bottom. The Wisconsin primary was the political end for Willkie and the Willkie-Stassen alliance, since the man from Indiana never really forgave the man from Minnesota for reneging on his promise. The public mind and the public press dismissed Willkie, but Stassen continued to attract favorable comment. Typical was a 1944 article in *Life* magazine which said in part: "There is no trace of doubt about his liberalism. Long before Tom Dewey . . . Stassen was speaking and writing in favor of a foreign policy of enlightened self-interest." Even among Stassen's critics, one confessed, "He certainly has been right on the international issue and his plan for the organization of the postwar world is the most forthright put out by any Republican candidate for the presidency." [16]

Stassen's opportunity to put some of his ideas to the hard test of international diplomacy came with his appointment by the president, shortly before Roosevelt's death, as a delegate to the San Francisco conference which wrote the United Nations Charter. The state department had recommended Stassen as a leading midwestern Republican, and Roosevelt accepted the recommendation. Stassen prepared himself for the task by consulting with Republican party leaders — a wise political ploy, and with academicians — a useful intellectual move. In the spring of 1945 Stassen, using various publicity outlets, tried to provide the American people with a basis of support for the new United Nations by reiterating the need for international organization and inveighing against old-fashioned concepts of national sovereignty. [17]

The conference opened on April 25, 1945, and the former governor joined his fellow delegates Secretary of State Edward R. Stettinius, Jr., chairman; former Secretary of State Cordell Hull, senior adviser; Senators Tom Connally and Arthur Vandenberg; Congressmen Sol Bloom and Charles A. Eaton; and Virginia C. Gildersleeve, dean of Barnard College. Dean Gildersleeve recorded her impression of Stassen as "a young man of great promise." She considered him a hard worker and a fast learner, handicapped only by his presidential aspirations. "He had to think of possible votes," she wrote. [18]

The discussions went on for nine weeks in some four hundred meetings. Stassen's chief responsibility was to chair a five-power group consulting on trusteeship. He put together the working paper and initiated a procedure of informal negotiations outside the regular meetings of the consultative group which greatly facilitated the proceedings. He proved useful in other ways. In her autobiography, Dean Gildersleeve described an occasion when Stettinius "failed to grasp the rather complicated question which was being raised. Mr. Stassen . . . got up from his chair at the end of the room, walked quietly along and sat down beside our Chairman to help straighten out the tangle." Senator Vandenberg alluded to this same ability in a diary entry in which he called Stassen "one of the ablest young men I have ever known; with not only a tremendous capacity for hard work but also with an equal facility for going to the heart of difficult and complex problems; with a fine personality and a superb earnestness in pursuing the highly important assignment which he has carried here; and with the greatest tenacity in his fidelity to his ideals." [19]

Experienced political journalists also offered the Minnesotan high praise. Among them were Walter Lippmann, who called Stassen "a recognized American national leader"; H. V. Kaltenborn, who remarked on his "sheer brainpower"; Thomas L. Stokes, who termed him the "most interesting new figure on the American political scene"; and William L. Shirer, who commented on his contribution at San Francisco in making the security organization "primarily a world body instead of a group of regional committees." James B. Reston referred to Stassen not only as outstanding but as "an able negotiator on complex and often unfamiliar subjects, patient, courteous but firm." [20]

The Charter was signed in an impressive ceremony by representatives of fifty nations on June 26, 1945. By October 24 the Big Five (China, France, the United Kingdom, the Union of Soviet Socialist Republics, and the United States had acquired this special stature because of their permanence and veto power on the security council) as well as a majority of the other governments had duly ratified the Charter. The United Nations became a living entity. A few days after the close of the San Francisco conference, Stassen admitted that the Charter was a "human document," realistic but not perfect. He singled out as deficiencies the one nation-one vote arrangement in the General Assembly; the veto power in the security council; the optional jurisdiction of the World Court; the limitation of powers (to recommend but not to legislate) in the General Assembly and in the economic and social council; the lack of taxing power; the failure to spell out its bill of rights; the omission of an international police force; and, finally, "The organization will not have direct jurisdiction over the airways of the future nor over the gateways to the seas." [21] In retro-

Stassen signing the United Nations Charter as President Truman, Secretary Stettinius, Senators Connally and Vandenberg, and Representatives Bloom and Eaton look on. Associated Press Wirephoto.

spect, the incisiveness of Stassen's critique is impressive. The weaknesses of the Charter, as Stassen saw them, have been in large part the continuing impediments to the organization's effectiveness. The growth, development, and correction he hoped for have not been fully realized.

After San Francisco, Stassen turned to a serious quest for the presidency. Hoping to enlarge his constituency he wrote, spoke, and traveled. He returned to Minnesota in 1946 to help his old friend, Governor Thye, win a primary victory over Henrik Shipstead for the GOP nomination of United States senator. The outcome confirmed the fact that isolationist policies and attitudes were losing their pulling power in the state. Thye has explained that while he disagreed with Shipstead and thought he should be challenged, he wanted Stassen to do the job. Stassen thought he could better prepare himself for high office by improving his qualifications, especially in international affairs, through extended travel abroad. Thye was convinced that Stassen could have been elected easily and that he made a great mistake in not filing for the Senate. Another close associate suggested that Stassen was reluctant to put himself in the position of explaining votes, feeling that he could be more effective as an outside man.[22]

The Minnesotan had impressive credentials as a presidential contender in 1948. His outstanding record as governor, his military service and veteran status, his wide travels which included a personal interview with Joseph Stalin, and his role as a delegate to the United Nations conference at San Francisco all militated in his favor. His political acumen had served his party well in Minnesota, and state Republicans endorsed his candidacy. In their opinion he had been a dynamic governor, and they identified with his view of the world.[23] Stassen's greatest appeal seemed to be among those who thought that world problems were more critical than domestic ones.

Unlike his friend Senator Ball, who in the beginning spoke for but in the end voted against the Marshall Plan, Stassen remained its enthusiastic and consistent supporter. The tragic condition of Europe in 1947 was eloquently described by Winston Churchill as "a rubble heap, a charnel house, a breeding ground of pestilence and hate." It was in this context that Stassen, speaking in Iowa on May 21, 1947, came up with an idea which he called "Production for Peace." He recommended that the United States set aside 10 per cent of the "total national production of goods and food" for ten years to build "world-wide peace and plenty and freedom." He held that the United States should not look for monetary returns, but should provide this assistance in exchange for raw materials, liberal trade policies, abolition of censorship, agreements to curtail nationalization of industry, and other political and economic objectives. Like Shipstead who was willing to invest dollars for a return of disarmament, Stassen was interested in utilizing the economic strength of the United States to achieve specified ends.[24]

His proposal received support. The *St. Paul Pioneer Press* commented, "The Stassen doctrine thus is the Truman doctrine, without any specific anti-Russian aim, and the [Henry A.] Wallace doctrine, without appeasement." The *Des Moines Register* praised the Stassen program as the only one that offered any real hope. Such diverse commentators as Arthur Krock, Max Lerner, Thomas Stokes, and Dorothy Thompson gave it their benediction. The *New York Herald Tribune*, while admitting that it was easy to tear Stassen's proposal apart, criticized "those who will blindly attack him without bringing up any other answer to the desperately practical human and economic issues to which he points and of which all responsible leaders are growing more and more acutely aware."[25]

Joseph M. Jones, a state department participant in the origin of the Marshall Plan, has intimated that Stassen's peace plan may have helped pave the way for Secretary of State George C. Marshall's memorable speech at Harvard University's commencement exercises the following month: "no atmosphere," Jones wrote, "is more conducive to official action than that created when public figures on the Right and on the Left happen to agree . . . that a daring, even 'visionary' course of action should be taken. The effect upon government officials is almost tangible: it raises their sights; it opens the psychological and political doors to action and invites them to pass through, bearing official proposals which, although more imaginative and effective than would otherwise have been the case, are nevertheless modest and conservative compared with those of their more daring public allies." [26]

Later Stassen was to say on behalf of the Marshall Plan that America's future and the future of freedom in Europe and around the world demanded definite, prompt, and sound action. He viewed the contest between the Soviet Union and the United States as one of ideological and economic competition. He urged the American people to support the Marshall Plan as the agent of free men and free markets. [27]

On a related foreign policy topic, Stassen had a seminal idea. In view of the continuing aggressive tactics of the Soviet Union in Latin America as well as in Europe, he suggested that the United States invite members of the United Nations to join in declaring that any violation of Article 2, section 4, of the Charter be viewed as a threat to their security. (The article stated that "All members shall refrain in their international relations from the threat or use of force against the territorial integrity or political independence of any state.") He specifically named the Brussels Pact nations — Belgium, England, France, Luxembourg, and the Netherlands — and described his proposal as a "collective security association." In effect, Stassen was outlining the kernel of what became the Atlantic Pact Treaty nearly a year later. He had earlier called for revision of the UN Charter to end the single power veto and develop the organization's police power. [28]

It seemed clear that his foreign policy pronouncements were advancing Stassen's campaign for the 1948 presidential nomination. While he gained only two delegates in the New Hampshire primary (Dewey got the other six), in Wisconsin he captured nineteen delegates, General MacArthur had eight, and Dewey had none. In the Nebraska primary Stassen led with 80,979 votes, followed by Dewey with 64,242 and Taft with 21,608. Even in Ohio Stassen won some support away from Senator Robert A. Taft. But Thye thought Stassen had made another serious tactical error by contesting Taft in his home state. Said Thye, "I disagreed with him at the time he . . . filed a slate of delegates in Ohio and I frankly told him that it was unwise. . . . He did not win as many as he had anticipated or hoped for and of course he did make . . . a lot of political enemies."

It is perhaps pertinent to note that Stassen apparently and with some frequency scorned the advice of others. A veteran Minneapolis reporter once observed, "Stassen has been accused of taking no counsel but his own. And it is true a little advice on some occasions would have saved him from mistakes that were embarrassing." [29]

Stassen reportedly based his campaign on four principles of political strategy: to attract young voters away from the New Deal and the Democratic party; to win over some of labor; to gain more support from minority groups; and to win back the western states. [30] Stassen's strategy was evidently upset by the need to capture conservative support from Dewey, the leading contender. As standard-bearer in 1944 against Roosevelt, Dewey had good reason to expect another opportunity, especially against Truman, a much less venerated president whose own party was talking of not nominating him. Still Stassen was a major threat to Dewey's aspirations, and the politicians, the press, and the people were taking him seriously.

In the belief that a direct confrontation with Dewey would work to his advantage, Stassen challenged him to debate the question of outlawing the Communist party. The place was Oregon but the nation eavesdropped through a nationwide radio hookup. Stassen argued that Russia's failure to outlaw the Communist party had been an important factor in allowing the party to come to power, but Dewey devastated Stassen by citing chapter and verse on the legislation and decrees of czarist Russia which had outlawed the party — measures that had not proved sufficient to stem the communist tide. In his history of the Republican party, Malcolm Moos commented, "No designated referees, of course, issued a decision on the Stassen-Dewey debate. The jury in this case was the American press and public." [31]

The jury found for Dewey. From that date Stassen seemed to lose momentum. Dewey won the Oregon primary and went on to challenge the Minnesotan's early commanding lead in the public opinion polls. Stassen's positions seemed inconsistent, and some of his champions cooled, notably Krock and Reston of the *New York Times* and Roscoe Drummond of the *Christian Science Monitor*. Years later in 1963 Reston wrote, "Harold Stassen started on the left and when he began to get the White House itch, he lurched over to the right." His apparent inconsistency was probably an attempt to garner votes from the more conservative wing of the Republican party. [32]

At the 1948 Republican National Convention, Congressman Walter Judd placed Harold Stassen's name in nomination. The demonstration for him was the convention's most exuberant, and it was clear that the young in heart were with the Minnesotan. Despite his toe-stubbing performance in Oregon, Stassen's supporters had reason to be greatly encouraged by a Gallup Poll of May 9, 1948, which revealed public sentiment for Stassen over Harry Truman by 56 per cent to 33 per cent. For two ballots Stassen trailed Dewey and Taft with 157 votes. This was the strongest showing for a Minnesotan since 1880, when the state's ten votes stayed for 28 ballots with Senator William Windom. In 1948 the holdouts were not so stubborn, and Stassen, failing in efforts to garner more delegate support and purportedly refusing to join forces with Taft as the vice-presidential candidate, realized that there was no hope. Minnesota delegates wept as he announced his withdrawal from the contest.[33]

After the election in which Truman scored a personal triumph by being elected president of the United States in a hairline contest over Dewey, Harold Stassen became president of the University of Pennsylvania in Philadelphia. His decision was probably shaped by his desire to have a more influential base than Minnesota from which to pursue the presidency. Pennsylvania, long a power in Republican political circles, afforded him that potential.

The period of the Truman presidency from 1948 to 1952 saw the development of the Korean War. After the invasion of South Korea by a "North Korean army — Russian-trained, Russian-equipped and presumably Russian-inspired" on June 25, 1950, Stassen was stern. He called for a foreign policy posture that would make it crystal-clear that other such probings by the Kremlin would result in direct American retaliatory action. Stassen's penchant for peace modified this strong stance, however, with a suggestion that "We must express a continuous willingness to meet in conference at any time, seeking the avenues for true peace." He continued to achieve public exposure by writing and speaking; in 1951 he took a trip around the world, an exercise that was fast becoming a *sine qua non* for presidential aspirants. On December 27, 1951, Stassen again announced his candidacy. This time a personality new to politics was to cost him the loyalty of Minnesota Republicans.[34]

In 1948 General Dwight D. Eisenhower, president *in absentia* of Columbia University and commander of NATO forces in Europe, had turned down an offer from the Republicans with the statement that he was "not available for and could not accept nomination to high political office." A Gallup Poll in 1950 indicated that the general would be far and away the most popular person the GOP could nominate for the presidency. His nearest rival was fellow educator Stassen, who trailed far behind.[35]

Despite the solicitations of important political figures, the general remained uncommitted. But early in 1952 two events occurred which he admitted were "persuasive." One was his considerable plurality in the New Hampshire primary, and the other was the March 18 Minnesota primary in which Ike's name did not even appear on the ballot. However, as Eisenhower recorded the story in his memoirs, "the state chairman of the 'Minnesotans for Eisenhower' . . . appealed to the voters . . . for a 'political miracle'. It appeared to have happened: more than one hundred thousand people wrote in varying versions of my name." [36]

The Minnesota results were a bitter blow to the favorite-son expectations of Stassen, who led by a slim 20,000 votes. Even though he won twenty-four of the twenty-eight delegates, Ike's write-in was clearly a personal "E-Day" victory that made the front pages around the world. With the Eisenhower band wagon beginning to roll, Stassen was urged by several of his supporters to throw his lot in with the general. No discernible ideological differences existed between them, and the progressive internationalists within the Republican party who supported Stassen would, it was said, turn to a man of like mind whose personality and heroic performance during World War II had captivated the American people. But Stassen carried on his own campaign, evidently in the expectation that there would be an Eisenhower-Taft deadlock out of which he might emerge as the nominee. Many, though by no means all, of the Minnesota delegates were champing at the bit. They could see Ike as a winner; of Stassen's chances, they were neither certain nor confident. They wanted to be sure that Minnesota would be recorded for Eisenhower on the crucial — and many expected it would be the first — ballot. [37]

The state's Republican national committeewoman, Elizabeth B. Heffelfinger, told Stassen that she and some other delegates wanted to go for Eisenhower on the first ballot. She has since said that C. Elmer Anderson, governor of Minnesota, was supposed to ask Stassen for their release, but he did not do it, so she did. Although there was dissension in the ranks, Thye, now Minnesota's senior senator and the chairman of the delegation, held nineteen of the twenty-eight delegate votes solid for Stassen on the first ballot. At the very moment the balloting ended, Congressman Judd ran down the aisle to catch the attention of Representative Joseph W. Martin of Massachusetts, the convention chairman. Another Minnesotan, Newell P. Weed, frantically waved the Minnesota placard, and Thye shouted over the nearest microphone, "Mr. Chairman, Mr. Chairman." Martin gave Thye the nod: "Minnesota wishes to change its vote to 28 for Eisenhower."

The band blared forth with the "Minnesota Rouser" in tribute to the votes that put the general over the top.[38]

Although his state went down in history as a winner, Stassen had lost once again. In the perspective of later years, he disavowed a serious run at the presidency, saying, "I was holding the ground for Eisenhower and it was the Stassen delegation that clinched his nomination." While the state's delegation may have "clinched" the nomination, conversations with delegates indicate that Stassen pleaded with the Minnesotans to stand firm for him.[39]

The former governor remained loyal to the Republican cause, campaigned for Eisenhower, wrote speeches and statements, and worked hard to bring leaders of organized labor into the Republican camp. In the election of 1952, Minnesota reflected the dissatisfaction with "Korea, Communism, and corruption," as one historian put it, and voted for Eisenhower and the Republican party for the first time since 1928. (The new president won all but fifteen of the state's eighty-seven counties.)[40]

Stassen's campaign efforts and his reputation as a pioneer midwestern internationalist won him consideration for a top appointment in the new administration. In 1953 Eisenhower chose Stassen to succeed W. Averill Harriman as director of the Mutual Security Administration, as the foreign aid agency was then called; he was one of the few presidential appointees with considerable experience in public affairs. Stassen stated that the primary objective of Republican foreign aid policy would be "to contribute to President-elect Eisenhower's top objective: peace and prosperity. . . . The Mutual Security program bears a vital relationship to . . . the underlying idea — that there can be no true security in the world without mutual security for the free peoples. . . . Our security depends on their security, theirs on ours. That is elementary but we can't restate it too often." Quick to recognize his talents, the president invited Stassen to attend cabinet meetings and made him a member of the National Security Council, the top policy-making body in defense and foreign relations.[41]

The new administrator was confronted almost immediately with a task of reorganization, for three previously independent agencies — the Mutual Security Agency, the Technical Cooperation Administration, and the Institute of Inter-American Affairs — had been regrouped by Congress into a new Foreign Operations Administration. Congress had also ordered a 10 per cent cut in personnel. Stassen asked the Civil Service Commission to give aptitude and public affairs tests to all FOA employees. The director himself took both tests and scored a rating of "excellent." Based on the test results, Stassen fired 350 of FOA's 1,750 Washington-based employees within one week. For this action he was praised and damned in equal measure, and for a time a new verb, "to Stassenate," had currency in the capital.[42]

Stassen's administration of the United States foreign aid program was vigorous; he began a thorough review of its aims, methods, and working activities. In this undertaking, he enlisted the help of fifty-five American businessmen who surveyed the program in the fourteen countries which accounted for the largest aid expenditures. He also secured the assistance of three outside experts to evaluate the efficiency and organization of the Washington agencies involved in the mutual security program. He elicited the co-operation of colleges, universities, and voluntary agencies to carry out programs of technical assistance overseas. He held regional conferences with mission chiefs in Africa, the Far East, Latin America, the Middle East, and Western Europe. Walter Judd has credited Stassen's effective administration of Judd's amendment to the 1953 foreign aid legislation with paving the way for the acceptance and invigoration of what came to be known as the "Food for Peace" program.[43]

As head of the Foreign Operations Administration, Stassen had occasion to tangle with Republican Senator Joseph R. McCarthy of Wisconsin, who was then riding the crest of a popularity wave as a result of his promise to root communists out of the Truman administration. Eisenhower hoped that with a Republican administration in power the senator from Wisconsin would put aside his wild accusations and wearying tirades. Trying to get along with McCarthy was one of the unwritten laws of the new administration. But when the senator constituted himself a foreign ministry of one and negotiated an agreement with Greek shipping interests in 1953 to stop trading at Soviet and satellite ports, Stassen called this a flagrant interference with the functions of the executive branch which had in reality "harmed" and "undermined" the government's efforts to curb strategic trade with the communists. Continuing his attempts to placate McCarthy, Eisenhower suggested that Stassen had probably meant "infringed" rather than "undermined" — and Stassen was forced to concur.[44]

McCarthy and Stassen had a second confrontation in 1954, when the senator scolded the administration for allowing Allied nations to send "the sinews of economic and military strength" to Communist China. Stassen called McCarthy's statements "untrue" and replied that the shipment of weapons of any type to the Soviet bloc "has been banned, is banned and will continue to be banned by the United States and its allies." "It is one thing," he added, "to have an honest difference of viewpoint and another thing to give false facts in order to reach a really vicious conclusion." This time there was no official backtracking. When Stassen asked the president, "'Did I get out of line at all yesterday?' Ike replied, not a bit, that all Stassen did was call the man a liar to his face."

Despite efficient administration by Stassen and despite Eisenhower's evident appreciation of his energy and abilities, the foreign aid program suffered from continuing congressional displeasure. Another reorganization was instituted in 1955 as a sop to congressional pressures, and John B. Hollister, a lukewarm supporter of the concept of economic assistance, was appointed administrator of the newly named International Cooperation Administration. By then Stassen had a fresh assignment.[45]

In March, 1955, Eisenhower appointed Stassen as his disarmament assistant, a job created by the president and sometimes described as "Secretary of Peace." His task was to conceive a new disarmament policy. Although it was certainly not Eisenhower's purpose, the new post was expected to intensify the existing distrust between Stassen and Secretary of State John Foster Dulles. One commentator noted that the recent statements of the two had been at cross-purposes, adding "Now matters will surely be worse. Mr. Dulles will be threatening war, and Mr. Stassen will be threatening peace, and neither, naturally, will be happy about what the other is saying." The prediction turned out to be accurate.[46]

After World War II the United States had turned its attention to the difficult problems of disarmament in a nuclear age. In 1946 the Americans proposed, in what came to be known as the Baruch Plan, that atomic weapons be placed under international control with the United Nations owning, managing, and licensing all atomic materials and facilities from mine to finished product. Bernard M. Baruch, adviser to presidents, made the United States proposal, which was based on a study and report jointly composed by David E. Lilienthal and Dean G. Acheson, to the twelve-nation UN Atomic Energy Commission on June 14, 1946. It was up to that time the most generous offer ever made in disarmament negotiations. No nation in recorded history had volunteered, as the United States then did, to give up an exclusive monopoly on weaponry of such terrifying magnitude. The Soviet Union rejected out of hand in 1946 the notion of UN control and responded with a proposal to prohibit the production and employment of weapons based on the use of atomic energy. Negotiations since 1946 have consisted of proposals and counterproposals with some small, but not unimportant, agreements concluded before 1968, to ban nuclear tests in the atmosphere, prohibit the proliferation of nuclear weaponry to other nations, and declare the Antarctic and outer space off limits to nuclear weapons. But no comprehensive arms control or disarmament agreements were settled upon.[47]

Nevertheless, by 1955 the time seemed propitious and forward movement seemed possible. With Stalin's death in 1953, the customary Soviet rigidity appeared to have been replaced by a new fluidity of ideas and actions, and the Cold War tensions between East and West were relaxing. A July summit meeting had been scheduled. This era of good feeling was initially upset by Stassen's reservation "withdrawing" all previous United States arms control proposals — in effect announcing that the slate had been wiped clean. In doing so, Stassen reflected the administration's collective opinion that technology had outpaced policy. The control of production was no longer the key to control of nuclear arms; both sides, it was known, had more than sufficient nuclear weapons to wreak havoc on one another. The new problem was one of devising methods to prevent the use of these weapons in a sudden nuclear attack.[48]

Under Nelson A. Rockefeller, who was then the president's special assistant for Cold War strategy, a group of experts had designed a plan to detect military build-ups through aerial surveys. On the first day of the 1955 summit talks, Soviet Premier Nikolai A. Bulganin resurrected his country's shopworn proposal to ban nuclear weapons and limit Chinese, Russian, and United States forces to 1,500,000 men, with a maximum of 650,000 for the British and the French. Eisenhower felt he must counter lest the Russians "steal the propaganda spotlight," and he put on the table Rockefeller's "open-skies" plan, whereby the United States would permit aerial photo reconnaissance if the Russians did the same. The Russians were surprised, the world was pleased, but the disarmament talks continued as before, with the Americans calling for inspection and control first and the Russians insisting on arms reduction prior to inspection. The French and the British sought to reconcile these contrary demands with a formula set forth by the French representative, which called for "Neither control without disarmament, nor disarmament without control, but, progressively, all the disarmament which can be controlled." Still the stalemate continued.[49]

In 1956 the Russians suffered a serious ideological and political setback in the Hungarian revolution. The use of violence and repression in quelling the rebellion seriously damaged the Soviet image around the world. In an effort to restore their prestige and primacy as peacemakers, the Russians made their first positive response in the perennial disarmament discussions. They offered, as part of the new proposal, to "consider" aerial inspection in Europe in a zone of about five hundred miles on either side of the Iron Curtain, on the condition that the West agree to a form of disengagement which would reduce pressures on the Soviet bloc. Ground inspection in this thousand-mile area was also provided for, although its exact boundaries were never made explicit. Eisenhower told Stassen to undertake a serious examination of the proposals. The president's decision was not unanimously supported in his administration. The secretary of state, the Pentagon, and the Atomic Energy Commission were known to have reservations about complying with Russian initiatives at this stage. Despite the inability of either the United Nations or the United States to help liberate the Hungarians, Dulles and his like-minded colleagues evidently hoped that similar revolts in the Eastern European satellites would put such pressure on the Soviet Union that it would be forced to bend to Western will.[50]

The president, however, had the last word. Officially in both the United Nations and its disarmament subcommittee, the United States and the Soviet Union moved closer together: "East-West negotiations have never been as near to fruition before or since," wrote a later observer. One feature of this fruition was a near consensus on aerial inspection in parts of both the United States and the Soviet Union. In the early spring of 1957, Stassen, feeling that agreement was imminent, flew from London, where the UN disarmament subcommittee was meeting, to Washington to confer with the president. Opposition to the proposed terms of the agreement was strenuous both at home and abroad. Admiral Arthur W. Radford, chairman of the joint chiefs of staff, and Lewis L. Strauss, chairman of the Atomic Energy Commission, said that the Russians were not to be trusted. Dulles was less vehement but neither was he enthusiastic. Chancellor Konrad Adenauer of West Germany let it be known that he was definitely against disengagement and all its implications. Britain and France had some reservations. In the end Eisenhower sided with Stassen, telling a press conference that "the United States must be ready to meet the U.S.S.R. half way on a first-step disarmament agreement."[51]

Stassen returned to London with what he believed to be a mandate for agreement. Almost immediately he made a critical diplomatic error. William R. Frye has described the denouement: "On May 31, in his eagerness to establish a bridge of confidence with the Russians, he gave them a memorandum of United States policy at the same time he showed it to the allies, without previously having cleared it with them. . . . The allies, suspecting Stassen of seeking direct negotiations with the Soviets behind their backs, and of bringing pressure on them to accept positions to which they objected, were furious. Britain, France, and West Germany protested to Washington; Stassen was rebuked with the president's approval; Dulles first sent a 'watchdog,' then flew to London himself to take charge." The upshot of this near-agreement was no agreement. For Stassen it was the end of his usefulness to the Eisenhower administration. Sherman Adams, the president's onetime aide and confidant, said that "Stassen's impromptu experiment might have been hailed with praise if it had succeeded," adding that "everybody, including Dulles, had to admit that it was Stassen who had brought the United States and Russia closer to an understanding on many issues than they ever were before or since, no matter how naïve or undiplomatic his methods may have been." A biographer of Dulles noted, however, that because of Stassen's known political ambitions, some government officials feared he would commit the nation to an unsound position simply to gain a reputation as the man who made peace with the Russians.[52]

The Minnesotan was not a man who gave up easily. Before his resignation early in 1958 but after his enforced absence from the UN disarmament talks, he presented a paper to the National Security Council in December, 1957, that directly challenged "almost the entire fabric of Dulles's foreign policy," reported *Newsweek*. Taking issue with the premise that Russia must first demonstrate its good will before the United States would take disarmament negotiations seriously, Stassen called for the suspension of nuclear weapons tests backed by a ground inspection system. This might be followed by "open-skies" aerial inspection and possibly a pullback of troops in Europe, establishing a buffer zone between East and West. He suggested that serious consideration be given to the reunification of Germany along the lines of the Austrian settlement, making that divided nation a neutral entity in the Cold War. He also urged that the cultural exchange program between East and West be greatly expanded. Stassen lost this "last-ditch fight for new negotiations with the Russians." It was his final gasp as a member of the Eisenhower team; he resigned on February 15, 1958. But his effort had made some impression. The reputable *Christian Century* observed that shortly after Stassen bowed out, Secretary Dulles "outlined a program which included without credit many planks of Mr. Stassen's platform for peace."[53]

The foreign policy differences between Dulles and Stassen were once explained by Robert E. Matteson, a long-time aide to the latter, who said that Dulles felt increased pressure could force the Soviet leadership to agreements that would cause the collapse of the communist system without resort to war; Stassen, on the other hand, believed a "relaxation of tension" with the United States would encourage the Soviet Union in the direction of greater freedom. Stassen himself summarized his differences with the secretary of state by saying, "Dulles simply had a different concept of the world picture. . . . He would speak in terms of maximum pressure on the Soviet Union. He would oppose neutrality. I felt we should open up contacts, encourage the evolution of people in Communist areas, recognizing the necessity of nationalism and neutralism." [54]

Assessments of Stassen's accomplishments in the Eisenhower administration by critics within and without the government were much alike. Chalmers M. Roberts, a distinguished diplomatic reporter for the *Washington Post*, wrote sharply of his egotism and his inability to admit error. He praised Stassen's courage and his understanding of "the nature of today's world and the meaning of today's weapons," pointing out that the Minnesotan had struggled with the "most complicated of international subjects, in a jungle of bureaucratic infighting." Roberts concluded that Stassen's departure was "a grievous blow to the chances for an arms agreement." Sherman Adams called him "forceful" and "energetic" but criticized his "unpredictable independence" that "left him few friends among the more conservative people in the administration." [55]

Ostensibly Stassen had resigned as disarmament adviser in 1958 to run for governor of Pennsylvania. Though he had acquired residence there through his five years as president of the university, he was still regarded as an outsider and a carpetbagger. Failing to win the governorship, he opened an office in Philadelphia and continued the practice of law, punctuated by seemingly endless political campaigns for governor (1958), mayor of Philadelphia (1959), and president (1960, 1964, and 1968). [56]

In Minnesota editorial comment on Stassen's presidential quest in 1964 ranged from serious and sorrowful to satirical. Walter Mickelson, an early supporter but later an isolationist opponent in the 1942 Minnesota gubernatorial primary, wrote in the *New Ulm Journal* of January 23, 1964, " 'Childe Harold' who once showed such great promise, now . . . is a national tragedy and a nuisance." A day earlier the *Mankato Free Press* commented, "There are few who do not view his unquenchable thirst for attention as a pitiful, almost tragic, chapter in a frustrated career." In a lighter vein a "breakfast ballad" in the *Minneapolis Tribune* of December 29, 1963, had referred to the permanence of

Stassen's ambition, concluding with the lines, "Thus when the universe is perilled/It finds stability in Harold."

Despite the browbeating he took in election after election, Stassen continued to speak out. On disarmament, China, the United Nations, and Berlin, he had vigorous opinions and new ideas. In 1958, for example, he thought the United States should express "willingness to join in creation of an atomic-armed United Nations police force and a UN agency to send the first man into space." His "Food over the Fence" plan in 1965 offered a peaceful means of reopening the barricaded border between East and West Berlin. In that year, too, he suggested abolishing the security council and substituting a general council of UN members elected by world regions. The votes of these members would be weighted to reflect population, economic status, and other factors, while the General Assembly would remain a "town hall of the world." A panel of mediators and arbitrators would be appointed to settle international disputes.[57]

During the administration of John F. Kennedy, Stassen applauded the nuclear test ban agreement of August, 1963, but he was critical of the proposal for a multilateral force — surface ships armed with Polaris missiles and manned by a mixed force from the NATO countries — as increasing the danger of wars, raising the threat of greater insecurity, and contributing in no meaningful sense to a sound defense or deterrent program. (The proposal was permitted to die under the administration of Lyndon B. Johnson.) One of Stassen's more provocative ideas was to isolate the Bering Strait as a geographic area of arms control. In this region between Russian Siberia and Alaska, no nuclear weapons would be permitted, and the United Nations, using the most advanced detection mechanisms, would be in charge of inspection and control.[58]

In 1967 Stassen came forth with a twelve-point list of causes and cures relating to the struggle in Vietnam, the six-day war in the Middle East, and the failure of the United Nations to mediate these conflicts. He suggested the Arab-Israeli crisis could not be permanently resolved as long as the United States continued its current course in Vietnam. Both the crisis and the war, Stassen argued, demonstrated the urgency of modernizing and strengthening the United Nations — a process which he felt could come about only if the United States took the initiative. The Suez Canal and the Gulf of Aqaba should be placed under UN jurisdiction until a political settlement could be effected. With respect to Vietnam, Stassen advocated unilateral and unconditional United States de-escalation while maintaining a powerful defensive presence until a properly equipped UN police force was authorized to replace the American troops. Accompanying the quieting-down of the war should be a stepping-up of humanitarian and development programs in Vietnam and throughout the world. Finally, Stassen said, "The United States must continue to be very powerful and very alert, but must be restrained by moral principles in the combat use of that force." [59]

Stassen's foreign policy views have been marked by a notable continuity and consistency. He has never lost his faith in the need for international organization. While he did not eschew national preparedness, he sought the alternative routes of disarmament and arms control to ensure national security. Assistance to less fortunate nations, Stassen has argued, could be justified morally, economically, and politically. He has been willing to give America's potential adversaries the benefit of the doubt. As both candidate and public official, he did not equivocate on his foreign policy positions in order to appeal to the voters or to please an administration.

He has continued to press his views on officialdom, party leaders, congressmen, and leading citizens. "I'm trying to move the foreign policy of this country. . . . If you move these men [opinion leaders], you finally move the policy of the country," he said in 1967. Dissatisfied with the results of his efforts, Stassen sought the presidency for the fourth time in 1968 as a way of getting a hearing. "I couldn't move any other Republican candidates on Vietnam so I decided to run myself," he said. "What happens to me as an individual is of no consequence. The important thing is to get my ideas across, and I can do that best as a Presidential candidate." This effort was undistinguished in its impact and distinguished in its content. Though Stassen plumped for peace, few took him seriously; other events and other individuals had a far greater influence in bringing Vietnam to the peace table. In the New Hampshire primary, Stassen collected 407 votes; in Wisconsin, where he made his best showing, 28,453; in Nebraska 2,587; and in his old nemesis, Oregon, "about five." His nephew, J. Robert Stassen of South St. Paul, put his name into nomination at the Republican convention, counting it "a signal honor to place in nomination . . . the name of a man who has dedicated his life to the cause of world peace and the freedom of man." Stassen got only two delegate votes. [60] In his belief that he could best command attention by being a candidate, Stassen was apparently impervious to the reality that his constant candidacy so alienated people that his words fell on deaf ears.

His commitment to international organization was an early one formed in his college years and cemented by his association with

Wendell Willkie. In carrying out this aim, he helped lift his state and his nation out of what he has termed "the dark groove of isolationism." His labors at the creation of the United Nations were notable and his efforts on its behalf and for disarmament were strenuous. His choice of an epitaph, "He laid the foundation for a lasting peace," may be an inflated one, but his dedicated work has earned him more than a footnote in the twentieth-century history of American foreign policy.[61]

Chapter 8

THE FOREIGN POLICY MISSION
OF WALTER H. JUDD

*"We . . . supported the administration's strong policy
of resisting the Communists in Europe; we opposed its
weak policy of trying to appease and bring in the Communists in Asia. The policy in Europe was sound. It
succeeded. The one in Asia was unsound. It failed."*
WALTER JUDD, 1953.

IN 1943, as Harold Stassen took temporary leave of politics to go to
war, one of the congressmen elected as a result of the incipient internationalist outlook the governor helped to foster in Minnesota took
his seat as the new representative from the state's fifth district. When
Walter Henry Judd walked into the House of Representatives as a
freshman congressman in 1943, the United States was in the midst
of a war he had predicted. On the morning of the attack on Pearl
Harbor on December 7, 1941, Dr. Judd, a practicing Minneapolis
physician, had given yet another of his innumerable speeches warning
Americans of the aggressive intentions of the Japanese. His personal
observations as a medical missionary in China had convinced him that
Americans must be alerted to the conflict in the Far East, which put
national security and international peace in jeopardy. His accurate
forecast of the imperialist intent of Japan catapulted Dr. Judd from
medicine to politics. The new congressman's field of expertise was
Asia, but his interests were world-wide. His skills in oratory and persuasion helped to change the fabric of foreign policy thought in the
state and nation.[1]

Like Joe Ball, Judd was indifferent to the minutiae of politics, but
he shared with Harold Stassen an unswerving loyalty to the Republican
party. The foreign policy judgments of the three coincided. Though
Judd, like Stassen, parted company with Ball over the Marshall Plan
and though he and Stassen came to disagree in later years over
Vietnam, all three men championed the cause of international
organization. As Joe Ball in the United States Senate represented the
Minnesota break with the isolationist tradition in the 1940s, so, too,
did Walter Judd in the House. Though Harold Stassen had chosen

a political career, Ball and Judd were wrenched from their primary occupations of journalism and medicine, the senator by appointment, the congressman by the importunings of citizens. This trio of Minnesota Republicans was among the leaders of the internationalist wing of the GOP. Ball's internationalism was marred by his refusal to vote for the Marshall Plan and Judd's by his equation of America's involvement in the world with intervention in Asia. Walter Judd's political success — and his defeat — devolved from attitudes and judgments shaped by his ten years as an American medical missionary in China from 1925 to 1931 and from 1934 to 1938.[2]

Judd was born on September 25, 1898, in the tiny community of Rising City, Nebraska. He attributed his interest in mission work to his mother — "the only educated woman in town" — who taught school and Sunday school and insisted that visiting missionaries and lecturers stay in the Judd home, so that the seven children would have some exposure to talk of "faraway places with strange sounding names." A map in church showing the travels of Saint Paul also excited Judd's interest and determination to see something of the world.[3]

After receiving his degree in medicine from the University of Nebraska, he was assigned in 1925 by the Congregational Foreign Mission Board to Fukien Province in south China. There he had two close brushes with death — one at the hands of the communists who had occupied the area around his hospital and were about to execute him as a hated English "colonialist" (he persuaded them in the nick of time that he was an American), and the other with malaria. The latter forced him to return to the United States, where he moved to Minnesota to take a surgical fellowship at the Mayo Clinic in Rochester. While Judd refined his surgical techniques at the clinic, he also began, in his infrequent spare time, to make speeches about China to Minnesota audiences. After an interim of three years, he returned to the Far East in 1934, this time to Fenyang in the dry nonmalarial climate of Shansi Province in northeastern China. In 1936 when the communists moved into that area, the doctor evacuated his wife and daughter but returned himself and remained throughout a long communist siege. After the Japanese invasion began in 1937, forcing a shaky united front between the contending forces of Chiang Kai-shek and the communists, Dr. Judd ministered to many communist leaders, including Lin Piao, later defense minister of the People's Republic of China and, for a period, rumored heir apparent to Mao Tse-tung. Judd was still in Fenyang when the Japanese captured the city on February 17, 1938. Five months later he left China and rejoined his family in the United States.[4]

It was then that the doctor took up the educational cudgel in earnest. Forsaking medicine, he wrote and lectured for two years in an effort to warn the American people of the "immediate danger from Japanese imperialism and the long-term threat of Communism in Asia." He returned to the United States, as one historian has noted, "to become Chiang Kai-shek's most devout supporter." In Minnesota, as in other states where he spoke, typical audiences included church groups, schools and colleges, civic organizations, businessmen's associations, and radio listeners. In all, he addressed about 1,400 audiences in 46 states from August, 1938, to the latter part of 1940.[5]

The essence of Judd's message was that the United States should cut off trade and stop supplying war materials to Japan. He described his personal experiences as an American sharing the terror of the Chinese during Japanese air attacks using planes largely built, fueled, and armed with raw materials supplied by the United States. A skillful speaker, the medical missionary told his listeners that "their own scrapped automobiles were converted into Japanese bombs."[6]

Judd was no friend of neutrality legislation, claiming that it sterilized the United States by making no distinction between aggressor and victim. In his view, this country should have taken preventive non-military action. Specifically, he wanted the nation to place an embargo on the sale and shipment of all war materials to Japan and to refuse to buy Japanese goods, thereby denying the ingredients of battle and the dollars which helped finance the war effort. In answer to the fears, spoken and silent, that such actions would lead to war, Judd responded that since they would curtail the means of combat, these moves could serve to prevent war.[7]

Called to testify before the Senate foreign relations committee in 1939, the doctor elaborated on his contention that in the interests of peace, security, and prosperity, the United States should impose an economic blockade on Japan. He insisted the reprisals he advocated did not include sending over "an American son or a ship or a dollar to carry on a war against Japan." In an exchange with Senator Vandenberg, who raised the question of Japanese reprisals against the Philippine Islands, Judd said that if the United States decided not to defend the islands, "they ought to be told that now and not strung along as Czechoslovakia was and left at the last ditch" in World War II.[8] The positions Judd took then remained constant: do not aid the aggressor; define and keep your commitments.

The doctor's admiration and sympathy for the people of China were an outgrowth of his experiences and his expectations that, given a breathing spell of peace, the Chinese could build upon their impressive progress in the years from 1932 to 1937. He regarded China's achievements in that period as unexcelled by any other nation in history. The great tragedy, Judd thought, was that China's faith in the leadership and protection of the United States was being undermined by American indifference to Japanese aggression. Again and again the medical-turned-political missionary called for measures to prevent Japan's acquisition from the United States of the military and industrial means of aggression. He held no brief for the wishful thinkers who hoped they could be insulated from the whole unpleasant business. Technology which "jammed us into one neighborhood with the rest of the world" had rendered isolationism obsolete, he said. "The world cannot be wrecked and we go unscathed." [9]

After more than two years of political missionary work carried on at considerable personal sacrifice, Walter Judd moved to Minneapolis and resumed the practice of medicine early in 1941. Even though he was filled with a sense of his failure to alter public policy, he enjoyed some success with respect to private action in Minneapolis. There a group opposed to helping Japanese aggression was formed to write letters on the subject to Washington officialdom and to persuade American women to wear cotton rather than silk stockings as a way of denying dollars to the Japanese. Public attention was aroused by the slogan, "American legs will defeat Japanese arms." A number of prominent citizens lent their names, their time, and their money (and the women, their legs) to the cause. [10]

Dr. Judd continued to use the speaker's platform to air his views, and increasingly he attracted a following among influential Minneapolitans, who realized that the United States could not stand apart from events in Europe and in Asia. Some he had converted or convinced; others, reaching similar conclusions independently, rallied around Judd's leadership. Less than a month before Pearl Harbor, Representative Richard P. Gale of the third congressional district agreed with Harold Knutson that "the feeling in Minnesota is still predominantly anti-war," but he also believed that "the feeling is stratified, the nearer you get to the social and economic top, the stronger is the feeling for intervention." It was this group, in large part, that coalesced around Walter Judd. [11]

The Japanese attack on Pearl Harbor made the doctor a prophet with honor in his own land. With the oncoming of the 1942 election, he was approached by Minneapolitans of the "social and economic top" who urged him to run for Congress. Oscar Youngdahl, the Republican incumbent from the fifth district, which embraced most of Minneapolis, was a consummate, though ineffective, isolationist. A victory

Walter H. Judd, 1968

by Judd would be a shift from that tradition. He resisted the importuners with the plea that his profession was medicine, not politics. They replied that he could not ignore his civic responsibilities and that he should "put up or shut up." When Judd asked the advice of his father in Nebraska, he was reminded that members of the Judd family had fought in the Revolutionary War, the War of 1812, the Civil War, and World War I. The implication was clear to Walter Judd — who himself had emerged from World War I as a second lieutenant in the field artillery — running for public office could be his contribution to the prosecution of this war and to the creation of peace. In announcing his candidacy in June, 1942, Judd said in part, "It had never occurred to me that a situation might arise where it would appear that I could best serve my country by leaving my profession for public office. But these are no ordinary times."[12]

In making the decision to run for Congress, Judd set down a number of conditions which were readily agreed to by his partisans. They would raise the money, provide the materials, and manage the campaign. He would do what he had been doing all along — discuss and debate the issues. In his fifteen-plank platform, winning the war and winning the peace were high on the list. A "declaration of principles" published in the *Minneapolis Sunday Tribune and Star-Journal* of July 26, 1942, called for successful prosecution of the war and for a peace built on individual rights and opportunities as well as teamwork among nations, whose differences could be accommodated in the mutual admission that working together "for the good of all is the true way to promote the good of each." [13]

In calling for world order, Judd refuted the arguments of isolationism and emphasized that nations, like neighbors, cannot escape the consequences of contagious incidents. Furthermore, the United States, which was, he said, "inescapably part of the world," had to be more than a good neighbor; it must be a *good citizen* and carry its rightful share of the world's load." In Judd's opinion, there could never be future security and prosperity until "a decent world order" was established. These foreign policy pronouncements would have been even more jarring in Minneapolis, which was "relatively isolationist," had Judd not had a powerful helper in his corner reinforcing his arguments. [14]

Gideon D. Seymour, editorial head of the *Minneapolis Star-Journal*, was, according to Judd, the single person who "did the most to change the thinking of Minnesotans during the crucial period of the late thirties and through the forties." The two men had come to know and respect one another for their kinship of views, and Seymour galvanized the power of the press on Judd's behalf. The challenger won over Youngdahl in the GOP primary in a fairly close contest and went on to a triumph of no mean proportions in the general election, garnering 60,883 votes to 18,566 for the Farmer-Labor candidate, Joseph Gilbert, and 15,976 for the Democratic candidate Thomas P. Ryan. After the primary, which was the critical contest, Judd wrote to a prominent Minneapolitan, saying, "I am perfectly aware that without the assistance and support of yourself and several others who astounded the routine political dopesters by going out on a limb for one so totally a newcomer, we could not have been successful." [15]

As Judd took office, he was convinced that only three types of security existed in the world's history: individual armaments typified by the gun on the hip; balance-of-power arrangements which sometimes led to "perversions of justice, to vigilante groups," and ultimately to lynch law; and collective security which implied organization and order under law. Man, he said, had come to know that he was his brother's keeper, but "Our generation refused to learn that lesson when it came to relations between nations." Throughout his adult life, Judd kept that lesson as the touchstone of his foreign policy beliefs. [16]

His maiden speech in Congress on February 25, 1943, reflected his primary interest in Asian affairs. While he argued then (but not later) for the importance of Russian co-operation to win the war against Japan, he understood the provocations which had led Japan to follow a militaristic course. Fundamental Japanese insecurities — which Judd defined as an inferiority complex, a lack of creativity and originality, and a hazardous geography beset by typhoons and earthquakes — were reinforced by the League of Nations' insult in denying Japan's request for a statement in the Covenant affirming the principle of the equality of races. This international affront was further compounded, Judd explained, by the American immigration act in 1924, which among other restrictions denied the right of citizenship to Asian aliens. Although directed at all Orientals, the Japanese were the largest group affected, and this expression of discrimination, abrogating a long-standing gentlemen's agreement to the contrary, inflated their sense of inferiority and outrage.[17]

Judd asserted that the American people "are reaping today in bloodshed what we sowed then in arrogance," and he gave continuing attention to the repeal of laws excluding Orientals from immigrating to the United States and denying them eligibility for citizenship. In 1952 Judd was to earn the gratitude of both the Chinese and Japanese by his successful legislative efforts to include in the McCarran-Walter Immigration Act provisions removing racial discrimination from United States immigration and naturalization laws and lifting the ban on the right of first-generation Orientals to become citizens. In 1953 he succeeded in upping the quota allotment for both Chinese and Japanese immigrants.[18]

During his first year in Congress, Judd, like Ball and Stassen, repudiated the old Minnesota notion shared by Republicans and Farmer-Laborites that protectionism favored Minnesota farmers. As he argued for the extension of the Reciprocal Trade Agreements Act, he said, "I believe the trade agreements are one of the best weapons yet devised for carefully, progressively, building up better relations and trade with other nations." In a major speech on the floor of the House, Judd compared the economic interdependence of Minnesota with other states to the mutual commercial dependency of the United States and other countries.[19]

In support of the Fulbright Resolution — a more modest expression of the Senate's B_2H_2 resolution — favoring the creation of international machinery to maintain peace and justice after the war, Judd spoke of the nation's four choices. The first of these was isolationism, which Judd rejected out of hand; the second was imperialism, which he termed suicidal; the third possibility was to buy the world's good will, which Judd called self-defeating. "If we cannot escape the world, or rule the world, or buy the world, is there any course left except a genuinely cooperative effort to achieve with our allies an organized security?" he asked. This fourth option was the path he deemed imperative.[20]

During his freshman year, the new congressman from Minnesota did not neglect the educational process which had first brought him national attention, crisscrossing the country and addressing groups. In the summer of 1943 Judd was among the foremost spokesmen for the B_2H_2 and Fulbright resolutions. His speeches and those of Ball and Stassen sounded the same theme: the shibboleth of the past — that what happened abroad was none of America's business — was no longer relevant; if World War II had any lesson for this nation, it was that Japan's invasion of China and Germany's attack on its neighbors was tantamount to aggression against "the main street of every city and town in America." Like Stassen, Judd concluded that if the United States had the wisdom to work with others in war, surely Americans could perceive the benefits of co-operative efforts to secure peace. It was not only in the country's best self-interest, it was also the responsibility of the United States to do so, for, said Judd, "no other nation has such a heritage of trust and good will," to exert leadership to that end.[21]

With the passage of the compromise Connally Resolution in 1944 and the ending of the war the following year, a new chapter opened for international organization. The United Nations took shape in the San Francisco conference in April, 1945; the Bretton Woods agreement establishing the International Monetary Fund and the World Bank was approved in the summer of that year. Of the eighteen representatives who voted against the monetary agreement, two were from Minnesota — Harold Knutson and Joseph P. O'Hara; a third, H. Carl Andersen, was announced in opposition. Judd voted for both, as well as for participation in the United Nations Educational, Scientific, and Cultural Organization (UNESCO). Later he was to author legislation affiliating the United States with the World Health Organization (WHO) and the International Children's Emergency Fund (UNICEF). Judd's clear-cut support of international machinery derived from his four-point definition of the minimum conditions of peaceful coexistence: no peace without order; no enduring order without justice; no justice without the machinery of justice; and no machinery of justice without the good will to make it work.[22]

What was lacking in the first years of the new United Nations was the good will to make it work. The ambitions and negativism of the

Soviet Union were causing concern that the infant machinery of the United Nations would go down the drain and an already shaky peace would be shattered. In 1947, when the congressman's influence on these issues was enhanced by his appointment to the House foreign affairs committee, and again in 1948, Judd joined other Republicans and Democrats in both houses in urging President Truman to call a conference to reorganize and strengthen the United Nations. (Harold Stassen was urging much the same course outside the halls of Congress.) Judd and his colleagues had in mind reforms which would strengthen the security council, especially by eliminating the veto on issues of planned or actual aggression, by providing for inspection of and control of nuclear weapons, and by establishing an international police force recruited from the ranks of smaller nations. If the Soviet Union should refuse to co-operate, the way would then be open for other nations to organize for their collective self-defense under the authority provided in Article 51 and to pursue, if they chose, regional arrangements authorized by Article 52. Judd claimed that "To call such a general conference to revise the United Nations Charter is not a vote of nonconfidence, a condemnation of the United Nations idea. Rather, it is a reavowal of our faith in that idea and an expression of our determination to achieve it in practice."[23]

After the invasion of South Korea by North Korea on June 25, 1950, Judd was one of thirty-four Republicans and Democrats in both houses (including Richard M. Nixon of California), who again urged in a concurrent resolution the establishment of a United Nations police force made up of volunteers from small nations. Judd maintained that while United Nations machinery had seemed to work in the Korean crisis, its responsiveness was actually a coincidence of conditions not likely to be repeated. In the first place, the Soviet Union had vacated its seat on the security council (in protest against that body's failure to act favorably on the representation of Communist China), and thus was not able to exercise its veto against the UN decision to act. In the second place, four American divisions stationed in nearby Japan were put at the service of the United Nations, allowing an effective military response to the political decision to counter North Korea's incursion. The international force had been improvised (it was supplemented later by small contingents from fifteen other nations). To Judd, this underlined the importance of a permanent United Nations police authority which could operate in similar emergencies, saving American lives and money, increasing American security, and providing greater protection for smaller nations.[24]

Judd's efforts to secure adequate funding for the United Nations and its associated agencies were rewarded in 1957 by President Eisenhower, who appointed him one of five American delegates to the twelfth General Assembly. Judd's credentials as a supporter of international organization could scarcely be challenged. He once confessed on the floor of the House that even though he came "from a staunchly Republican family," he had cast his first vote for the Democratic slate of James M. Cox and Franklin D. Roosevelt in 1920 because he thought the overriding issue of that campaign was the League of Nations. (Cox and Roosevelt had endorsed the league without compunction; Warren Harding, the GOP nominee, had been one of the "strong reservationists" in the Senate.) [25]

The congressman's devotion to the necessity of international organization did not blind him to the limits and defects of the United Nations. While some Americans argued that the crisis in Greece in 1947 should be referred to the world body, Judd opposed the proposal on the grounds that it was contrary to the Charter provision prohibiting UN involvement in matters of domestic jurisdiction, that the UN did not have the tools in men or money to do the job, and that the Russians would veto any effort to counter the communist insurrection. However, when President Truman recommended that the United States furnish aid of considerable magnitude to Greece and Turkey to enable them to resist the Russian-backed threat, Judd reacted favorably. The Truman proposal became the subject of heated debate in Congress with some claiming that the insurgents were not communists but rather rebels against the Greek monarchy, and others arguing that such aid would be provocative and dangerous. Judd was not in either group. "It is not because I want war with Russia; it is precisely because I don't want war with Russia that I beg us not to pursue further the fallacious notion that we can get peace with her by sacrificing our principles and other people's territory," he told the House. To a question from another congressman about the apparent inconsistency of a missionary advocating military assistance for Greece and Turkey, Judd replied that such action was "right and proper" in order to help threatened people "retain their independence instead of allowing them to be murdered or enslaved as people have been wherever Communists have taken over. . . . I think that is a worthy cause for a missionary, especially a missionary doctor, to support." [26]

Judd foreshadowed the domino theory, later invoked by some to rationalize United States support of South Vietnam, with the ninepin theory, predicting that other Middle Eastern countries would fall under communist domination if the United States did not take a stand in Greece and Turkey. Always mindful of China, he posed this question to Secretary of State Dean Acheson in 1947: "If it is a wise policy to urge . . . the government of China to unite with organized Communists there, why is it a wise policy to assist the Greek government to fight against the same sort of armed Communist minorities in Greece?" In his reply, Acheson contended that the situation was very different — that the Chinese Communists had for twenty years controlled a large contiguous land area, and that the United States had provided large amounts of economic and military aid to the Chinese government, which was not on the verge of collapse as was the government of Greece. Although he supported the Greek-Turkish aid plan, Judd insisted, "It is difficult for me to believe that we do not have obligations there [China] almost as great — perhaps greater — than those in Greece, from the point of view of the security of the United States." He never forgot or forgave the failure of the Truman administration to apply the policy of containment in Asia before it was forced to move in that direction by the onset of the Korean War in 1950. In 1953 he remarked, "In Europe it [the government] said, 'We will help you if you keep the Communists out of your government.' In China it said, 'We will help you only if you take the Communists in.' " 27

A consistent champion of military and economic aid programs, Judd referred to the Truman proposal of aid to Greece and Turkey as "merely . . . a furrow," but extolled the Marshall Plan in 1948 as a means to "resist further expansion of the area of tyranny and dictatorship" and simultaneously to "assist expansion of the area of freedom and federation." The various components of assistance — military, economic, and technical — fell into place under the aegis of the variously named mutual security programs administered by Stassen from 1953 to 1955. 28

When the Eisenhower administration took office in 1953, Walter Judd found that one of his major tasks in this Cold War period was to generate support among his fellow party members for the Republican aid program. In general, the congressman from Minnesota appealed to his colleagues' fears of growing communist influence. "I believe we have a good chance to turn back this avalanche of tyranny which threatens to sweep over the rest of the world, and then over us, too," he said in 1953. "What other policy provides a better chance?" As the increasing unpopularity of assistance to the less developed countries was reflected in the American public's frustration at a complex, ungrateful world and in congressional votes, Judd did constant battle with those who proposed reductions in programs of aid for Africa, India, Indochina, Latin America, and the Middle East,

Walter Judd welcoming President Eisenhower to the Twin Cities during the campaign of 1956

or in the contributions to United Nations programs of economic and technical assistance. In protest over the cuts made in President Eisenhower's request in 1957, Judd said, "Mr. Speaker, during this debate several Members have emphasized with satisfaction how much has been cut from the President's request for funds for mutual security. I want to speak for the many Members who believe these reductions are too deep and we want to register our dissatisfaction." Although Judd protested against cuts and argued for increases, he disappointed foreign aid advocates by refusing to go along with proposals for long-term financing. He was not a blind devotee but rather a devoted critic, on occasion finding fault with both the administration and management of the programs. It was because Judd was both champion and critic that he must be judged among the most effective Republican spokesmen for foreign aid.[29]

He was not merely a defender of foreign aid, but an initiator as well. He counted as one of his three most significant contributions in the international field his idea for the Joint Commission on Rural Reconstruction in China. This proposal, adopted in the Economic

Cooperation Act of 1948, was an attempt to organize Americans and Chinese in a co-operative effort to aid in rehabilitating the predominantly rural communities of mainland China. Judd was persuaded that its tardy implementation by the Truman administration denied the program a fair trial. He told Congress that the areas of strongest resistance to the 1949 communist take over could be found in those communities where the program was in operation. The commission was transferred in 1949 to Formosa, where it enjoyed a distinguished success. Famed China scholar, John King Fairbank, has referred to it as "One creative instance of Chinese-American collaboration." Fairbank shared Judd's assessment of the commission's later effectiveness. "Like our own Tennessee Valley Authority, the Joint Commission on Rural Reconstruction on Taiwan has set an example of great interest to developing countries," he wrote in 1971.[30]

The second idea cited by Judd as "probably" among his most important contributions to the content of American foreign policy was his amendment to the Mutual Security Act of 1951 "to further encourage the economic unification and political federation of Europe." A review of the legislative experience of this amendment suggests how the determination of a single congressman can influence public policy. When Judd first offered it in 1948, it was defeated. (It was more moderate but not entirely dissimilar to Senator Ball's proposal in the same year that dollar aid be made contingent on the formation of a union of Western European nations.) In 1949 and 1950 the House foreign affairs committee accepted the somewhat less explicit phrases "unified direction and effort" and "to encourage the further unification of Europe." After congressional acceptance of the amendment in 1951, the administration bill in 1952 included the wording: "The Congress welcomes the recent progress in political federation, military integration, and economic unification in Europe." This, with the administration's addition of "military integration," had been Judd's exact wording in 1948. As a consequence of his interest in European unity, Judd was appointed in 1951 as one of the official United States delegates to a conference at Strasbourg, France. Out of these talks with Lord Michael John Layton of Britain, Paul Henri Spaak of Belgium, and other leaders of Western Europe came the thrust toward unity which later resulted in the organization of the European Economic Community, more widely known as the Common Market.[31]

The third foreign policy initiative which Judd considered of more than passing significance was his proposal, adopted as a section of the Mutual Security Act of 1953, which provided for the transfer of surplus agricultural products from the Commodity Credit Corporation to the Mutual Security Agency to be sold in friendly countries for local currencies. This money would then be used "to increase the security of the United States and to promote its foreign policy by giving military and economic and technical assistance to friendly countries." The congressman credited Stassen's effective administration of this provision as being instrumental in securing the support of the farm bloc and the sponsorship of the agriculture committee in the following year. Entitled Public Law 480, it was nicknamed "Food for Peace" in 1958 by Don A. Paarlberg, an expert in the department of agriculture. The new name did not gain currency until President Kennedy "gave it glamour in his usual dramatic way." [32]

Though his insistence in 1947 that he had worked harder for a world organization than for any other cause was probably accurate, it cannot for Walter Judd be a comment in perpetuity. [33] His preoccupation with Asian affairs and his pro-Chiang Kai-shek anticommunism proved more durable both in depth and in time. The Japanese aggression against China in the 1930s, the ultimate take over of the Chinese mainland by the communists in 1949, the Korean War in the early 1950s, the conflicts in Indochina — especially the escalation of American involvement in the 1960s — these and other Far Eastern issues, inspired the rhetoric for which Judd has been best known. Over the years, he has more often than not been critical of American sins of omission or neglect of Asia. Previously distracted by troubles in Europe and in Latin America where national interests seemed more pressing to policy makers, the United States reaped the unhappy consequences of what Judd regarded as American misunderstanding of Asians in general and misjudgment of the Chinese Communists in particular.

During his twenty years in Congress, Judd traveled widely — to Europe seven times and to the Far East eight times to study and report to his colleagues on conditions. The earliest of these trips in 1944, when he flew over the Himalayas into wartime China, reinforced his earlier impressions. The former missionary was convinced that the Chinese Communists were not, as some argued, democratic-agrarian reformers. He cautioned against their coalition with the Chiang Kai-shek government, maintaining that the primary allegiance of the mainland communists was to the Soviet Union and that their chief aim was to make Russia a power in Asia as well as in Europe. Admitting that Chiang was no democrat in the American sense, Judd nevertheless urged support of the general's administration as the only viable countervailing power to the communists. [34]

Specifying that "There are few subjects about which American thinking is more confused today than it is about China," Judd asked in 1945 that the United States moderate its criticism, provide material and political assistance, and make an effort at greater understanding of the non-Communist Chinese. America's failure to act, he warned, might find the United States in a racially taut world, in which the colored majority can "outwork and undereat the white man, they will outsuffer him, they will outwait him, and they will outbreed him." Taking issue with those who criticized the central government of China because it was undemocratic, corrupt, and inefficient, Judd maintained in 1947 that "We have got to put first things first. And the first thing is not that China have a better government but that she have a free and independent and Chinese Government." Judd's perception that the United States should not have applied Western standards to an Oriental culture was doubtless correct, but his perception did not extend to the hard reality that postwar America was not willing to commit the resources necessary to "save" China — if, indeed, that could have been achieved. In 1948 he countered the apparent American insistence on democracy, unity, and efficiency in China as preconditions for assistance by quoting a "great American out in the Far East" (whom he later identified as General Douglas MacArthur): "For the first time in the history of our relations with Asia, we have endangered the paramount interests of the United States by confusing them with an internal purification problem in China. It may prove to be the greatest single blunder in the history of the United States." [35]

Judd mounted his crusade with vigor. Between 1945 and 1948 he gave, as he said a decade later, "one speech, with variations, scores of times." In this speech Judd maintained that America's involvement in the Pacific during World War II was predicated on the belief that the United States could not afford to let one totalitarian, militarist nation — Japan — get control of the manpower, materials, and potential markets of China and Asia. Yet a good many Americans were evidently ready to abandon China to the control of another totalitarian, militaristic nation — Russia. To Judd, this was "an almost incredible performance." [36]

In fact United States policy was not as cavalier as Judd made it out to be. President Roosevelt had, for all practical purposes, elevated China to kingpin status in his hope for its wartime success and postwar greatness. He persuaded Congress to remove the humiliation of extraterritoriality and the discrimination of exclusion. He tried to accommodate the demands and the temperaments of the Chiang Kai-sheks. Though both China and the Soviet Union thought they were being shortchanged in strategic decisions and in the allocation of materials, differences among the Allies in the conduct of the war had to be compromised. No single nation was content with every decision. In his determination to involve Russia in the war against Japan, Roosevelt agreed at the Yalta conference in February, 1945, to the *status quo* of Outer Mongolia as Russian domain and to a joint Sino-Soviet occupancy of Manchuria won back from Japan. In turn, Stalin acquiesced in Roosevelt's hope for China's survival by concluding on August 14, 1945, a pact in which the Yalta agreements were cemented. In it the Soviet Union promised to aid the established Nationalist government rather than the Communist revolutionary party and to refrain from meddling in China's internal affairs. In a variety of ways, the Soviet Union abrogated its promises and the Chinese Communists became stronger, the Nationalists weaker. [37]

Throughout this period the United States supplied Chiang Kai-shek with $2 billion in military supplies and other forms of assistance. General George Marshall went to China in 1946 to try to mediate the differences which threatened civil war and to effect some kind of compromise political settlement. When that effort failed and when Chiang finally fled to Formosa in 1949, the policy of the Truman administration remained passive and neutral. This continued even with the beginning of the Korean War in 1950 when the American seventh fleet was interposed between Formosa and the mainland to insulate each from the other and prevent a contagion of the conflict. A subsequent decision to renew military and political aid to Chiang Kai-shek committed the United States to support the Nationalist regime. When the Eisenhower administration took office in 1953, the unleashing of Chiang Kai-shek for possible forays against the mainland became official policy. From that moment until the late 1960s, the United States course vis-à-vis the People's Republic of China was, with a few modest exceptions expressed in the 1960s, one of containment and isolation.

Even though it is generally agreed that aid from Washington to the Nationalists in 1945–47 exceeded that from Moscow to the mainland Chinese, Judd viewed the Chinese Communists as dominated by the Kremlin. He could not countenance American diplomatic efforts to gain a Russian promise to come into the Pacific war theater. In 1950 he said, "I was seized with the most intense feeling of dismay I have ever known . . . we were inviting in another potential enemy, Russia, and starting to build it up in Asia." The doctor recalled that he had sent a personal appeal to Truman the day before he went to the Potsdam conference in July, 1945, urging that the United States keep Russia out of the Pacific war. But Truman, six months after Yalta, was eager to get a confirmation of the Russian pledge to enter the Pacific war.[38]

It had become usual to hear Judd described as "the man who certainly knows most about the Far East" — a description used by *Time* magazine in the June 18, 1945, issue. Two months earlier on the floor of the House, the congressman had predicted that "if America gets into another war, almost certainly it will also be through Asia." Both the Korean War and the Vietnam conflict verified his analysis. Of Korea, Judd said in 1953 that it was more than a struggle of arms; it was a fundamental contest between philosophies and systems at variance. Korea deepened Judd's conviction that in the confrontation with communism, the United States had abandoned the will to win. He interpreted Truman's sending of the seventh fleet in 1950 to act as a kind of buffer between Formosa and the mainland as having the effect of keeping the Chinese Nationalist forces prisoners on the island. He was particularly exercised in April, 1951, by Truman's dismissal of General MacArthur from command in Korea when he wanted to strike at the sources of North Korean support in China. The dismissal constituted a decision to confine the dimensions of the war, which Judd regarded as disastrous. He told Congress it was "the abandonment of a policy of trying to win victory in Korea and the adoption of a policy of trying to made [*sic*] a deal with the Communists, to accommodate ourselves, to accept, to adjust to Communist control of North Korea and mainland China."[39]

Judd and William F. Knowland of California were popularly regarded as the House and Senate leaders of the so-called "China lobby." (Knowland was often referred to as the "Senator from Formosa.") Outside the Congress, Alfred Kohlberg, head of the American China Policy Association, William Loeb, a New Hampshire publisher, and Frederick C. McKee, spokesman for the China Emergency Committee, were the most prominent leaders. In and out of Congress they pressed for greater support for Chiang Kai-shek's Nationalists, attacking those who doubted the latter's ability to man a triumphant return to the mainland. In 1953 with Judd as one of the founders, the group organized the Committee of One Million Against the Admission of Communist China to the United Nations to collect a million signatures of those opposed to seating the communists in the United Nations. Later the committee was re-formed and renamed the Committee of One Million and took credit in the 1950s for preventing any significant modification in the policy to support the Republic of China on Taiwan and to isolate the People's Republic of China.[40]

With the Eisenhower administration in power in 1953 and with the famed "unleashing of Chiang Kai-shek," Judd hoped that Formosa could be a launching pad for the liberation of the mainland. When Harold Stassen appointed Harry A. Bullis, president of General Mills, to investigate the mutual security program on Formosa, Judd wrote that "Such an act will upset the Kremlin's balance of power and lead, I am confident, to a relatively quick crumbling of this whole world movement. That is, there are risks and difficulties in a positive program looking toward the liberation of the mainland of Asia, again principally from within coupled with effective assistance from without — but there is hope in such a program." [41]

"I have been a salesman for one idea: that Communists act like Communists," Judd said frequently, and he meant communists Kremlin-style. As late as 1959 he reported that he told a "very important official in Washington," who indicated little concern about Red China "because he was sure the interests the Chinese Communists have as Chinese would lead them into conflict with the Soviet Union," that "This proves, sir, only that you don't know anything about communism." Pointing out that the communists used tactics that Judd described as the five "T's" — truce, talks, trade, trust, and time — for their own ends, he proposed that the United States employ four "P's" — "power in support of principles, pledges, and peoples." His experience as a delegate to the UN General Assembly in 1957 had convinced him that the communists were afraid, most of all, of man's yearning for freedom. They feared the aspirations of the people behind the Iron Curtain, and before they dared initiate actions against the outside world, they must first break the "will-to-resist" at home. Though subsequent events have discredited Judd's assessment of the cohesion of communism, they have supported his judgment concerning internal dissent and unrest. [42]

Judd's reputation as the major spokesman for the China lobby in the House of Representatives devolved in large part from his firm stance against the seating of the People's Republic of China in the United Nations. At least six times Judd offered congressional resolutions, taking issue with the justifications for admitting China. He could not accept the argument that the United Nations was meant to be a universal organization embracing all nations. It was clearly limited in the Charter, he asserted, to "peace-loving nations." To those who claimed the right of membership for Communist China because the Soviet Union was in, Judd replied that two wrongs did not make a right; that while the Russians had pretended to be peace-loving, mainland China did not even volunteer such a pretense; that the government was not representative of the people, only of the Kremlin; and that China would be more powerful and dangerous in the United Nations than out. "We do not argue, in the name of realism, that . . . the FBI should take the gangsters in," he told the House in 1956.[43]

By 1959, however, the previous unanimity of congressional sentiment against the seating of the People's Republic was beginning to break down. When some exasperation was expressed on the House floor in 1961 that the same resolution had been passed on many previous occasions, Judd countered by asking, "is the gentleman suggesting that if a man, on his 17th wedding anniversary, tells his wife he loves her, it does not make any difference because he has said it 17 times before?" But the Minnesotan vigorously argued the case against the Communist Chinese for twenty years, and it is little wonder that he sometimes wore patience thin. Even one of his partisans, Republican Representative Clare E. Hoffman of Michigan, commented, "I admit that the gentleman from Minnesota is intellectual, very intelligent, well able to use words, but he spent the formative years of his life in China as a doctor and missionary and, figuratively speaking, he cannot see anything but a Chinese queue." In all fairness, it must be said that Judd did see more than "a Chinese queue" — he saw a diminution of human freedom. China was important to him, not just because he had lived and worked there but because it had become an issue in the postwar ideological conflict between communism and democracy. In his view of the world, areas permitting man a free choice of his own destiny had been greatly diminished since the Japanese invasion of Manchuria in 1931. He felt that it was the responsibility of the United States to proclaim a new doctrine which would obligate it, first and foremost, to support man's freedom whenever and wherever it might be denied or jeopardized.[44]

Recognizing the inherent cautiousness of the leadership of the People's Republic on the mainland, Judd urged a policy of unbending strength in opposing UN representation and United States recognition, and in resisting pressures to resume trade relations. Although he had consistently supported expanding trade with other nations, he drew the line at the communists. The United States must weigh, he said, the possible but uncertain economic benefits of trade with communist tyrannies against the certain political and psychological losses. In the congressman's book, trade with the People's Republic of China would aid that country's interests, not those of the United States. In clear contrasts, according to Judd, wisdom would dictate that every effort be made to enlarge the military, economic, and political well-being of the Republic of China on Formosa.[45]

In 1966 when Judd, then out of office, testified before the Senate foreign relations committee, the *Minneapolis Tribune* of March 29, 1966, termed his "the most dogmatic stand against changes in United States China policy of any witness to appear." Reminding the senators of his first appearance before the committee in 1939 when he warned against the threat of Japan's aggressive expansionism, Judd said that the experience should have taught that "no great expansionist movement has ever stopped until it was checked." He insisted that delays exacerbated the difficulties — the time to act was before aggression escalated. The former congressman took issue with what he called unjustified assumptions. He argued that the communist regime in China was not entrenched — rather it had an uncertain security as did Hitler in Germany, Ahmed Sukarno in Indonesia, Nikita Khrushchev in Russia, Kwame Nkrumah in Ghana, and other like despots. He contended that China's hostility and belligerency had caused its isolation in the international community, and he refused to concur in the belief that diplomatic recognition, trade, and representation in the United Nations would cause China to change its attitudes and activities. Finally he maintained that changes in United States policy would not necessarily produce an evolutionary process more compatible with American interests. The People's Republic took its seat in the United Nations in 1971. At this writing, with trade and diplomatic relations opening up between the United States and mainland China, Judd holds to his position opposing such exchanges. [46]

On the question of Vietnam it was predictable that Judd, given his set of premises, pin pointed the problem as communist expansion, the stake as the future of Asia, and the issue as whether or not jungle law would prevail in the settlement of international disputes. Paraphrasing Franklin Roosevelt in 1967, he argued that "if the lawless elements are not checked at the neighbor's house, we will have to check them later at our own house." The United States must, he said, resist "that sort of behavior while striving patiently to build effective machinery for civilized settlements of international disputes." In Judd's view, if America faltered in Vietnam, the United States would indeed be a paper tiger. If America withdrew from Vietnam, it would be, at least to other Asian nations, an untrustworthy ally. The United States should have more effectively protected American fighting men. He approved the bombing of North Vietnam but would have preferred an open announcement of United States military targets so that the populace could be removed from those areas. Judd had also proposed a "Kennedy quarantine" of Haiphong Harbor, the port of access for outside aid destined for North Vietnam. To weaken the North by air power and supply interdiction and to strengthen the South were Judd's 1967 prescriptions for the successful prosecution of the war in Vietnam.[47]

It must be pointed out that Judd's personal resolve to stand up to communism had been tempered by an equal concern to reduce the dangers of war. In 1961 he initiated legislation in the House proposing a disarmament agency for world peace and security and said that he would have voted for ratification of the treaty to ban nuclear testing had he been a senator in 1963.[48] His record in favor of forms of regional and international organization was clearly established. His fidelity to foreign aid was probably less an instrument of compassion than a means of correcting conditions which, in his mind, served to foment communism.

In these convictions, Judd was in tune with his constituency. He periodically sent questionnaires to persons in his district asking for their views on current issues such as continuing American aid abroad and support of the United Nations. In general Minnesotans favored these measures, but they were less affirmative on issues which touched their pocketbooks. By 1958 the state's Republicans who responded to Judd's polls were backing Eisenhower's foreign aid program by a slightly higher percentage than did Democratic-Farmer-Laborites. Other measures of opinion confirm the results of Judd's questionnaires.[49]

Judd's efforts for the United Nations included a successful 1962 bond proposal under the terms of which the United States would underwrite the international organization for $100 million to help bail it out of a financial crisis. He led a handful of Republicans in the House who joined Democrats and succeeded in fighting off restrictive amendments. Secretary of State Dean Rusk sent a "Dear Walter" letter which said in part: "I want to express my thanks for your great contribution to the success of the United Nations loan legislation. You have really been a workhorse for us on foreign policy matters in the house, and I am deeply grateful." (It was a sore point with Minnesota Republicans that two weeks later President John F. Kennedy was in Minneapolis campaigning for Donald M. Fraser, Judd's opponent for the fifth district seat in the 1962 election. Kennedy, however, did not attack Congressman Judd, probably out of deference to his bipartisan co-operation on foreign policy.)[50]

Only two years before, Judd's political future seemed secure. In 1960, when he gave the keynote address at the Republican National

Convention, his oratory won more than sixty bursts of applause, and the candidate, Richard Nixon, praised his outstanding speech. The general acclaim generated brief support for him as a vice-presidential prospect, backing that came to him as "a traditional Republican" from delegates "of a more conservative nature." At the 1964 convention the congressman was nominated as a favorite son candidate for the presidency by liberal Minnesota Republicans trying to insulate themselves from the candidacy of Arizona Senator Barry M. Goldwater.[51]

Judd had never suffered any real difficulty in the ten election campaigns which preceded 1962. His closest contest had been in 1948 when Marcella F. Killen trailed him by 11,000 votes. In 1962, however, Judd had an effective opponent in Donald Fraser, whose father, Everett M. Fraser, had been the respected dean of the University of Minnesota law school. The son was associated with a law firm of prominent Democrats (most particularly former Minnesota Governor Orville L. Freeman); he had served in the state senate, was an active participant in DFL politics, and projected an attractive and modest personality.[52]

A combination of factors contributed to Judd's defeat. The lines of congressional districts in Minnesota had been redrawn to conform to population shifts within the state, and it was commonly thought that the newly designed fifth district favored Fraser and hurt Judd. The incumbent congressman also suffered because of his conservative stands on domestic issues. And supporters and opponents alike were weary of his unchanging views on United States China policy. His seeming rigidity and his reputation as a one-man China lobby in the House served to change his reputation from "expert" to "fanatic." He was so closely identified in the public mind with intransigence on the China issue that his activities in other foreign policy matters were overlooked. Fraser may also have benefited from Kennedy's presence in his behalf, and some of the glow of the president's handling of the Cuban missile crisis in October may have rubbed off on the challenger, who defeated Judd in November by 6,137 votes.[53]

Over the years Walter Judd had been solicited for other offices. In 1954 Minnesota Republicans wanted him to run for the Senate against Hubert Humphrey. He refused, no doubt largely because of the seniority and the influence he enjoyed in the House, especially on the foreign affairs committee where he served for sixteen of his twenty years in Congress. Had he moved to the Senate he would have been merely a freshman at the bottom of the seniority ladder. President Eisenhower revealed in his memoirs that the Minnesotan was one of five names on his personal, private list of vice-presidential possibilities in 1952. After Eisenhower's election, Judd had been recommended for consideration as assistant secretary of state for Far Eastern affairs.[54]

For a while after his political fortune cookie crumbled in 1962, there was talk of his appointment as a foreign policy adviser to the Kennedy administration. Judd's record of support merited such consideration. He had voted with that administration on 89 per cent of all foreign policy roll-call votes, and his record was more in accord with the president than 165 of 261 House Democrats. From 1949 to 1959 Republican Congressman Judd and DFL Senator Humphrey had no voting differences on seventeen foreign policy issues. His successful opponent, Donald Fraser, suggested that his talents should not be lost. But his clear-cut identification with the Republican party and the postcampaign bitterness, in which he charged Fraser with using the "Big Lie" technique to create a "false image," caused the idea to be dropped. Several years later in 1966 he was appointed by Secretary of State Rusk to a nineteen-man advisory panel on East Asian and Pacific affairs.[55]

In his enforced retirement from Congress, Judd has pursued an active life, involving radio broadcasting, lecturing, and writing. The attitudes of men about the affairs of the world are inevitably shaped by events in the world. But the same events can be read differently. Judd's interpretations have continued to command public attention even as they have taken on an increasingly conservative coloration. Most Americans, certainly those who had not lived through the periods of origin and climax of the Cold War in the 1950s, were coming by the late 1960s to accept a world in which diverse forms of communism existed in the Soviet Union, in Eastern Europe, in Cuba, in China. They reasoned that the superpowers, though still capable of irrational acts which could destroy civilization, were no longer so super, that their ideological dispute had been moderated, and that it was therefore essential for the foreign policies of both the United States and the Soviet Union to move in the direction of live and let live. Walter Judd did not see it that way. He argued in 1967 that the basic goal of world domination by international communism had not been modified, and "anybody who relaxes in the thought that Communism is changing is engaging in self-deception."[56]

Sustaining his belief that the Cold War was not obsolete was the Soviet intervention in Czechoslovakia on August 20, 1968, to control its deviations from communist doctrine, Kremlin-style. "*Czecho-*

slovakia has proven that the Cold War is *not* over, because Soviet leadership has not changed its basic objectives," Judd wrote in 1969. He thought any evidence to the contrary must be manifested in actions by the communists to take down the Berlin Wall, to let the people of Eastern Europe vote, to stop using Cuba as a base for subverting the western hemisphere, and to declare officially that the Soviet Union would abandon its policy of world domination. Judd never lost his conviction that United States decisions to stand firm in Europe, Latin America, and Southeast Asia had infinitely more influence on communist attitudes than any probings for agreements. While he continued to protest United States recognition, other Americans protested the artificial political isolation of mainland China. While he objected to trade with the People's Republic of China, other Americans objected to the closed door of commerce and communication. And while Judd argued against admitting Communist China to the United Nations, these Americans argued that it was better to run the risk of a dissident in the international community than to have an outlaw impervious to the influence of world public opinion. As the 1970s dawned these differences in specific policy prescriptions separated Walter Judd from many other influential persons who gave their time and attention to foreign affairs.[57]

A man who was a prophet on the prospects of war with Japan was defeated in part by his prophecies on China. Whatever the final verdict of history, Judd will be remembered largely for his views on Asian affairs. If with the passage of time, he is proved wrong in his perception of the aggressive intentions of the communists, his support of the United Nations, his compassion for the plight of the world's underprivileged, his concern that weaponry be controlled, and his interest in the cohesion of politically free nations must also be weighed in any accounting of debits and credits. Walter Judd's stance cannot be dismissed as simplistic or totally one-issue oriented. He was obviously influenced by his personal encounters with Chinese Communists in the 1930s and by the justification of his position on Japan. But in Minnesota he helped to transform a previously isolationist tradition into an internationalist one. In the House of Representatives, he was a recognized Republican leader on foreign policy matters. In the nation, he educated Americans and provoked useful controversy and debate.

In a very real sense, Judd's interventionism may be considered an extension of Cushman Davis' imperialism. The potential of the Pacific area fired Davis' imagination. For Judd, the region's importance was a stark reality. Davis' arguments for the "civilizing" mission of the

United States were fulfilled by Walter Judd — medical missionary to China. That two Minnesotans — one a nineteenth-century Republican senator, the other a twentieth-century Republican congressman — made Asian affairs their prime concern, and as a consequence exerted a marked influence on American foreign policy in the Far East, is a matter worthy of some note.

Chapter 9

A TALE OF TWO DEMOCRATS: HUBERT H. HUMPHREY AND EUGENE J. MC CARTHY

"Let's not sit back, stagnate, let's not worry lest we make some move. We need to get our foreign policy in movement, to make it an active foreign policy."

HUBERT H. HUMPHREY, 1963.

"I believed the people of the country had the right to be given the opportunity to make an intellectual and moral determination on the war in Vietnam."

EUGENE J. MCCARTHY, 1969.

TWO MINNESOTANS — Hubert H. Humphrey and Eugene J. McCarthy — jousted for the Democratic presidential nomination in 1968. That year of convulsion and dissent focused upon United States involvement in the Vietnam War. In one sense the struggle between them was a classic one for political power; in another it was a unique expression of an issue which had cleaved the nation. The two men took part in a debate which transcended partisanship but was waged primarily within the Democratic party. Eugene McCarthy's challenge to Lyndon B. Johnson over the direction of United States policy in Vietnam was widely judged as a contributing factor in the president's decision to withdraw from the political campaign of 1968. Hubert Humphrey, the vice-president, stepped into the breach, and two Minnesotans, who had long been comrades at arms, were at political war with each other. In the end, they both lost — McCarthy, the nomination, and Humphrey, the presidency.[1]

There are striking parallels and perpendiculars in the background, experience, and character of these two men from Minnesota. Both were born in small communities where agriculture ruled. Their families encouraged their intellectual curiosity. Both earned bachelor's and master's degrees and worked as teachers; for varying reasons neither saw service in World War II. Both were involved in the successful effort to purge the Democratic-Farmer-Labor party of Marxist elements in the 1940s, and both were subsequently elected to Congress in 1948. Both became respected leaders in the House and Senate. A combination of ambitions, issues, and circumstances brought them into conflict — first in 1964 for the office of vice-president and again in 1968 for the office of president. Their voting records on foreign policy issues varied only on rare occasions, and when they did, their differences were for the most part in degree rather than in kind. Both were confirmed internationalists in that they supported the concepts of interdependence and containment. Both enriched their knowledge and understanding with extensive travel to various parts of the world. And on domestic issues both were markedly attentive to the problems of Minnesota's farmers; both were reformers, less radical than Lindbergh, more liberal than their Republican predecessors or contemporaries, in their advocacy of programs enlarging the commonweal.[2]

Yet if their interests and attitudes were parallel, their personalities were perpendicular. Humphrey was an extrovert who reveled in the political game. McCarthy was an introvert for whom politics was not the end-all — he could be content with poetry and philosophy. Jack Ludwig, a visiting lecturer at the University of Minnesota, once equated Humphrey with Minneapolis and McCarthy with St. Paul, not because one had been mayor of the former and the other congressman from the latter, but because, as Ludwig put it, "Were I to write an allegory about the two cities I could never sum them up with greater allegorical exactness than in the personalities of these two men." St. Paul was the established city — more eastern than midwestern in tone and temper. It was the older of the Twins, heavily populated by Irish Catholics but dominated by railroad and lumber magnates of conservative persuasion. Minneapolis was the newer but larger community where grain was king, with a brash and aggressive middle class. St. Paul seemed remote, detached. Minneapolis was involved. Or, as Ludwig distinguished between the two cities, "Minneapolis, like Chicago, is a modern Midwestern town of this century; St. Paul is a Boston that never made it out to San Francisco." He concluded his description of the duo with this peroration: "Humphrey is a Protestant reforming friar; McCarthy, an introspective Roman Catholic monk. . . . Humphrey is a Minneapolitan Midwesterner bringing good cheer and good hopes to the world; McCarthy, a St. Paul cosmopolite implying moral test and intellectual challenge."[3]

By 1968, six years after this article was written, the mode of Hubert Humphrey had become for some the "old" politics. In contrast, the manner of Eugene McCarthy became the "new" politics. In the pre-convention campaign novice politicians were attracted by McCarthy's restraint rather than Humphrey's exuberance. As the nation's conscience tuned into the tragedy of Vietnam, it was a time seemingly more appropriate for the cool critique voiced by McCarthy, a critique which served, some have argued, to calm the passions of dissent and demonstrate the capacity of the system to listen and to change. Humphrey was caught up in the dilemma of his past and present. His earlier radicalism was dismissed; his status as vice-president in an administration attacked by friend and foe limited his options, since he chose to stay in office during the period of his candidacy and to remain loyal to the measures and the men of an officialdom of which he was a part. He could only hint at the new directions he might pursue were he to become his party's nominee.[4]

It is not hard to identify the sources of the Humphrey ideology. According to Humphrey himself, his father was a great influence. One commentator observed that the politics of Hubert Humphrey, Sr., were "a potent mix of Wilsonian internationalism and the radical spirit of Populism." Another biographer noted that the elder Humphrey was "the only Democrat or internationalist in sight in Republican, isolationist South Dakota," where the family lived. William Jennings Bryan and Woodrow Wilson were the Humphrey heroes. As other families read the Bible, the Humphreys shared the words of Bryan and Wilson. Unlike other agrarian radicals, the junior Humphrey never flirted with isolationism. In every other respect he matched the agrarian profile in both ideology and in bitter experience. His family was an early victim of the 1930s depression, a circumstance which forced him to leave college. His lifelong identification with the interests of agriculture came, first, from his belief that Americans generally underrate the important contributions of farmers to the national well-being, and, second, from his conviction that any future depression would begin in the agricultural community. His heritage and his environment fostered Humphrey's devotion to economic and social reform and to an internationalist outlook. He was a new Democratic breed combining the instincts of the radical agrarian with the foreign policy tradition of Woodrow Wilson.[5]

Humphrey was born in Wallace, South Dakota, on May 27, 1911. In the course of time his family moved to Doland and then to Huron, South Dakota. When his family's economic plight caused him to drop out of the University of Minnesota in 1931, he seemed destined to follow in his father's footsteps as a drugstore proprietor. He received a pharmacy degree but was clearly discontented with the opportunity afforded by a vocation reluctantly chosen. After an interim of six years, Humphrey, with few assets except the earning power of his recent bride, Muriel Fay Buck, resumed his studies at the University of Minnesota. He earned a B.A. with the accolade of Phi Beta Kappa in 1939 and won an M.A. the next year at Louisiana State University with a thesis on the New Deal. The Humphreys returned to the North Star State, where he held a succession of jobs at the university, in the Work Projects Administration, with the War Manpower Commission, and at Macalester College in St. Paul. As early as 1942 he showed his internationalist bent, saying, "Either we cast aside our political isolation, or we must prepare for a more devastating conflict. Either we cast aside our indifference to the fate of other people, or these 'other people' will threaten our own security."[6]

Walter Judd has said that Humphrey came to see him after Judd's initial congressional campaign victory in 1942, implying his Republicanism by virtue of his statement that he had supported Willkie, Stassen, and Ball (though it may have been more accurately an expression of Humphrey's internationalism) and indicating his interest in entering politics. Humphrey did so the next year in an unsuccessful effort to become mayor of Minneapolis, a nonpartisan office. After rejecting the supplication of prominent Minneapolitans to cast his fate with the Republicans, he earned his spurs by tending the Democratic-Farmer-Labor party's fences and managing the Minnesota campaign for the Roosevelt-Truman presidential ticket in 1944. Some sources credit him with the key role of marriage counselor in the union of the Minnesota Democratic and Farmer-Labor parties in 1944, although one expert observer minimized Humphrey's contributions, saying that the pressures for fusion were such that "the merger would have gone through if he hadn't raised a finger." Nevertheless, his attention to party affairs undoubtedly served him well in his second and successful try for mayor in 1945. In office, he was active and effective, diminishing crime and corruption in Minneapolis. With the establishment of a human relations council and the first municipal Fair Employment Practices law in the United States, his city moved to reduce some of the more blatant forms of discrimination.[7]

Meanwhile there was bickering between the newly wedded parties. The same left-wing forces which had discredited the Farmer-Labor party and enabled Stassen to win the governorship for the Republicans in 1938 rose to positions of power and leadership. Humphrey, aided by young men and women like Orville L. Freeman and Eugenie M. Anderson, who became a national committeewoman and later was ambassador to Denmark, led the successful 1946–48 fight to purge the communists from the DFL party. The vanquished formed a "People's Party," which soon died. Humphrey has said of the experience that "We just outmaneuvered, outworked and outvoted the Communists." This personal confrontation with communist tactics cannot be discounted as another influence on his later attitude and outlook.[8]

Humphrey was not an early champion of the policy of communist containment later typified by John Foster Dulles in the 1950s — quite the contrary, in fact. In 1945 before the Minnesota intraparty tussle, Humphrey showed an interesting perception of Russian territorial aspirations as a need to establish conditions promoting and guaranteeing Soviet security. Later in the same year he led a group of Minneapolitans in urging that President Truman recall United States troops from China, arguing that "a policy of armed intervention in the domestic affairs of nations can only lead to another, more devastating war than the one just concluded." The ensuing coincidence of the local intraparty conflict and the outbreak of the Cold War hardened the Humphrey sentiment against communism. Although he, like many others, viewed the external communist challenge of the post-World War II era as dire and dangerous, he also tempered his firm stance as he sought possible paths of accommodation.[9]

In 1948, well established as the leader of the DFL party, he challenged Joe Ball for his Senate seat and scored a smashing success. Ball admitted that Humphrey's personality and his facility in debate were contributing factors in the defeat. Ball also believed that the population shift from farm to city had diminished GOP support and that his own increasing conservatism was not in tune with the temper of the people. Labor support, aroused by Ball's active endorsement of the Taft-Hartley Act, gravitated to Humphrey. Ball's opposition to the Marshall Plan was generally considered another factor in his defeat; Humphrey took the opposite tack in approving it as "a broad, dynamic plan which was meant to lift up the people of Europe, to nourish democracy everywhere, to obtain a just, prosperous and lasting peace." Humphrey did not then regard the plan as an expression of containment but rather as "competition" with the Soviet Union. More than once in his campaign, he protested the policy of containment and argued that America must search out new means of negotiation. He did not believe that containment was the opposite side of the coin of appeasement.[10]

The new Minnesota senator's first years in Washington were not easy ones. He had commanded public attention at the 1948 Democratic National Convention by virtue of his now-famous speech advocating a strong human rights plank — a speech which triggered a walkout of dissident southern delegates who subsequently ran their own third-party candidate, J. Strom Thurmond of South Carolina. Humphrey also possessed a meritorious reputation as a mayor. But his brashness, his cosmopolitan interests, and his rhetoric were counterproductive. He was generally regarded as a radical, engaging the support of labor and the left-wing (but anticommunist) Americans for Democratic Action (ADA) and engendering the opposition of the geographic community of the South and the interest community of American business. In time he learned the ways of Washington and the Senate, and in 1953 he earned "the prize of all prizes" when he was asked to take a seat on the Senate foreign relations committee.[11]

According to one account, in a meeting before the new Eisenhower administration took office, President Truman, Secretary of State Dean Acheson, Mutual Security Administrator W. Averill Harriman, and Senate majority leader Lyndon Johnson expressed concern over the strong isolationist representation on the committee. Truman and Acheson suggested Humphrey to counteract that sentiment, and Johnson subsequently engineered the appointment. Though he had to give up his seat on the important labor and welfare committee, Humphrey reportedly was predisposed to do so because of the possible entry of Judd, a foreign affairs expert, into the 1954 senatorial campaign.[12]

As a member of the foreign relations committee, the senator from Minnesota was a staunch advocate of foreign aid, expanded trade, and a strengthened United Nations. He was not bashful about his accomplishments, and often cited his efforts to keep developmental appropriations from being cut and to protect reciprocal trade legislation from crippling amendments. In 1953 after the Korean conflict, when the foreign aid emphasis shifted from development to containment, Humphrey protested that the technical co-operation explicit in Point Four of Truman's 1949 inaugural speech was "being smothered to death under a massive military aid program." His support of the United Nations intensified in 1957 with his appointment as a delegate to the twelfth session of the General Assembly. He was an active and effective member of the United States delegation, and representatives from other countries found him a willing channel of communication in the years that followed.[13]

Though Humphrey gave full support to defense appropriations as the highest national priority, he had misgivings during the 1950s over the concept of "massive retaliation," which placed singular reliance for national security on nuclear deterrence. He was fearful that probable aggressions in the Far East or Near East would be limited in scale and that the American response, under such a defense posture, would necessarily have to accept aggressions "nibbling away at the Free World" or plunge the world into nuclear holocaust. He considered the Middle East the "hot spot" in the Cold War, but he voted for the Eisenhower Doctrine reluctantly. (The doctrine was designed to give the president authority to provide economic aid and armed support to any communist-threatened nation requesting it.) Humphrey, typically, sought alternative policy routes to pacify that troubled region, suggesting both a Middle East development agency and a regional disarmament arrangement.[14]

The senator flitted back and forth among the concepts of containment, competition, and co-operation with respect to United States policy vis-à-vis the Soviet Union. Like Judd, there was much of the missionary in his zeal to meet the communist challenge. The United States, Humphrey said, should inspire and lead. "Only in a unity of peoples who want to prosper and be free can we find an enduring peace. We can build that unity by sharing with others our own heritage of freedom and progress," he wrote in 1960. His concern over Soviet achievements in space and missile development prompted him to comment in 1958 that in a race with the Soviet Union the United States should meet the competition on every front. There was need, he noted, to be alert to Russia's Cold War "inroads" and he viewed trade and aid as necessary instruments in combating these advances.[15]

The Soviet problem was not all black or all white to Humphrey. He also proposed initiatives to co-operate with the Soviet Union in joint programs and projects for economic development. If the terms "dove" and "hawk" had been current in the 1950s, Humphrey would have been labeled a dove. Although he considered the defense shield "imperative," he placed greater emphasis on expanding the works of peace in the world. He did not consider it inconsistent to strengthen domestic defenses and those of free nations allied with the United States while pursuing arms-control agreements. As late as 1968 he wrote that "there is nothing contradictory about striving for peace and at the same time being determined to defend our nation and our national interests. . . . In a world of imperfect men and imperfect nations, individuals and nations must be prepared to defend themselves."[16]

With the waning of the Cold War in the 1960s, disarmament received more nearly equal attention with defense, revealing the administration's awareness of the need for both containment and accommodation. The senator from Minnesota had previously "invented the 'field' of disarmament as a Senate speciality," and it might be said that it was in this area that he made his greatest foreign policy contribution. Convinced that "It is the duty of a leader to get just a bit ahead . . . on an issue . . . [and] to educate the people," he had reacted to President Truman's announcement in 1949 that the United States would build a hydrogen bomb by calling for unilateral disarmament. In 1951 he had been one of several senators sponsoring a resolution urging the president to obtain the agreement of all nations to a complete inventory of armaments and to a universal arms reduction under safeguards. But it was not until 1955 that he determined on a practical, realistic effort to halt the arms race. He proposed that Congress organize a disarmament committee to be composed of representatives from other established committees — foreign relations, armed services, and joint atomic energy. It seemed an appropriate legislative balance to Eisenhower's appointment of Harold Stassen as disarmament assistant to the president. With the passage of the Humphrey Resolution, Senator Walter F. George of Georgia, chairman of the foreign relations committee, offered Humphrey the chairmanship of the new subcommittee, and he accepted it.[17]

The committee held hearings which brought to the public's attention the risks involved in unrestrained nuclear tests. One committee report, issued in October, 1956, approved of Democratic presidential candidate Adlai E. Stevenson's proposal for a voluntary one-year cessation of H-bomb testing. In the heat of that year's election contest, however, the Republican administration reacted negatively; President Eisenhower termed the notion "dangerous," and Vice-President Richard Nixon called it "catastrophic nonsense." There is some evidence to suggest that the incumbents had given serious consideration to the idea — indeed they may have actually decided in principle to adopt it — but once the matter became a partisan issue, they abandoned it.[18]

The Humphrey subcommittee did not give up. It continued to search out and encourage research for devices capable of detecting at long range violations of any agreement. In the process, the senator, his staff, and his colleagues kept the question before the public eyes and ears. One observer noted that "Humphrey performed a unique service in getting important segments of the national community to begin giving serious attention to the problem of controlling and reducing armaments" and thereby "helped to build a climate of public opinion in which actual progress became possible." [19]

In 1959 Humphrey introduced another resolution urging that any savings from disarmament should be diverted to programs which would expand peace in the world. "Our goal should be the achievement of an international arms control agreement which would allow us to devote the major portion of our national budget, not to defense, but to constructive peaceful pursuits," he told his constituents in a June newsletter. In October he said that while "the economy would in the long-run benefit enormously by a cutback in arms expenditure," the United States should be ready for the transition, should plan ahead, and be prepared. Very little public or private attention was given at that time, however, to the need he emphasized for long-range planning, for programs of diversification or conversion.[20]

Efforts to reach some kind of agreement on a test ban or a disarmament arrangement suffered from the ups and downs of Cold War tensions. Prospects seemed especially bleak in 1961 as conflicts in Berlin and Laos became acute and both the Soviet Union and the United States resumed nuclear testing. (On March 31, 1958, the Soviets had voluntarily proclaimed a moratorium on nuclear tests but resumed them on August 31, 1961.) The senator protested to President John Kennedy that the informal test ban had been "a ray of hope to millions of worried people" and counseled against a retaliatory resumption by the United States. Nevertheless, Kennedy reluctantly authorized a response in kind.[21]

Meanwhile, with the establishment of the United States Arms Control and Disarmament Agency, the government was tooling up for a more systematic examination of the related issues. Initially introduced by Humphrey on February 3, 1960, as a proposal for a national peace agency, the name was changed to the "U.S. Disarmament Agency for World Peace and Security" in new legislation submitted to Congress by the Kennedy administration on June 29, 1961. As one of the four chief authors, Humphrey played a prominent part in the week-long debate in which the Senate narrowly defeated an amendment to strip the agency of funds for research by a vote of 46 to 43. On September 8, 1961, the establishment of the Arms Control and Disarmament Agency was approved by a 73 to 14 margin.[22]

In the aftermath of the Cuban missile crisis which raised the very real specter of nuclear war in October, 1962, both the Americans and the Soviets reappraised and reconsidered means which might render that threat less probable. Kennedy, who had been greatly disappointed by the collapse of the test ban talks in the first year of his presidency, proposed in 1963 to Premier Nikita S. Khrushchev a new round of discussions, and the Russians accepted. In a historic congressional initiative in 1963, the Senate affirmed a resolution sponsored by Humphrey and thirty-two other senators calling for a limited ban covering all nuclear tests in the atmosphere, under water, and in outer space. The resolution, according to one writer, "helped to revive the dying negotiations." Once the treaty had been agreed to by British, Soviet, and United States representatives, Humphrey did a monumental job of helping to pave the way for its acceptance by Congress and the country. The Senate ratified the treaty on September 24, 1963, by a vote of 80 to 19.[23]

The senator, who had been a witness to the signing of the treaty in the summer of 1963 in Moscow, was on hand to see the president sign the official instrument of ratification. Reportedly, Kennedy said to him on that occasion, "Hubert, this is your treaty. And it had better work."[24] In a certain sense it was. With his initiation of a committee in Congress and an agency in the executive branch, Humphrey had provided the government with an organization which permitted a more effective basis for study and analysis. Both publicly and privately he helped to establish an acceptance on the part of citizens and officials alike of the rationale for the Test Ban Treaty as a first step in the progression of other possible agreements which could similarly serve the national interest. In was no mean achievement.

Two other programs in whose establishment Humphrey took special pride were Food for Peace and the Peace Corps. He first broached the idea of using the country's agricultural resources as a positive arm of American foreign policy rather than as a farm relief program before a conference of the Grain Terminal Association in 1952. On February 25, 1954, he introduced legislation "to use agricultural commodities to improve the foreign relations of the United States, to relieve famine and for other purposes." The core of his idea rested in a provision authorizing the sale of food in exchange for local currencies which would be loaned back to countries for various projects to assist their economic development. The Agricultural Trade Development and Assistance Act of 1954, better known as Public Law 480, did not implement the Humphrey concept but rather served simply to dispose of unwanted agricultural surpluses abroad. It was mistrusted by some countries as a disguised dumping operation; others thought they were being used by the United States to absorb its embarrassing excess of food and fiber.[25]

In 1959, Humphrey introduced the International Food for Peace bill to give Public Law 480 the more positive emphasis he and others thought it deserved. After a hard battle he won a moral victory by persuading the Senate to adopt strengthening amendments. Even President Eisenhower, who had rejected the words "Food for Peace" in the title of the new legislation, finally succumbed and used the term in a speech in New Dehli, India, in 1959. But it was not until President Kennedy appointed a task force in 1961 (with Humphrey as one of the members) that the concept was transformed from disposal to development. The result was a separate organization for the Food for Peace Program with Representative George S. McGovern of South Dakota as the first director. Even though McGovern and Walter Judd had championed the legislation in the House, the new director called Humphrey "the Congressional father of the program."[26]

The other measure in which the Minnesota senator took personal pleasure was the Peace Corps. He had been speaking to student groups for three years about an idea for a "Youth Peace Corps" and on June 15, 1960, he introduced the first bill to send young American volunteers overseas to teach and to participate in other programs of economic development. In the fall of that same year, presidential candidate John Kennedy also mentioned the idea in addresses at the University of Michigan and in San Francisco. Shortly after he took office, the new president issued an executive order establishing the first stage of the Peace Corps. Humphrey noted at the time that this was "a dream come true for me" and promised that legislation would be introduced providing the new agency with a permanent and expanded authority. The subsequent legislation differed in only two essentials from Humphrey's original bill — it was coeducational and it imposed no age limits.[27]

Toward the end of the first phase of his congressional career, Humphrey took a special interest in Latin America. He did so in part because, as he wrote in July, 1964, "Although the United States must continue to be concerned with developments in many parts of the world, it is no longer either necessary or possible for the United States to become deeply involved in every area of the world and to undertake the massive political, military and economic commitments that such involvement entails. The break-up of the bipolar world of the postwar era and the emergence of independent centers of power in the noncommunist world should in the decade ahead allow the United States greater freedom to concentrate its resources in areas of primary concern to our national interest." While he considered Europe still a crucial area, he argued that "obvious geopolitical factors of proximity, size and population" rendered Latin America especially important to the United States. He visited the region several times and was an enthusiastic champion of the Alliance for Progress, a kind of Marshall Plan for South America.[28]

By the mid-1950s Humphrey had clearly made his mark in the Senate. Enjoying the respect of his colleagues and a measure of national prominence, it was not surprising that a man of his ambition would cast his eye on higher political office. From the moment he became mayor of Minneapolis he sought new fields to conquer, not entirely out of ambition but because of his own convictions about his country and the world. Humphrey was a politician who wanted to make possible what he considered necessary, and obviously the presidency offered the foremost opportunity to do just that. The Minnesota senator possessed attributes which would not make such an expectation out of the question. He had garnered a national press with his eight-hour-long dialogue with Premier Khrushchev in 1958; he was well known in politically important circles within the Democratic party and had the support or respect of some segments of the business community, minority groups, labor unions, farm organizations, and civic associations with a special interest in foreign policy; he was articulate, liberal, and personable — even his political enemies liked him — and no hint of scandal or corruption had touched him.

Humphrey first decided to bid for higher office in 1956; breaking precedent, he formally announced his candidacy for the vice-presidential nomination. He had reason to believe, he thought, from previous conversations with Adlai Stevenson that he would be the latter's choice for a running mate, and he was consequently dismayed when Stevenson declared an open convention, permitting the delegates to choose the vice-president. Humphrey was unprepared for the tactic, and the convention nominated Senator Estes Kefauver of Tennessee in an exciting contest over John Kennedy. The Minnesotan made his next move on December 30, 1959, when he became the first announced candidate for the 1960 Democratic presidential nomination. He carried the campaign through two primaries in Wisconsin and West Virginia and lost both to John Kennedy. Theodore H. White, impressed by the "very simplicity, the clarity, the homely sparkle he could bring to any issue," mused that Humphrey failed because "There was no distance about him, no separation of intrigue, none of the majesty that must surround a king." A president, White argued, must be different from everyone else, but the friendly, unrestrained senator from Minnesota "was just like everybody else." The ultimate election of Kennedy forecast a four-year, possibly an eight-year moratorium on Humphrey's ambitions until the tragic assassination of the president intervened on November 22, 1963.[29]

Humphrey's former colleague, mentor, and friend, Lyndon Johnson, succeeded Kennedy. As he prepared to run for the office in his own right in 1964, the choice of a running mate became a subject of intense speculation. In the end Johnson narrowed the choice to the two senators from Minnesota, Humphrey and McCarthy. As the days went by, McCarthy, becoming impatient with the president's

Humphrey (right) and President Johnson (center) at Minnehaha Falls, Minneapolis, 1964. *Minneapolis Star* photo.

games, took himself out of the running. To prolong the suspense Johnson found an unlikely substitute in the person of Senator Thomas J. Dodd of Connecticut, but in the end Humphrey was the man he tapped. On two earlier occasions Johnson had communicated to Humphrey through intermediaries that the first condition of the office was loyalty; a third time, the president did it himself.[30]

A central but not crucial issue of the 1964 presidential campaign between challenger Barry Goldwater and incumbent Lyndon Johnson was the then limited engagement of the United States in Vietnam. In the following years, Vietnam was to swell in dimension until protest and contention made it a crucible in the contest between the two Minnesota senators for the Democratic presidential nomination in 1968. And it was McCarthy, the lesser known of the two, who first joined the battle.

Eugene J. McCarthy was born on March 29, 1916, in Watkins, Minnesota, a community only slightly larger than the birthplace of his confrere, Hubert Humphrey. After attending the parochial school of his home town, McCarthy went on to St. John's Preparatory School and was graduated from St. John's University in Collegeville, Minnesota, in 1935. He earned a Master of Arts degree in sociology and economics from the University of Minnesota in 1938 and taught in public high schools and private colleges for ten years. He gave some thought to becoming a monk and served as a novice in the Benedictine order for nine months. During World War II, he worked for a time as a civilian technical assistant in the military intelligence division of the war department. In 1945 he married Abigail Quigley, a brilliant young woman then teaching English at the College of St. Catherine in St. Paul, and they settled on a farm he had purchased near his home town. At the time of his election to Congress in 1948, McCarthy, who earlier had responded to a request to help teach the influx of returning veterans, was acting head of the sociology department at the College of St. Thomas, St. Paul's male counterpart of St. Catherine's.[31]

A faculty colleague had persuaded him to become actively involved in Democratic-Farmer-Labor politics at the time of the friction between the two segments of the party, and McCarthy supported Humphrey's leadership in ridding the DFL of communist influence in the late 1940s. In 1947 he became chairman of a previously moribund DFL party in Ramsey County (which includes the city of St. Paul), and as part of the new order of young men and women exercising the rites of leadership, he ran that year for Congress. He won the 1948 primary by a narrow margin of less than 500 votes, but he was an easy victor in the general election and in four subsequent elections to the House and two to the Senate.[32]

Though it caused some amusement that McCarthy, who represented an urban constituency, served on the House agriculture committee, it was in fact an appropriate assignment for a congressman who owned a farm and who had evidenced his concern for the problems of small farmers by espousing the cause of co-operatives. Like his predecessors and his newly elected contemporary in the Senate, McCarthy felt strongly about the nation's agricultural sector. "It is important that our agricultural economy be kept healthy and strong," he said in 1954, "not only to assure the future supply of food and fibre, but also because it is important that the economic base for the social and cultural life of our farm population remain high enough to allow these people to maintain and improve their standard of living. There is a very close relationship between the health of our agricultural economy and the related health of our industrial and trade economy of our towns and cities."[33]

Although McCarthy maintained a liberal, internationalist record in Congress, he was less an innovator than an organizer. He took the lead in bringing together liberal Democrats to state positions and to plot strategy. They were variously called "McCarthy's Marauders" or "McCarthy's Mavericks." But his was a more responsible dissent than those names might imply; in 1955 he would be rewarded for his diligence by Speaker Sam Rayburn with a seat on the prestigious House ways and means committee. In 1959 when he crossed over to the Senate, the McCarthy-led band evolved into a more formal organization with the dignified title of Democratic Study Group.[34]

McCarthy was a consistent supporter of freer trade, larger aid, and varying forms of international organization. His enthusiasm was generally understated, less fervent, and sometimes less firm than Humphrey's. In the context of the 1950s, McCarthy, like Humphrey, viewed the foreign aid program not solely as a humanitarian instrument but also as a stratagem of the Cold War. On one occasion in 1955, for example, he said that a three-year extension of the Reciprocal Trade Agreements Act was necessary "in order to give some help to the government in improving the international situation." He wrote in 1960 that American economic competition with the Soviet Union required programs of trade and aid, selective private overseas investment, technical assistance under Point Four, surplus food disposal, and a continuing participation in the United Nations and other international agencies. He also cautioned that America's responsibility in improving the economic well-being of other nations must be "free of taint of commercial exploitation, of imperialism, or of colonial domination. We must whenever possible work with other nations through international organizations."[35]

Believing that as a senator he would have a better rostrum from which to speak out on the nation's problems — and particularly its foreign policy — McCarthy decided to challenge the incumbent senator, Edward Thye, in 1958. Despite state convention opposition from Eugenie Anderson, who fought hard for party endorsement, and despite a primary contest with former Farmer-Labor governor Hjalmar Petersen, McCarthy defeated his opponent by a modest margin. He was the first Catholic to be elected to the Senate from Minnesota.[36]

In the Senate McCarthy was soon labeled as an intellectual and a loner. He first emerged on the national scene with his eloquent nominating speech for Adlai Stevenson at the Democratic National Convention in 1960. Otherwise his performance seemed less inspiring that it had been in the House. He appeared to be bored and frustrated with the tedium and rigidity of the Senate routine. He made offbeat moves such as voting for the Goldwater amendment denying research funds to the new agency on arms control and disarmament. In 1965, upon Humphrey's elevation to the vice-presidency, McCarthy was appointed to the Senate foreign relations committee where he served variously on the subcommittees dealing with European affairs, the

American republics, economic and social policy, international organization, and as chairman of the subcommittee on African affairs.[37]

One of his chief concerns was with legislative supervision of the Central Intelligence Agency (CIA). Beginning in 1954, he had introduced bills and resolutions — four times in the House and five in the Senate — to extend the congressional prerogative beyond the armed services and appropriations committees. He did so in the conviction that the committees of Congress dealing with foreign policy should have a central place in overseeing the CIA. The legislation was never enacted, but McCarthy won a modest victory in 1966 when Senator Richard B. Russell, Democrat of Georgia (who may have been influenced by the McCarthy resolution of that year calling for a "full and complete" study of the effect of the CIA on United States foreign policy) invited three members of the foreign relations committee to join with members of the armed services committee in its considerations of agency affairs.[38]

In 1957 Representative McCarthy voted against the Eisenhower Doctrine because he thought the authority requested for presidential use of military force already existed, making it unnecessary. Moreover, if the situation in the Middle East were as dire as described by administration spokesmen, the resolution was inadequate. In 1965 Senator McCarthy was critical of America's intervention in the Dominican Republic, partly because he thought the accounts of communist influence were exaggerated. In addition, he believed it to be more in keeping "with the traditional foreign policy objectives of the United States and with our obligations under the United Nations Charter and the Rio Treaty to conduct our policy in terms of an attack on the causes of economic, social and political unrest, rather than, as seems to have been the case recently, to apply radical surgery when the disease risks getting out of control." Though he was among the first — as early as 1966 — to question United States policy on selling arms abroad, he generally supported defense appropriations, military assistance programs, and, until Vietnam, the general direction of American foreign policy. In short, he conformed.[39]

But Gene McCarthy had the makings of a nonconformist. In his first book entitled *Frontiers of American Democracy*, which was published in 1960, he pointed out two conditions that justified civil disobedience. The first was enterprise by the state in fields beyond its jurisdiction — "if it usurps the authority of the family or religion or if it trespasses on areas reserved for individual and personal decision and choice." The second — which was later to influence his own decisions — was "when the government, acting in its proper sphere, orders actions which are wrong and contrary to right reason, an extreme example of which would be either an unjust war or an unnecessary one." In a book published four years later, McCarthy quoted approvingly Reinhold Niebuhr's critique of conservatism in American foreign policy: "the distinctive trait appears to be a curious ambivalence between isolationism and imperialism, between a disavowal of the response of our power and an exercise of that power without a sense of its limits." He also cited Adlai Stevenson's remark: "There are limits to the effectiveness of our nation's foreign policy. For foreign policy is concerned with problems which lie beyond our jurisdiction and about which we cannot legislate. There are only two means available for influencing the actions of other states: persuasion and coercion. As a free society, we must rely primarily on persuasion." These concepts — an unjust or unnecessary war, the limits of power, and a prime reliance on persuasion — provided the philosophical framework for McCarthy's decision announced on November 30, 1967, to enter certain presidential primaries.[40]

The war in Vietnam crept up upon the American people. There is more truth than fiction in the assertion by an English trio who wrote of the 1968 presidential campaign that "one of the most important political points about America's war in Vietnam was that, to an unusual degree, involvement preceded rationale: the war was well advanced before there was any structured national debate about its purpose."[41]

The story of America's seduction is well known. First, there was President Truman's decision in 1952 to aid France in its colonial war against the communist-led forces; then military advisers were dispatched by Eisenhower in 1954, soldiers by Kennedy in 1962. A giant step toward involvement was precipitated in Lyndon Johnson's presidency by an alleged North Vietnamese attack on two American destroyers in the Gulf of Tonkin in August, 1964. The United States retaliated with an air raid against North Vietnam, and the president asked for congressional support "for action to deal appropriately with attacks against our armed forces and to defend freedom and preserve peace in Southeast Asia." The Gulf of Tonkin Resolution was opposed by only two United States senators — Democrats Ernest Gruening of Alaska and Wayne L. Morse of Oregon. In February, 1965, systematic bombings of the North began, and that summer 100,000 American troops were dispatched to Vietnam. All this was only a beginning. While there had been some initial opposition to the war from "peace groups," pacifists, and certain Protestant church leaders, they were politically impotent. But then the young people became aroused. As early as April, 1965, 15,000 students picketed the White House. By the middle of 1967 the students had picked up allies in influential circles and the protest was nearing rebellion.[42]

McCarthy's concern began, he said, with doubts about the validity of statements emanating from the Johnson administration. At a White House meeting on February 18, 1965, Secretary of State Dean Rusk assured his listeners that the government of South Vietnam was strong and stable. The next morning it was announced that the government had been overthrown. It became increasingly clear to the senator from Minnesota that the nature of the conflict was different from that presented by administration spokesmen. It seemed to him that the issue was not a clear-cut case of aggression against people willing to defend themselves. McCarthy became persuaded that Vietnam was not comparable to Ethiopia in 1936, Czechoslovakia in 1939, Greece in 1947, or Korea in 1950. He refrained from a public break until January 27, 1966, when he joined fourteen other senators in a request that the president extend the bombing pause then in effect. On March 1, 1966, he was one of five senators who supported Wayne Morse's attempt to repeal the 1964 Gulf of Tonkin Resolution. Later McCarthy was depressed and alarmed by the statement of Nicholas deB. Katzenbach, undersecretary of state, who imprudently told the Senate foreign relations committee on August 17, 1967, that Johnson did not need a declaration by Congress to conduct the war. By October, 1967, according to the senator's recollection in his book *The Year of the People*, his judgment was firm. The military difficulties were evident, the political problems had been exposed, and the morality of the whole sorry affair was at issue.[43]

Why did he decide to run? His readiness to respond to the search by Allard K. Lowenstein and others for a challenger to President Johnson evinced his belief in the importance of alternatives in the democratic process of government. In this respect his beliefs assuredly overcame, at least for a time, his aversion to the pedantics of politics. (One journalist estimated that McCarthy's normal attention span for the "nuts and bolts" of campaigning was a meager seven minutes.) Possibly his boredom with the Senate also helped to propel him into another adventure. McCarthy himself said in 1968: "I run because this country is now involved in a deep crisis of leadership — a crisis of national purpose — and a crisis of American ideals. It is time to substitute a leadership of hope for a leadership of fear. This is not simply what I want, or what most of us want. It is, I believe, the deepest hunger of the American soul." He was moved also by the antigovernment sentiment evident among the young; he was assured

McCarthy greeting supporters in New Haven, Connecticut, 1968

of organized support from the "dump Johnson" group; he was convinced of the intransigence of the administration on the issue; and, finally, no one else stepped forward. In his own words, "My decision was strengthened by indications that the Administration has no plans for Vietnam other than continued escalation and intensification. It seems to have set no limits on the price it will pay for military victory. The war in Vietnam is the most crucial issue before the country today. . . . It involves a deep moral judgment with reference to national policy and the future of the nation. It is a case that must be taken to the people." [44]

McCarthy took his case first to New Hampshire, where he won 20 of 24 delegates in the primary election of March 12, 1968. Robert F. Kennedy then entered the race. Victory was forecast for McCarthy in Wisconsin, and on the eve of that primary on March 31, 1968, President Johnson took himself out of contention and moved toward peace talks in Paris. The junior senator from Minnesota attracted large numbers of alienated students, and his youthful campaign organization was popularly termed "The Children's Crusade." They kept "clean for Gene," shaving beards and putting on ties so that their appearance and manners would open doors and gather votes. Their candidate's victories raised their hopes that an alternative was possible. McCarthy moved on with an incoherent primary campaign organization, winning some and losing some, but the core of his message was cogent. The war was "no longer defensible . . . [it] had not gained support of what is generally accepted as the decent opinion of mankind." The nation must begin to develop a restrained attitude toward the rest of the world and accept the fact that the United States was part of the movement of history, not apart from it. The war had escaped public review, he said, because the Pentagon and the CIA had grown beyond civilian control; the militarization of American life and American foreign policy had become unacceptable. The McCarthy campaign legitimatized an open attack on the military institutions by respectable politicians. [45]

Another recurrent theme was his concern over the personalization of the presidency: "If I am elected," McCarthy said in April, "I will never regard the presidency as a personal office. . . . the office belongs not to the man who holds it but to the people of the nation." The president, McCarthy continued, "must know the limitations of power . . . and understand that this country cannot be governed by coercion." Although his was not a one-issue campaign — he also spoke of civil rights and the need to reorder national priorities — the war was clearly the core of it. As a consequence, he did not attract the poor or the minorities who surged around Robert Kennedy, nor did McCarthy appeal to professional followers of Kennedy who viewed his concept of a passive presidency with alarm. *Time* magazine quoted one "prominent Kennedyite" as commenting "From what he says, he'd turn the conduct of the office over to a committee and go off and read books. That scares the hell out of me." [46]

McCarthy came to the Democratic National Convention in Chicago on August 25, 1968, knowing that he had lost. For whatever reasons, the campaign had wound down in the last month. (Some observers said because of his own indifference; others suggested his fear of failure.) Only a miracle could overcome the Humphrey delegate count secured from the party loyalists. The Soviet invasion of Czechoslovakia on August 22 had hardened the president's hand in manipulating the "peace plank" in the platform, and the McCarthyites lost that fight. There was one small victory — the credentials contest in which McCarthy insurgents arrayed against party regulars paved the way for the subsequent establishment of a commission on party reform chaired by Senator George McGovern. Humphrey won the nomination decisively with 1,761¾ votes to 601 for McCarthy, 146½ for McGovern (a Robert Kennedy stand-in), and 67½ for Channing Phillips, a Black candidate from Washington, D.C. The McCarthy cam-

Hubert H. Humphrey, 1966

paign ended in the three tragedies which seared the soul of America in 1968 — the assassinations of Martin Luther King and Robert Kennedy and the Chicago street battles between protestors and police. On the morning after the decision and the dementia, McCarthy told his supporters, "I am happy to be here to address the government in exile." [47]

In the aftermath the two nominees, Hubert Humphrey and Richard Nixon, both promised to end the war. McCarthy correctly noted, "More important than politics and power was the substance of the challenge and the response of the people . . . before California [in the primary campaign], judgment was passed by the people of this country against the war." Journalist Thomas G. Wicker agreed that the effect of the McCarthy effort was to give millions of Americans a chance to vote against the war. McCarthy "believed people preferred orderly and democratic change to assault on the Pentagon," wrote Wicker, "and he gave them hope for that, too. He gave a powerful but smothered sentiment an opportunity to find expression and make a difference, and that alone is no small contribution." [48]

And what of Humphrey? He almost did the impossible by coming from behind to within half of one per cent of Nixon's total vote. He began his campaign, as Charles W. Bailey reported in the *Minneapolis Tribune* of November 10, 1968, "with an incredible collection of handicaps — a long and frustrating war, an unpopular president, a terribly divided party, an empty campaign treasury, a late start, an increasingly bitter racial conflict, a total lack of organization — and an all too vivid public memory of the riot and bloodshed at the party's convention in Chicago, Illinois." On September 30, 1968, Humphrey publicly shook himself free from the Johnson line on Vietnam and promised to stop the bombing of the North if he became president. This move seemed to energize latent support and lessen overt hostility. Even so, it was said that McCarthy could not endorse his former political ally and maintain credibility with his supporters, who saw little difference between the Democratic and Republican nominees. Both the content and timing of his modest endorsement on October 29, only a week before the election, probably had little effect. McCarthy said that Humphrey had "a better understanding of our domestic needs" and seemed more likely than Nixon to scale down the arms race and reduce "military tensions in the war." [49]

In the 1968 debate over American foreign policy, Humphrey was inhibited by his double role of vice-president and candidate. The Minnesotan himself once said that "Humphrey's law on the vice presidency" stemmed from the fact that the office's authority derived from the president rather than from the Constitution. Later he commented that the office did not have autonomy. Humphrey fulfilled its first condition — loyalty to the president. What he counseled on the Vietnam issue in the inner sanctums of the Johnson administration, future researchers may be able to ascertain more clearly. The general tenor of his advice was revealed in 1971. Before Humphrey was picked for vice-president, he had written a memorandum to the president in which he opposed American withdrawal from Vietnam but contended that "direct U.S. action against North Vietnam, American assumption of command roles, or the participation in combat of U.S. troop units, are unnecessary and undesirable." After taking office, the vice-president sent another memorandum to Lyndon Johnson on February 17, 1965, in which he argued against the decision to initiate a sustained bombing raid against North Vietnam. Following a trip to Vietnam in 1967, his private report to the president counseled de-escalation, and in the discussions preceding Johnson's famous withdrawal speech of March 31, 1968, he urged that the bombing halt should be complete, not partial as the president announced. Before the Democratic convention of August, 1968, Humphrey was twice dissuaded by Johnson from issuing a policy statement advocating a total bombing halt on the grounds that it would "harm and confuse" the Paris peace talks. If he seemed more of a champion and less of a protester on Vietnam in 1968, it was probably because, as he has confessed, "I honestly felt he [Mr. Johnson] was doing his damnedest to end the war."

Perhaps for this reason he was reluctant to break into the Johnson position during the campaign. Once he did so, however modestly, his fortunes improved. Had he done so earlier, he might have won. His public statements, however, seemed to suggest an unrestrained enthusiasm for the American purpose in Vietnam. There may be reason to believe that Humphrey, longer than McCarthy, equated Vietnam with Ethiopia, Czechoslovakia, Greece, and Korea.[50]

After 1968 Humphrey's enforced retirement from politics took him back to Minnesota and a dual professorship at the state university in Minneapolis and at Macalester College in St. Paul. Unlike many politicians who never return in defeat, choosing instead to retire in the familiar environs of Washington, D.C., Humphrey healed his wounds in the pleasant house he and his wife had built at Waverly, a small community not far from the Twin Cities. But a man of his experience and energy was not content with the life of the campus. He traveled extensively and spoke widely, castigating Republicans in general and Richard Nixon in particular. He did not, however, make political capital out of Vietnam. As he had with Lyndon Johnson, Humphrey credited Nixon with wanting to get out of the war and predicted that he would.[51]

Eugene McCarthy's decision to quit the Senate in 1970 was too rich an opportunity for Humphrey to resist. Even though electoral success would put him way down the senatorial seniority list, any chance for another presidential nomination would fall more gracefully on the mantle of a United States senator than on the shoulders of a private citizen. "Humphrey — you know he cares" was the slogan of his campaign, conveying his criticism of Nixon's economic policies and his own championship of liberal social programs. He won handily over Congressman Clark A. MacGregor and became the first majority whip, vice-president, and presidential contender to return to Congress as a freshman senator. Appropriately his maiden speech in 1971 was on disarmament and arms control.[52]

But Humphrey's eye was still on the White House, and after testing the waters of political sentiment, he launched his third campaign for the presidency in Philadelphia on January 10, 1972. He did reasonably well, coming in second in the Florida primary, third in the Wisconsin primary, and second in the California runoff. It became increasingly clear, however, that the momentum belonged to Senator George McGovern of South Dakota, and Humphrey withdrew his name before it was placed in nomination at the Democratic convention that year. Although his disappointment was profound, Humphrey, the complete political animal, could still call the United States Senate home.[53]

Eugene McCarthy, meanwhile, had returned to the Senate in 1968 without enthusiasm. He considered but turned down President-elect Nixon's offer of the United States ambassadorship to the United Nations. He surprised everyone when he resigned from the Senate foreign relations committee, permitting Senator Gale W. McGee of Wyoming, an avowed "hawk" on Vietnam, to replace him. It was part of a pattern of diminishing interest; on July 24, 1969, he announced his decision not to run for re-election. Like Humphrey, he returned to academe, this time at the University of Maryland, where he became a professor of poetry.[54]

A speech by McCarthy in Minnesota on May 23, 1971, stirred speculation that he might be receptive to assuming leadership of a third-party movement. James Reston of the *New York Times* was skeptical, pointing out that "leading third-party movements requires . . . animal energy and personal ambition . . . and this does not comport with McCarthy's lonely and melancholy life." The former senator, who was never impervious to political realities, understood that a third-party effort could be justified only after trying for the Democratic nomination. After calling together key 1968 supporters to assess his prospects, he proceeded with an uncertain campaign in 1972 that was deflated in the Wisconsin primary, where he received less than 1 per cent of the total vote and finished seventh among eleven Democratic contenders. McCarthy's opposition to the war had been largely usurped by Senator McGovern; his own supporters, weary of trying to understand an enigmatic man, were evidently willing to settle for a less ambiguous candidate. At the Miami convention McCarthy was ignored and Humphrey rejected. The Minnesota contest of 1968 was not to be replayed in 1972.[55]

The influence of the two senators from Minnesota on American foreign policy can be sketched in contrasts. Before the mid-1960s Humphrey's record was one of accomplishment and effectiveness, McCarthy's was one of more modest achievement. Humphrey used the Senate, it has been said, "for the incubation of policy ideas."[56] In his senatorial role he has been an innovator, educator, and advocate. He worked at translating his ideas into programs and policies. In contrast, McCarthy, as representative and senator, was noted for his keen intellect rather than for either creativity or energy. It was McCarthy the presidential candidate who made an enormous impact in a nine-month campaign, capturing the public mood, giving it voice and direction. He stimulated an extraordinary turnabout in American foreign policy by his critical and systematic explanation of the post-World War II assumptions underlying that policy.

Eugene J. McCarthy, 1968

Few states can lay claim to contending nominees for the presidency within a single party. Moreover, a contest like that of 1968, waged with foreign policy as the central issue, was a rarity in American history. John A. Blatnik, who has represented Minnesota's eighth congressional district since 1946, observed that the ultimate tragedy lay in the fact that if the split between the two men had not occurred in 1968, one of them would have been president. They began by sharing the idiom of internationalism. Although they parted public company over Vietnam, they also shared a common concern over the manner of the American presence in the world. McCarthy scorned those who attacked his position as a reversion to isolationism, or neoisolationism, pointing out that the issue was not subject to such a classification, that what was important was the development of a new and different approach to international responsibility. And Humphrey made the same point when he said that during the next decade the United States would continue to have "major responsibility for preserving world peace. But how we fulfill that responsibility will change." [57]

The foreign policy mood set by McCarthy in 1968 and in time echoed by Humphrey spurned intervention and called for a more modest presence in the world. Although it was labeled by some as "neoisolationism," the comparison fails in a number of crucial respects. For one thing some of the forces that supported isolationism, as we have seen in earlier chapters, had vanished by 1968, and America's place on the world scene was so transformed as to defy comparison with that of earlier times. Midwestern isolationism, once so central to the equation, no longer pertained. The American Middle West had become in many instances more "internationalist" than other regions. The anti-European bias was no longer invoked. It was replaced perhaps by an anti-Asian bias, or at least by a determination to have a "lower profile" in Asia. Another difference was the expressed opposition of the business community (defense contractors excepted) to the war in Vietnam, suggesting its awareness that United States involvement contributed to inflationary pressures and a sluggish economic performance; there was little profit to nondefense business from the American intervention in Southeast Asia. Nor were the old ideas of a "Fortress America" or a hemispheric defense applicable. They had been rendered obsolete by nuclear weapons and the superior performance of offensive missiles over defensive missile systems. The belief that man and nation could be self-sufficient was no longer seriously argued even as technology advanced the art of substitution or replacement. The "old safe distinction between internal and external" was no longer clear. The Jeffersonian notion that the United States could serve the world solely by example had grown weaker. While the United States can improve the imperfections of American society, prejudice, poverty, and pollution are world-wide problems and their amelioration in one nation seemed not to immunize their contagion from another. The technology which reduced distance, the communications which made news instantaneous, the travel which enhanced contact, and the internationalization of American business presented a substantially changed set of circumstances to those prevailing in the earlier years of the century.[58]

It also evinces a lack of semantic precision to apply the label of neoisolationism, as some do, to the great numbers of Americans who, in the late 1960s, expressed a wish for discrimination and selectivity in international dealings. The foreign policy debate which grew out of United States intervention in Vietnam was not an isolationist-internationalist polarization. Rather, as the two Minnesotans demonstrated, it was an argument over the manner and magnitude of the American presence in the world. The core of the debate, noted one critic, was "not whether the U.S. should return to the isolationist posture of the 1930s. Culture, communications and nuclear weapons have laid that ghost to rest. The real debate — to which the cry of 'isolationism' is a rhetorical diversion — is over the *extent* of American military and political involvement overseas." Although Americans began to insist on more modest foreign policy aspirations, they did not advocate "benign neglect."[59]

The political careers of Hubert Humphrey and Eugene McCarthy have spanned a period marking the end of isolationism after World War II and heralding a less conceited and aggressive participation by the United States in world affairs. At the outset of their careers they sustained the internationalism of their predecessor, Senator Joseph Ball, and paralleled the efforts of Harold Stassen and Walter Judd to build an operative community of nations. Like most Americans in the 1950s they perceived the aspirations of the Soviet Union for power and influence as threats which justified the policy of containment. Both extended this perception to Vietnam, but McCarthy, before Humphrey, was heard to protest this inflated intervention as a misreading of the national interest. As they called for a new look at America's role in the world — McCarthy more stridently than Humphrey — they did not reject the proposition that the United States, with a host of public and private relationships, had been swept up in a current of involvement. In concert and in debate, these two men of Minnesota advanced the state's tradition of issue-oriented politics as they addressed the nation on crucial foreign policy concerns of the mid-twentieth century.

REFERENCE NOTES

Introduction — TEN MEN AND THEIR MILIEU — pages 1 to 14

[1] Donald F. Warner, "Prelude to Populism," in *Minnesota History*, 32:129 (September, 1951).

[2] 90 Congress, 2 session, *Background Information on the Committee on Foreign Relations, United States Senate*, 58–70 (Revised edition, February, 1968).

[3] Recent examples include George Lichtheim, *Imperialism* (New York, 1971); Felix Greene, *The Enemy: What Every American Should Know About Imperialism* (New York, 1971); George Liska, *Imperial America* (Baltimore, 1967); Herbert S. Dinerstein, *Intervention Against Communism* (Baltimore, 1967); and Urs Schwartz, *Confrontation and Intervention in the Modern World* (Dobbs Ferry, N.Y., 1970). The entire issue of *Journal of International Affairs*, volume 22, no. 2 (1968), discusses the problem of intervention.

[4] E. Berkeley Tompkins, *Anti-Imperialism in the United States: The Great Debate, 1890–1920*, 2–5 (Philadelphia, 1970); Winks, "American and European Imperialism Compared," in Richard W. Miller, ed., *American Imperialism in 1898: The Quest for National Fulfillment*, 182–186 (New York, 1970); Lichtheim, *Imperialism*, 57; Richard J. Barnet, "The Illusion of Security," in *Foreign Policy*, 81 (Summer, 1971).

[5] Paul M. Sniderman and Jack Citrin, "Psychological Sources of Political Belief: Self-Esteem and Isolationist Attitudes," in *American Political Science Review*, 65:404 (June, 1971).

[6] Cooper, *The Vanity of Power: American Isolationism and the First World War, 1914–1917*, 217 (Westport, Conn., 1969.); Steel, "A Spheres of Influence Policy," in *Foreign Policy*, 107 (Winter, 1971–72). See also Barnet, in *Foreign Policy*, 85 (Summer, 1971).

[7] Quoted from Herbert McClosky, "Personality and Attitude Correlates of Foreign Policy Orientation," in James N. Rosenau, ed., *Domestic Sources of Foreign Policy*, 54 (New York, 1967); Herman, *Eleven Against War: Studies in American Internationalist Thought*, viii, 1, 2 (Stanford, Calif., 1969); Warren F. Kuehl, *Seeking World Order: The United States and International Organization to 1920*, viii (Nashville, 1969).

[8] Oran R. Young, "Intervention and International Systems," and Beloff, "Reflections on Intervention," in *Journal of International Affairs*, 22:184, 198; Dinerstein, *Intervention Against Communism*, 26.

[9] Dinerstein, *Intervention Against Communism*, 3, 4, 22, 26; James N. Rosenau, "The Concept of Intervention," in *Journal of International Affairs*, 22:165–176.

[10] Among the most useful publications analyzing the isolationist phenomenon are Selig Adler, *The Isolationist Impulse: Its Twentieth-Century Reaction* (New York, 1957); Manfred Jonas, *Isolationism in America, 1935–1941* (Ithaca, N.Y., 1966); Ray A. Billington, "The Origins of Middle Western Isolationism," in *Political Science Quarterly*, 60:44–64 (March, 1945); Ralph H. Smuckler, "The Region of Isolationism," in *American Political Science Review*, 47:386–401 (June, 1953). Samuel Lubell in *The Future of American Politics* (New York, 1952) makes much of ethnic considerations in attitudes about foreign policy. This thesis has been challenged by some scholars who doubt its relevance in the pre-World War II period. It is relevant for Minnesota in World War I. See, especially, Manfred Jonas, "Pro-Axis Sentiment and American Isolationism," in *Historian*, 29:221–237 (February, 1967). Materials about Minnesota include George W. Garlid, "Politics in Minnesota and American Foreign Relations, 1921–1941," Ph.D.

thesis, University of Minnesota, 1967; Arthur Naftalin, "A History of the Farmer-Labor Party of Minnesota," Ph.D. thesis, University of Minnesota, 1948 — copies in the Minnesota Historical Society; and Carl H. Chrislock, *The Progressive Era in Minnesota, 1899–1918* (St. Paul, 1971).

[11] Cooper, *The Vanity of Power*, 203, 204.

[12] Commager, ed., *Living Ideas in America*, 653 (New York, 1951).

[13] William B. Parker and Jonas Viles, eds., *Thomas Jefferson: Letters and Addresses*, 46, 137 (New York, 1908); John Quincy Adams to John Adams, July 27, 1794, and to Francis C. Gray, August 3, 1818, in Adrienne Koch and William Peden, eds., *Selected Writings of John and John Quincy Adams*, 240, 294 (New York, 1946).

[14] Jefferson to John Jay, August 23, 1785, in Parker and Viles, *Thomas Jefferson*, 40; Richard Hofstadter, *The Age of Reform: From Bryan to F.D.R.*, 24 (New York, 1955). Arthur M. Schlesinger, Jr., argues that Jefferson's ideas remain fertile and alive but his ideology is remote and irrelevant; see *The Crisis of Confidence*, 49 (New York, 1969).

[15] Hofstadter, *The Age of Reform*, 28; Seabury, *Power, Freedom, and Diplomacy: The Foreign Policy of the United States of America*, 48 (New York, 1967).

[16] Jefferson to Elbridge Gerry, January 26, 1799, in James Truslow Adams, *Jeffersonian Principles: Extracts from the Writings of Thomas Jefferson*, 7 (Boston, 1928); Richard Hofstadter, *The American Political Tradition and the Men Who Made It*, 39, 40 (New York, 1954).

[17] Thomas A. Bailey, *A Diplomatic History of the American People*, 181, 183 (quotation), 185 (Seventh edition, New York, 1964); Jefferson to President James Monroe, October 24, 1823, in Parker and Viles, *Thomas Jefferson*, 276; André Fontaine, "Has America Had Enough of Europe?" in *Interplay of European-American Affairs*, 2:6 (June-July, 1968); Council on Foreign Relations, *Basic Aims of United States Foreign Policy*, 1, a study prepared at the request of the Senate Committee on Foreign Relations, 1959.

[18] Albert E. Bergh, ed., *Grover Cleveland: Addresses, State Papers and Letters*, 62 (New York, 1909).

[19] Smuckler, in *American Political Science Review*, 47:390, 398, 400, 401 (June, 1953).

[20] *United States Census*, 1930, *Population*, 3:1194.

[21] Jonas, *Isolationism in America*, 277; Seabury, *Power, Freedom, and Diplomacy*, 15; Schlesinger, *The Vital Center*, 219 (Boston, 1949).

[22] Dorothy Dodge, *Internationalism-Isolationism in Minnesota: A Study of the Roll Call Votes of the Minnesota Congressional Delegation, 1940–60*, 47 (Minneapolis, 1961).

[23] Daniel J. Boorstin, *America and the Image of Europe*, 121, 122 (New York, 1960); Jonas, *Isolationism in America*, 277, 281.

[24] Sinclair Lewis, "Minnesota: The Norse State," in *Nation*, 16:627 (May 30, 1923).

Chapter 1 — CUSHMAN K. DAVIS — pages 15 to 31

[1] The opening quotation is from Davis, "The Foreign Relations of the United States," in University of Pennsylvania, *Alumni Register*, 11 (July, 1900), Davis Papers, Minnesota Historical Society. See also Frederick Lewis Allen, *The Big Change: America Transforms Itself, 1900–1950*, 3, 4, 27 (New York, 1952); John D. Hicks, "The Birth of the Populist Party," in *Minnesota History*, 9:219–247 (September, 1928). On Bryan and the silver plank in the Democratic platform, see Thomas A. Bailey, "The 1900 Election Was a Mandate for Partisanship, Not Imperialism," in Miller, *American Imperialism in 1898*, 169–175.

[2] United States Bureau of the Census, *Historical Statistics of the United States, Colonial Times to 1957*, 56, 72, 180 (Washington, D.C., 1960).

[3] See, for example, A. T. Mahan, "The United States Looking Outward," in *Atlantic Monthly*, 66:816–824 (December, 1890); *The Influence of Sea Power Upon History*,

1660–1783 (Boston, 1895); and *The Interest of America in Sea Power, Present and Future* (Boston, 1897).

⁴ Information in this and the succeeding two paragraphs is given in Barbara W. Tuchman, *The Proud Tower: A Portrait of the World Before the War, 1890–1914*, 131, 135, 149–151 (New York, 1966), and Bailey, *A Diplomatic History*, 451–456. See also Kennan, *American Diplomacy, 1900–1950*, 7 (Chicago, 1951).

⁵ Bailey, *A Diplomatic History*, 455; Miller, "Introduction," in *American Imperialism in 1898*, 6. Other essays in the same volume substantiate the thesis that the Spanish-American War was a manifestation of the American impulse to empire, an inevitable extension of continentalism that was motivated by a myriad of factors about which there remains healthy, scholarly disagreement. William A. Thayer, *The Life and Letters of John Hay*, 2:337 (Boston, 1915).

⁶ Billington, in *Political Science Quarterly*, 60:46.

⁷ Tuchman, *The Proud Tower*, 151, 152 (quotation), 153; Tompkins, *Anti-Imperialism*, 126; Adler, *The Isolationist Impulse*, 22. Both opponents and supporters of imperialism acted from complex motives. See, for example, David Healy, *US Expansion: The Imperialist Urge in the 1890s*, 213–231 (Madison, Wis., 1970).

⁸ *Minneapolis Tribune*, March 11, 27, 1898; *St. Paul Pioneer Press*, March 19, 1898. See also Peter Mickelson, "Nationalism in Minnesota During the Spanish-American War," in *Minnesota History*, 41·1–6 (Spring, 1968).

⁹ Historians disagree as to the position of the business community regarding the war. See, for example, Julius W. Pratt, *Expansionists of 1898: The Acquisition of Hawaii and the Spanish Islands*, 230–278 (Baltimore, 1936); Miller, *American Imperialism in 1898*, 8. On Minnesota attitudes, see Mickelson, in *Minnesota History*, 41:4.

¹⁰ Minnesota, *Legislative Manual*, 1901, p. 99; George M. Stephenson, *John Lind of Minnesota*, 134 (Minneapolis, 1935).

¹¹ Theodore Christianson, *Minnesota: The Land of Sky-Tinted Waters*, 2:242, 263 (Chicago and New York, 1935).

¹² Davis, *The Treaty of Paris*, 10 ([Chicago?], 1899), a speech before the Union League Club of Chicago, February 22, 1899, copy in the Minnesota Historical Society library.

¹³ James H. Baker, *Lives of the Governors of Minnesota*, 192 (*Minnesota Historical Society Collections*, vol. 13 — St. Paul, 1908); Henry A. Castle, "Cushman Kellogg Davis," 7, an address given at the unveiling of Davis' monument, Arlington National Cemetery, Virginia, May 30, 1903, in Davis Papers; Raymond A. Reinter, "Cushman Kellogg Davis, Expansionist," 59, B.A. honors thesis, Harvard University, 1952, copy in the Minnesota Historical Society.

¹⁴ Christianson, *Minnesota*, 2:48, 64; Harlan P. Hall, *H. P. Hall's Observations: Being More or Less a History of Political Contests in Minnesota from 1849 to 1904*, 123–128 (St. Paul, 1904).

¹⁵ Until 1916 United States senators from Minnesota were chosen by the state legislature. William W. Folwell, *A History of Minnesota*, 3:296 (Reprint edition, St. Paul, 1969); *Sauk Centre Tribune* quoted in Dwight Richard Coy, "Cushman K. Davis and American Foreign Policy, 1887–1900," p. 47, Ph.D. thesis, University of Minnesota, 1965.

¹⁶ Eleanor E. Dennison, *The Senate Foreign Relations Committee*, 99 (Stanford, Calif., 1942); Walter Wellman in *Chicago Times-Herald*, quoted in *Pioneer Press*, November 30, 1900, p. 1.

¹⁷ Dennison, *The Senate Foreign Relations Committee*, 99. Before 1968 Davis was the second Minnesotan to have served as chairman of the Senate foreign relations committee. William Windom held the post during the first and second sessions of the 47th Congress, 1881–82.

¹⁸ R. S. N. Sartz, "C. K. Davis," a manuscript evidently prepared for *Skandinaven* [1897?], in Davis Papers; Davis, quoted by Wellman, in *Pioneer Press*, November 30, 1900, p. 1; Kent Kreuter and Gretchen Kreuter, "The Presidency or Nothing: Cushman K. Davis and the Campaign of 1896," in *Minnesota History*, 41:314 (Fall, 1969).

[19] Reister, "Cushman Kellogg Davis," 103; *Congressional Record*, 53 Congress, 2 session, 621, 694. Davis renewed his efforts regarding Hawaiian annexation in 1897; see *Congressional Record*, 55 Congress, 2 session, 6140, 6188–6191, 6225, 6300, 6308, 6350, 6403.

[20] Davis, *A Treatise on International Law*, 120–135 (St. Paul, 1901); *Congressional Record*, 53 Congress, 2 session, 702 (quotation).

[21] Davis, "Our Relations with Spain," a speech reprinted in Robert I. Fulton and Thomas C. Trueblood, *Patriotic Eloquence Relating to the Spanish-American War and Its Issues*, 101, 102 (New York, 1900).

[22] Davis, *The Treaty of Paris*, 3; Davis, *A Treatise on International Law*, 101, 102.

[23] *Chicago Inter-Ocean* quoted in *St. Paul Pioneer Press*, November 30, 1900, p. 4; *Congressional Record*, 55 Congress, 2 session, 3773; Bailey, *A Diplomatic History*, 463; Davis to Cordenio A. Severance, April 20, 1898, Davis Papers.

[24] *Congressional Record*, 55 Congress, 2 session, 3820, 3993.

[25] One account blames Knute Nelson, then Minnesota's junior senator, for Davis' failure to get the appointment. According to Nils P. Haugen, "Pioneer and Political Reminiscences," in *Wisconsin Magazine of History*, 12:52 (September, 1928), Nelson was opposed to Hawaiian annexation and presumably to a pro-annexationist secretary of state. The report seems somewhat dubious. Nelson had voted for annexation in 1896, and in 1898 he supported intervention in Cuba and later championed acquisition of the Philippines. *Congressional Record*, 55 Congress, 2 session, 3993; 55 Congress, 3 session, 836; Kellogg to Davis, April 24, 1898, Kellogg Papers, Minnesota Historical Society.

[26] See, for example, Howard Schonberger, "James J. Hill and the Trade with the Orient," in *Minnesota History*, 41:178–190 (Winter, 1968); Davis to Severance, May 5, 1898, Davis Papers.

[27] James to W. M. Salter, November 18, 1898, and to the *Boston Evening Transcript*, March 1, 1899, quoted in Ralph Barton Perry, *The Thought and Character of William James*, 2:309 (Boston, 1935); Sara Norton and M. A. De Wolfe Howe, eds., *Letters of Charles Eliot Norton*, 2:290 (Boston, 1913).

[28] Kennan, *American Diplomacy*, 15; Healy, *US Expansionism*, 54; Hoar, in *Congressional Record*, 55 Congress, 2 session, 6665.

[29] Towne, quoted in Fulton and Trueblood, *Patriotic Eloquence*, 313, 317.

[30] Seabury to Davis, June 23, 1898; Davis to Kellogg and Severance, June 27, 1898; and undated notes, all in Davis Papers. On territorial acquisitions, see Bailey, *A Diplomatic History*, 109, 172, 262.

[31] Franklin F. Holbrook, *Minnesota in the Spanish-American War and the Philippine Insurrection*, 130 (St. Paul, 1923); Hill, quoted in Schonberger, in *Minnesota History*, 41:182, 186.

[32] 55 Congress, 3 session, *House Documents*, no. 1, p. 812 (serial 3743).

[33] Henry Cabot Lodge, ed., *Selections from the Correspondence of Theodore Roosevelt and Henry Cabot Lodge, 1884–1918*, 1:337 (New York, 1925).

[34] 55 Congress, 3 session, *House Documents*, no. 1, p. 908, 932, 934 (Gray quotation); Davis to Castle, October 30, 1898, Castle Papers, Minnesota Historical Society. See also Pratt, *Expansionists of 1898*, 332. Evidence documenting the proposition that in fact McKinley wanted all of the Philippines appears in H. Wayne Morgan, "McKinley Got What He Wanted," in Miller, *American Imperialism in 1898*, 114–120.

[35] 55 Congress, 3 session, *House Documents*, no. 1, p. 948, 950; Davis to Castle, November 23, 1898, Castle Papers, Minnesota Historical Society; H. Wayne Morgan, ed., *Making Peace with Spain: The Diary of Whitelaw Reid, September-December, 1898*, 221 (Austin, Tex., 1965); Pratt, *Expansionists of 1898*, 360.

[36] 55 Congress, 3 session, *House Documents*, no. 1, p. 966; *New York Times*, December 25, 1898.

[37] Quoted in *Pioneer Press*, November 28, 1900, p. 1.

[38] Margaret Leech, *In the Days of McKinley*, 355 (quotation) (New York, 1959); Davis,

quoted in Paolo E. Coletta, "Bryan Was Caught in Trap," in Miller, *American Imperialism in 1898*, 167.

[39] *Congressional Record*, 55 Congress, 3 session, 93 (quotation). In *Expansionists of 1898*, 357, Pratt argues that Bryan switched from his long-standing opposition to expansionism, hoping that the possibility of Philippine independence would be greater under the United States than Spain. Other interpretations minimize Bryan's influence. See Miller, *American Imperialism in 1898*, 162, 169–175, for Coletta and Bailey's opinions. On the vote, see 55 Congress, 3 session, *Journal of the Executive Proceedings of the Senate*, 1284 (serial 3724).

[40] Hay, quoted in Adams, *The Education of Henry Adams*, 374 (Boston, 1918); Lodge, *Correspondence of Roosevelt and Lodge*, 1:391; Worthington Chauncey Ford, ed., *Letters of Henry Adams (1892–1918)*, 209 (Boston and New York, 1938); Davis, *The Treaty of Paris*, 7. Ratification of the treaty had a high presidential priority because McKinley wanted the power to put down the insurgent forces on Luzon; see Leech, *In the Days of McKinley*, 330.

[41] The story of Davis' abortive effort to gain Minnesota support for his presidential ambitions is told by Kreuter and Kreuter, in *Minnesota History*, 41:301–316. A harsh epitaph was recorded in the *Belle Plaine Herald*: "Senator Davis' boom for the presidency is gone to keep company with St. Paul's ice palace." Undated clipping, Castle Papers. See also Castle, "Reminiscences of Minnesota Politics," in *Minnesota Historical Society Collections*, 15:594 (St. Paul, 1915); *Minneapolis Journal*, July 27, 1897.

[42] 56 Congress, 2 session, *Memorial Addresses on the Life and Character of Cushman Kellogg Davis, delivered in the Senate and House of Representatives*, 77 (Washington, D.C., 1901).

[43] Quotations in speech notes [1897?], p. 10, 11, and Davis, in *Alumni Register*, 11, both in Davis Papers. On the historical dichotomy of American attitudes toward Europe versus Asia, see Bernard Fensterwald, Jr., "The Anatomy of American 'Isolationism' and Expansionism," in *Conflict Resolution*, 2:113 (December, 1958).

[44] Davis, *The Treaty of Paris*, 3; *An Address by Senator Cushman K. Davis Before the Hamilton Club of Chicago*, 29 (August 29, 1900), in the Minnesota Historical Society library; Davis, in *Alumni Register*, 12, Davis Papers; Davis, *A Treatise on International Law*, 2.

[45] *Pioneer Press*, November 30, 1900, p. 1; *Minneapolis Tribune*, November 28, 1900, p. 1.

[46] Healy, in *US Expansionism*, 32, makes the point that "However broadly interpreted, the central focus of traditional expansionism was the North American continent and its environs." Even anti-imperialists saw merit in the annexation of Cuba and Canada.

[47] Testimony of Henry Steele Commager, 90 Congress, 1 session, *Hearing before the Committee on Foreign Relations, United States Senate, February 20, 1967*, 7 (Washington, D.C., 1967); Commager, *Living Ideas in America*, 660; William G. Carleton, "Isolationism and the Middle West," in *Mississippi Valley Historical Review*, 33:377–380 (December, 1946).

[48] John M. Gilman, in Ramsey County Bar Association, *In Memoriam: Cushman Kellogg Davis*, 18 (St. Paul, 1900); Castle, "Cushman Kellogg Davis," 10, Davis Papers.

Chapter 2 — CHARLES A. LINDBERGH — pages 32 to 53

[1] The opening quotation is from Lindbergh, *The Economic Pinch*, 222 (Philadelphia, 1923). See also Samuel Flagg Bemis, *A Short History of American Foreign Policy and Diplomacy*, 297–313, 345–358 (New York, 1959); Bailey, *A Diplomatic History*, 486–520.

[2] Lindbergh, *The Economic Pinch*, 222.

[3] Walter S. Ross, *The Last Hero: Charles A. Lindbergh [Jr.]*, 14 (New York, 1964).

[4] Helpful reference works for information on these reform movements are Russel B. Nye, *Midwestern Progressive Politics* (East Lansing, Mich., 1959); Chrislock, *Progressive Era in Minnesota*; Eric F. Goldman, *Rendezvous with Destiny* (New York, 1952); Hofstadter, *The Age of Reform*; and Naftalin, "A History of the Farmer-Labor Party." See also White, *The Autobiography of William Allen White*, 487 (New York, 1946).

[5] Nye, *Midwestern Progressive Politics*, 261; *New York Times*, April 5, 1913, p. 2.

[6] Lynn and Dora B. Haines, *The Lindberghs* (New York, 1931) is a useful contemporary source of biographical material. The Lindbergh Papers in the Minnesota Historical Society also provide valuable information. See also Bruce L. Larson, "Little Falls Lawyer, 1884–1906: Charles A. Lindbergh, Sr.," in *Minnesota History*, 43:159–166 (Spring, 1973).

[7] Charles A. Lindbergh, [Jr.], *Boyhood on the Upper Mississippi: A Reminiscent Letter*, 2, 6n (St. Paul, 1972); Bruce L. Larson, *Lindbergh of Minnesota: A Political Biography*, 18, 20, 28, 29 (New York, 1973).

[8] Kenneth S. Davis, *The Hero: Charles A. Lindbergh and the American Dream*, 409 (Garden City, N.Y., 1959) states that the younger Lindbergh's fight against intervention in what he considered "Europe's war" almost certainly had its roots in his father's isolationism during World War I. Contemporary commentators in the late 1930s and early 1940s made similar observations. See, for example, Dorothy Thompson, "As the Twig is Bent," in *Milwaukee Sentinel*, July 31, 1936. In his wartime journal Charles Lindbergh, Jr., recorded his rereading of his father's book, *Why is Your Country at War* on the evening of June 21, 1940, and recalled that, after a speech in Minneapolis on May 10, 1941, "I think the greatest satisfaction I have had at any of these meetings lay in the applause I received when I spoke of my father tonight. People are beginning to appreciate his vision and courage." Charles A. Lindbergh, *The Wartime Journals of Charles A. Lindbergh*, 360, 485 (New York, 1970).

[9] Nye, *Midwestern Progressive Politics*, 13.

[10] Quotations are from Lindbergh, *Why is Your Country at War and What Happens to You after the War and Related Subjects*, 83 (Washington, D.C., 1917); Lindbergh, "Agricultural Plans of King Emanuel," in *Law of Rights*, 1:45 (March, 1905); Lindbergh, *Banking and Currency and The Money Trust*, 195, 220 (Washington, D.C., 1913); Lindbergh, *The Economic Pinch*, 25. The Federal Reserve Act of 1913 and the Esch-Cummins Railway Act are examples of legislation Lindbergh thought served the profiteers. The latter established a rate system to ensure a fair return for carriers; as a result, freight rates increased, working a hardship on farmers. One of Lindbergh's final acts in Congress was to call for the impeachment of members of the Federal Reserve Board; see *Congressional Record*, 64 Congress, 2 session, 3126.

[11] Lindbergh, *Why is Your Country at War*, 136; Lindbergh, *Banking and Currency*, 29; Haines, *The Lindberghs*, 167. On the coalition, see Naftalin, "A History of the Farmer-Labor Party," 84.

[12] One of the persuaders was Charles Weyerhaeuser, who reportedly lived to regret his enthusiasm. Lindbergh at the time was retained as attorney for the Pine Tree Lumber Co. owned by the Weyerhaeuser family. Typescript of interviews with G. A. Raymond, 3–5, September 22, 24, 1936, Lindbergh Papers.

[13] *Wheaton Gazette-Reporter* and *Minneapolis Journal* quoted in *Little Falls Herald*, undated clippings, Lindbergh Papers; *Elbow Lake Herald* quoted in *Little Falls Herald*, April 27, 1906; a paid political advertisement for Lindbergh in *Little Falls Herald*, July 20, 1906; "To the People of the Sixth Congressional District of Minnesota," 1–10, campaign literature, 1906, Lindbergh Papers.

[14] Lindbergh received 16,752 votes, Tifft, 13,115; Minnesota, *Legislative Manual*, 1907, p. 491.

[15] Hofstadter, *The Age of Reform*, 168, 214, 230; *Congressional Record*, 62 Congress, 2 session, 13, 1910. On Lindbergh's reaction, see Ernest Lundeen, "Chas. A. Lindbergh, the First," 9, typed manuscript [1940], Lindbergh Papers.

[16] On the Mexican incident, see Bemis, *A Short History of American Foreign Policy*,

325–332. Bailey, *A Diplomatic History*, 555, points out that "Wilson's righteous attitude represented a sharp clash between idealism and legalism. From the days of Thomas Jefferson the United States had generally . . . pursued the policy of recognizing governments, regardless of how they had come into office." But Wilson said, "I am going to teach the South American Republics to elect good men."

[17] Minnesota ex-governor John Lind "played a pivotal role" in the Mexican situation, serving as Wilson's personal representative there from 1913 to 1914. See Deborah K. Neubeck, *Guide to a Microfilm Edition of The Mexican Mission Papers of John Lind*, 16 (St. Paul, 1971).

[18] Bailey, *A Diplomatic History*, 554; *Congressional Record*, 63 Congress, 2 session, 6951, 6952 (quotations); Lindbergh to his daughter Eva, April 27, 1914, Lindbergh Papers. Lindbergh's voluminous correspondence with his daughter was most informal, usually hastily typed letters on bits and scraps of paper. Upon her marriage in 1916, Eva Lindbergh became Mrs. George W. Christie.

[19] *Congressional Record*, 63 Congress, 2 session, 6958; Larson, "Charles A. Lindbergh, Sr.," 253–255.

[20] Samuel Lubell, "Who Votes Isolationist and Why?" in *Harper's Magazine*, April, 1951, p. 31; *United States Census, 1910, Abstract*, 86, 187; *United States Census, 1910, Population*, 1:877, 894.

[21] Charles S. Ward, "The Minnesota Commission of Public Safety in World War One: Its Formation and Activities," 3, 73, Masters thesis, University of Minnesota, 1965; Clifton James Child, *The German-Americans in Politics, 1914–1917*, 3, 117, 125 (Madison, Wis., 1939); George M. Stephenson, *A History of American Immigration, 1820–1924*, 207 (Boston, 1926). On German-American attitudes, see also Chrislock, *Progressive Era*, 95–99. An editorial in North Dakota's leading Norwegian-language newspaper, *Normanden* (Grand Forks), December 14, 1917, p. 4, claimed that "Anyone who has followed German-American journalistic activity over a period of years must be aware how craftily and systematically German-American papers have worked for Pan Germanism. . . . The Scandinavian press . . . has to a considerable extent followed German press leadership. This is particularly true of the Swedish-American press, though less so now than earlier." (Translation by Carl H. Chrislock.)

[22] Goldman, *Rendezvous with Destiny*, 234, 235 (quotation); *Congressional Record*, 64 Congress, 1 session, *Appendix*, 497 (quotation); Adler, *The Isolationist Impulse*, 45.

[23] *Plain Dealer* quoted in Bailey, *A Diplomatic History*, 563; Ray Stannard Baker and William E. Dodd, eds., *The New Democracy: Presidential Messages, Addresses, and Other Papers (1913–1917) by Woodrow Wilson*, 1:158 (New York, 1926).

[24] For the impact of the war on Minnesota, see Chrislock, *Progressive Era*, 66–76; for the quotation, see Franklin F. Holbrook and Livia Appel, *Minnesota in the War with Germany*, 1:2 (St. Paul, 1928).

[25] Holbrook and Appel, *Minnesota in the War*, 1:11, 26; Oscar W. Firkins, *Cyrus Northrop: A Memorial*, 570 (Minneapolis, 1925).

[26] Billington, in *Political Science Quarterly*, 60:55; Baker and Dodd, *The New Democracy*, 1:321.

[27] Republican Knute Nelson voted against the resolution. *Congressional Record*, 64 Congress, 1 session, 3465; Barbara W. Tuchman, "How We Entered World War I," in *New York Times Magazine*, March 5, 1967, p. 72. For the Minnesota reaction, see Chrislock, *Progressive Era*, 104.

[28] *Congressional Record*, 64 Congress, 2 session, 1742.

[29] For a full discussion of the telegram, see Barbara W. Tuchman, *The Zimmermann Telegram* (Bantam edition, New York, 1971). On the arming of merchant ships and Lindbergh's attitude, see *Congressional Record*, 64 Congress, 2 session, 4499–5502, 4692, *Appendix*, 701.

[30] On the Minnesota reaction, see Holbrook and Appel, *Minnesota in the War*, 36–38, 39 (quotation), 42, 43 (quotation).

[31] Robert L. Morlan, *Political Prairie Fire: The Nonpartisan League, 1915–1922* (Min-

neapolis, 1955) and Carol E. Jenson, "Agrarian Pioneer in Civil Liberties: The Nonpartisan League in Minnesota during World War I," Ph.D. thesis, University of Minnesota, 1968, offer comprehensive accounts. See also Chrislock, *Progressive Era*, 111, 147; Nye, *Midwestern Progressive Politics*, 291–295.

[32] Haines, *The Lindberghs*, 253; *Congressional Record*, 64 Congress, 1 session, 4731, *Appendix*, 66; 2 session, 78, 3240, 3734, 4202 (quotations), 4962, *Appendix*, 700 (quotation).

[33] Lindbergh's campaign statements with his positions on issues are in the Lindbergh Papers. See, for example, newspaper clippings from the *St. Cloud Daily Journal*, undated, fall, 1908, and the *Cass Lake Times*, March 10, 1909.

[34] On withdrawing from the gubernatorial contest, Lindbergh explained that he was satisfied that his views and those of J. A. A. Burnquist (who became governor on the death of Winfield S. Hammond) were compatible; *St. Cloud Daily Journal-Press*, February 21, 1916. On May 22, Magnus Martinson, Lindbergh's secretary, wrote to ex-governor Adolph O. Eberhart that Lindbergh would have stayed in the gubernatorial primary had Hammond lived; Kellogg Papers. The 1916 contest was the first direct vote for senators in Minnesota, and Kellogg profited by the divided opposition. Folwell, *Minnesota*, 3:298; Chrislock, *Progressive Era*, 119.

[35] Lindbergh, *Why is Your Country at War*, 12, 13 (quotation), 31, 75 (quotation). According to Larson, "Charles A. Lindbergh, Sr.," 333–338, about 300 copies of the book had been printed before the plates were destroyed by "government agents." Lindbergh assigned the copyright to his associate, Walter E. Quigley, in 1923, and it was reissued by Dorrance and Co., Inc., of Philadelphia in 1934.

[36] Interviews with G. A. Raymond, 6 (quotation), and Lundeen, "Chas. A. Lindbergh, the First," 15, both in Lindbergh Papers. See also Quigley's introduction to the 1934 edition of *Why is Your Country at War*, 7.

[37] Morlan, *Political Prairie Fire*, 136–141; Chrislock, *Progressive Era*, 165.

[38] On Nonpartisan League procedures, see Naftalin, "A History of the Farmer-Labor Party," 41.

[39] Minnesota, *Laws*, 1917, p. 373–377; O. A. Hilton, *The Minnesota Commission of Public Safety in World War I, 1917–1919*, 1–3 (Oklahoma Agriculture and Mechanical College, *Social Science Series*, vol. 48, no. 14 — Stillwater, Okla., 1951); Chrislock, *Progressive Era*, 131.

[40] Theodore C. Blegen, *Minnesota: A History of the State*, 473 (Minneapolis, 1963); Ward, "The Minnesota Commission on Public Safety," 76; Holbrook and Appel, *Minnesota in the War*, 2:74 (quotation), 76.

[41] Holbrook and Appel, *Minnesota in the War*, 2:85, 86.

[42] Ward, "The Minnesota Commission of Public Safety," 136; Hilton, *The Minnesota Commission of Public Safety*, 17, 18.

[43] Ward, "The Minnesota Commission of Public Safety," 138. Chrislock, *Progressive Era*, 149–153, has a good account of this episode and its aftermath.

[44] H. C. Peterson and Gilbert C. Fite, *Opponents of the War, 1917–1918*, 69 (quotation), 72 (Madison, Wis., 1957); *Congressional Record*, 65 Congress, 1 session, 7491, and 3 session, 1527.

[45] Testimony of McGee, 65 Congress, 2 session, *Hearings before the Committee on Military Affairs, United States Senate, April 19, 1918*, 54, 56, 57, 60 (Washington, D.C., 1918).

[46] Quoted in Peterson and Fite, *Opponents of the War*, 193. The *Public*, a weekly journal of opinion from 1898–1919, was the predecessor of the *New Republic*.

[47] For a full account of the primary campaign, see Morlan, *Political Prairie Fire*, 187–201; Chrislock, *Progressive Era*, 164–171.

[48] Ernest Lundeen claimed that 575 of Minnesota's nearly 600 newspapers were "bitter in opposition"; "Chas. A. Lindbergh, the First," 16, Lindbergh Papers.

[49] "Let the People Rule in Minnesota," campaign literature of the Nonpartisan League, Lindbergh Papers; Walter E. Quigley, "Out where the West Begins," 47, manuscript in the collections of the Minnesota Historical Society. See also Lindbergh,

Why is Your Country at War, 87; Lindbergh to Eva L. Christie, April 14, 18, 1917, February 1, 1918, Lindbergh Papers.

⁵⁰ Knud Wefald, ninth district congressman from 1923 to 1927, described the violence toward Lindbergh supporters in a letter dated May 24, 1927, to "Editor, Daily Star," a Minneapolis newspaper, Knud Wefald Papers, in the Minnesota Historical Society; Haines, *The Lindberghs*, 282; Naftalin, "A History of the Farmer-Labor Party," 47, 49 (quotations).

⁵¹ Lindbergh to Charles Jr., June 12, 1918; to Eva L. Christie, undated, both in Lindbergh Papers; *Martin County Sentinel* reprinted in *Redwood Falls Sun*, June 14, 1918.

⁵² *Congressional Record*, 65 Congress, 2 session, 7542–7544; Haines, *The Lindberghs*, 279. Wilson showed confidence in Lindbergh by asking Bernard M. Baruch to appoint him to the War Industries Board, where his knowledge of economics would be an asset. After he was sworn in, objections came from the enemy camp and he resigned. See Haines, 286–288. In a note appended to a Lindbergh letter written in the summer of 1918, Eva L. Christie observed, "The whole thing was disgraceful and I *know* it hurt father keenly, tho' he would not admit it." Lindbergh Papers.

⁵³ Lindbergh speech, March 21, 1918, Lindbergh Papers; undated memorial, in the Joseph A. A. Burnquist Papers, in the Minnesota Historical Society. Haines states that the memorial was presented on May 16, 1918; *The Lindberghs*, 293.

⁵⁴ Morlan, *Political Prairie Fire*, 198; *Congressional Record*, 64 Congress, 1 session, Appendix, 1839, 1840 (quotation). Walter Quigley, a Catholic himself, did not consider Lindbergh anti-Catholic but thought the wording of the resolution "unfortunate." Quigley, "Out where the West Begins," 58, 63, 95.

⁵⁵ Lindbergh to Eva Christie, May 31, 1918, Lindbergh Papers; *Legislative Manual*, 1919, p. 252; *Minnesota Leader* (St. Paul), June 22, 1918; Christianson, *Minnesota*, 2:366; Chrislock, *Progressive Era*, 179–181.

⁵⁶ Walter E. Quigley, "Like Father, Like Son," in *Saturday Evening Post*, June 21, 1941, p. 36; Christianson, *Minnesota*, 2:370; Nye, *Midwestern Progressive Politics*, 292.

⁵⁷ *Report of Minnesota Commission of Public Safety*, 32 (St. Paul, 1919).

⁵⁸ Blegen, *Minnesota*, 473; Amaury de Riencourt, *The American Empire*, 37 (New York, 1968); Christianson, *Minnesota*, 2:402.

⁵⁹ Lindbergh, *Why is Your Country at War*, 214 (quotation); Lindbergh to Eva Christie, August 13, 1918, March 22, 1920 (quotation), Lindbergh Papers.

⁶⁰ Lindbergh, "Terrorism in Russia," in *Lindbergh's National Farmer*, May, 1919, p. 8; Lindbergh to Eva Christie, [1918], Lindbergh Papers.

⁶¹ Robert K. Murphy, *Red Scare: A Study in National Hysteria, 1919–1920*, 33, 40–45 (Minneapolis, 1955); Bailey, *A Diplomatic History*, 636. Lindbergh's opinion is in a letter to Eva Christie, [January 20, 1920], Lindbergh Papers.

⁶² *Legislative Manual*, 1921, p. 527.

⁶³ "World War Veterans Indorse C. A. Lindbergh for United States Senator, Farmer-Labor Ticket," campaign literature, 1923; Lindbergh to Eva Christie, July 3, 1923, both in Lindbergh Papers; *Legislative Manual*, 1925, p. 297.

⁶⁴ Note by Eva Christie attached to letter from Lindbergh, January 31, 1924, and notes on conference with state Senator Victor Lawson, July 1, 1937, both in Lindbergh Papers; George H. Mayer, *The Political Career of Floyd B. Olson*, 28 (Minneapolis, 1951).

⁶⁵ *Minneapolis Tribune*, May 28, 1924, p. 3; Pederson, "Lindbergh as I knew him," 2, Lindbergh Papers; Pederson, "Reminiscences," 70, Thomas Pederson Papers, Minnesota Historical Society. Ernest Lundeen, for example, called Lindbergh "the most distinguished Congressman Minnesota ever had"; *Congressional Record*, 74 Congress, 2 session, 9697.

⁶⁶ Quigley, in *Saturday Evening Post*, June 21, 1941, p. 27, 42; Lindbergh to Eva Christie, undated, Lindbergh Papers; Haines, *The Lindberghs*, 225 (quotation).

⁶⁷ Nye, *Midwestern Progressive Politics*, 247; Cooper, *The Vanity of Power*, 173.

⁶⁸ Lindbergh to his publisher, Dorrance and Co., Inc., Philadelphia, November 21,

December 26, 1922, suggesting jacket copy for his new book, *The Economic Pinch*, Lindbergh Papers.

[69] Lindbergh, *The Economic Pinch*, 235.

Chapter 3 — HAROLD KNUTSON — pages 54 to 75

[1] The opening quotation is from *St. Cloud Daily Times*, November 5, 1948. For general historical background information in this chapter, the following works have been especially helpful: Bailey, *A Diplomatic History*; Allen, *The Big Change*; John Kenneth Galbraith, *The Great Crash, 1929* (Boston, 1961); Cushing Strout, *The American Image of the Old World* (New York, 1963); Warren I. Cohen, *The American Revisionists: The Lessons of Intervention in World War I* (Chicago, 1967); Lubell, *The Future of American Politics*, 129. As a result of the 1913 reapportionment, the sixth congressional district included the counties of Aitkin, Beltrami, Benton, Cass, Crow Wing, Hubbard, Morrison, Sherburne, Stearns, Todd, and Wadena. In 1933 it was enlarged by the addition of Kanabec, Pine, Mille Lacs, Meeker, and Wright counties (Beltrami was made a part of the ninth congressional district).

[2] *New York Times*, December 1, p. 4, December 11, p. 1, 1920, August 22, 1953, p. 15; *Congressional Record*, 71 Congress, 2 session, 3894; 80 Congress, 2 session, 8904, 9776 (quotations). Biographical information here and below is from the *Biographical Directory of the American Congress, 1774–1971*, 1247 (Washington, D.C., 1971).

[3] Minnesota, *Legislative Manual*, 1917, p. 519.

[4] Knutson's platform appears in a campaign advertisement in the *Wadena Pioneer Journal*, November 2, 1916, p. [6].

[5] *Congressional Record*, 65 Congress, 1 session, 413, *Appendix*, 22; George F. Authier in *Minneapolis Tribune* reprinted in *St. Cloud Daily Times*, April 16, 1917, p. 4.

[6] *Congressional Record*, 65 Congress, 1 session, 362, 412, *Appendix*, 11 (quotation); Holbrook and Appel, *Minnesota in the War with Germany*, 1:52, 55.

[7] Bailey, *A Diplomatic History*, 593 (quotation); Paul S. Holbo, "They Voted Against War," Ph.D. thesis, University of Chicago, 1961, quoted in Cohen, *The American Revisionists*, 13; *United States Census*, 1920, *Population*, 3:504, 509–517.

[8] *Congressional Record*, 65 Congress, 1 session, *Appendix*, 23.

[9] *St. Cloud Daily Times*, April 6, p. 4, April 16, p. 4 (quotation), 1917.

[10] *New York Times*, September 17, 1918, p. 2; *Congressional Record*, 65 Congress, 2 session, 10346, *Appendix*, 383; letter from Nelson to N. K. Hunt, in *Sauk Centre Herald*, May 23, 1918, p. 2.

[11] *Congressional Record*, 65 Congress, 1 session, 1705; 2 session, 10346; *Legislative Manual*, 1921, p. 527. Knutson voted against the espionage bill; *Congressional Record*, 65 Congress, 1 session, 1841.

[12] *Congressional Record*, 67 Congress, 1 session, 2522, 2523.

[13] Walter R. Sharp and Grayson Kirk, *Contemporary International Politics*, 332 (9th printing, New York, 1947); *Congressional Record*, 67 Congress, 4 session, 3710-3712 (quotations); *New York Times*, February 16, 1923, p. 3.

[14] *Congressional Record*, 68 Congress, 2 session, 2596 (quotation); 71 Congress, 1 session, 5587; 2 session, 690, 8868; *St. Paul Pioneer Press*, November 26, 1929, p. 10.

[15] *Congressional Record*, 71 Congress, 2 session, 690; 72 Congress, 1 session, 720, 7405; Bailey, *A Diplomatic History*, 674.

[16] Galbraith, *The Great Crash, 1929*, 173.

[17] Bailey, *A Diplomatic History*, 664; *Congressional Record*, 71 Congress, 2 session, 6204 (quotation), 9964–9966, 10831.

[18] *Congressional Record*, 72 Congress, 1 session, 2361; 73 Congress, 1 session, 5943.

[19] Bailey, *A Diplomatic History*, 673; *Congressional Record*, 73 Congress, 2 session, 5347; 75 Congress, 1 session, 34; 76 Congress, 3 session, 1647; 78 Congress, 1 session, 67; 79 Congress, 1 session, 4884.

[20] Information on the war debt and reparations issues here and in the following three paragraphs is from Bailey, *A Diplomatic History*, 655–671.

[21] See, for example, *Congressional Record*, 71 Congress, 1 session, 3242; 72 Congress, 2 session, 475; 73 Congress, 1 session, 172, 173.

[22] Knutson's satire was read into the record by Representative Hamilton Fish of New York. One interesting comment ascribed to the ambassador from Hipigon (Japan) was "Under the new deal all men are brothers. There is to be no color line, except for the Negro, and he is a domestic problem that we know how to handle." *Congressional Record*, 73 Congress, 2 session, 5923.

[23] *Congressional Record*, 75 Congress, 1 session, 1625.

[24] Cohen, *The American Revisionists*, 159, 234–239; the Hemingway quotation is in Strout, *The American Image of the Old World*, 205.

[25] *Congressional Record*, 72 Congress, 2 session, 5344; 74 Congress, 2 session, 2218; 75 Congress, 1 session, 3200; 3 session, 165; 77 Congress, 1 session, 590, 7985 (quotation); 2 session, *Appendix*, 2230.

[26] *Congressional Record*, 75 Congress, 3 session, *Appendix*, 1373; 77 Congress, 1 session, 590; 79 Congress, 1 session, 4878.

[27] Minnesota Department of Education, "War or Peace," Unit One: 4–6 (quotation), Unit Three: 6, 20, copy in Minnesota Historical Society.

[28] Knutson's support of the Ludlow amendment is in *Congressional Record*, 75 Congress, 2 session, 243, and 3 session, 165. Knutson to Olga Selke, August 5, 1935, in the Central Council of District Clubs (St. Paul) Papers, Minnesota Historical Society. The Gallup Poll is cited in Allen, *The Big Change*, 159.

[29] *Congressional Record*, 74 Congress, 1 session, 14369 (quotations), 14434.

[30] *Congressional Record*, 75 Congress, 1 session, 98, 5695; 76 Congress, 1 session, 36.

[31] Bailey, *A Diplomatic History*, 714; *Congressional Record*, 76 Congress, 2 session, 1202 (quotation).

[32] Bailey, *A Diplomatic History*, 715; *Congressional Record*, 76 Congress, 1 session, 8311; 2 session, 1375.

[33] Knutson's vote on 1922 naval appropriations is recorded in *Congressional Record*, 67 Congress, 2 session, 5753. See also *Congressional Record*, 67 Congress, 4 session, 584; 75 Congress, 1 session, 1931, 1993; 3 session, 794, 3433, *Appendix*, 1476.

[34] The bill was introduced on February 15, 1939; *Congressional Record*, 76 Congress, 1 session, 1422 (quotation), 1446.

[35] *Congressional Record*, 76 Congress, 3 session, 7997.

[36] An account of the lend-lease transaction appears in Bailey, *A Diplomatic History*, 721; *Congressional Record*, 76 Congress, 3 session, 11437; 77 Congress, 1 session, 119, 534.

[37] *Congressional Record*, 77 Congress, 1 session, 590, *Appendix*, 4758. Bruce M. Russett, *No Clear and Present Danger: A Skeptical View of United States Entry Into World War II* (New York, 1972), a revisionist study, agrees with Knutson's position.

[38] Knutson discussed arming merchant ships in a radio address, October 17, 1941, reprinted in *Congressional Record*, 77 Congress, 1 session, *Appendix*, 4757–4759 (quotation), 8042.

[39] Bailey, *A Diplomatic History*, 713.

[40] *Congressional Record*, 76 Congress, 3 session, 2063, 2105.

[41] Garlid, "Politics in Minnesota," 469.

[42] *Congressional Record*, 76 Congress, 3 session, 2064.

[43] *Minneapolis Tribune*, December 8, 1941, p. 2; *Congressional Record*, 77 Congress, 1 session, 9506, 9536.

[44] *Congressional Record*, 77 Congress, 2 session, *Appendix*, 2937; 78 Congress, 1 session, 1815, 1969; 2 session, 695, 3516, 3554–3557, 3582. See also "Observations from Washington," April 30, July 9, 1942, February 10, August 31, 1944, a collection of mimeographed weekly newsletters from Knutson to his constituents, in Minnesota Historical Society library.

[45] *Congressional Record*, 77 Congress, 1 session, 1456, 7730; "Observations from Washington," September 21, 28, October 5, 1944.

[46] "Observations from Washington," March 15, May 24, October 18, 1945.

[47] *Congressional Record*, 79 Congress, 1 session, 4878; "Observations from Washington," November 15, 1945.

[48] *Congressional Record*, 79 Congress, 1 session, 8512 (quotation), 8513, 8581; "Observations from Washington," December 13, 27, 1945.

[49] *Congressional Record*, 80 Congress, 1 session, 1981, 4641. For general background information on the Truman doctrine and the Marshall Plan here and below, see Bailey, *A Diplomatic History*, 796–800; Hans J. Morgenthau, *Truth and Power: Essays of a Decade, 1960–70*, 258 (New York, 1970).

[50] *Congressional Record*, 80 Congress, 1 session, 4640, 4641; 2 session, 3875.

[51] *Congressional Record*, 79 Congress, 1 session, 5723; 80 Congress, 2 session, 9896 (quotation); "Observations from Washington," March 29, 1945.

[52] *Congressional Record*, 80 Congress, 1 session, *Appendix*, 4614.

[53] *Congressional Record*, 76 Congress, 1 session, 1421 (quotation); 80 Congress, 1 session, 11151, *Appendix*, 4616.

[54] *Congressional Record*, 73 Congress, 2 session, 636; 75 Congress, 1 session, 2153; 79 Congress, 1 session, 4729.

[55] *Business Week*, February 22, 1947, p. 16 (quotation); *Minneapolis Star*, August 23, 1953, p. 8.

[56] National Progressive League, news release, October 23, 1932, in Wefald Papers; Will Chasan, in *Nation*, 155:438 (October 31, 1942).

[57] *Life*, November 18, 1946, p. 34; *Business Week*, February 22, 1947, p. 16.

[58] *New York Times*, August 22, 1953, p. 15.

[59] *St. Cloud Daily Times*, November 5, 1948, p. 10, October 29, 1948, p. 12.

Chapter 4 — HENRIK SHIPSTEAD — pages 76 to 98

[1] The opening quotation is from a radio address on April 2, 1939, printed in the *Congressional Record*, 76 Congress, 1 session, *Appendix*, 1317. For biographical data here and below, see "Senator Henrik Shipstead: His Boyhood and Youth," in the *Friend*, July, 1930, p. 12, copy in the Henrik Shipstead Papers, in the Minnesota Historical Society; St. Cloud State Normal School, *Catalogue*, 17 (St. Cloud, 1899); Martin Ross, *Shipstead of Minnesota*, 21, 22, 24–26 (quotation), 34, 35 (Chicago, 1940), a laudatory biography written before Shipstead returned to the Republican party. On Shipstead's beginning political career, see Sister Mary René Lorentz, "Henrik Shipstead: Minnesota Independent, 1923–1946," 7, Ph.D. thesis, Catholic University of America, 1963, copy in the Minnesota Historical Society; *Biographical Directory of the American Congress*, 1692; *Glenwood Herald*, September 6, 1912, p. [4].

[2] Ross, *Shipstead of Minnesota*, 39; Minnesota, *Legislative Manual*, 1919, p. 225.

[3] Morlan, *Political Prairie Fire*, 279; typescript of a taped interview with J. A. O. Preus conducted by Lucile M. Kane and June D. Holmquist, 1960, p. 79, in the collections of the Minnesota Historical Society; Naftalin, "History of the Farmer-Labor Party," 76 (quotation); Folwell, *History of Minnesota*, 3:549; Ross, *Shipstead of Minnesota*, 41.

[4] Lorentz, "Henrik Shipstead," 12; Preus interview, 79. For election returns, see *Legislative Manual*, 1921, p. 101, 526. On the campaign fund, see Ross, *Shipstead of Minnesota*, 42; George Creel, "The Radical Humorist," in *Collier's*, September 14, 1935, p. 26, totaled the fund at a somewhat more modest $750,000.

[5] Minnesota, *Laws*, 1921, p. 53; Naftalin, "History of the Farmer-Labor Party," 84.

[6] Folwell, *History of Minnesota*, 3:550; Ross, *Shipstead of Minnesota*, 44.

[7] Ross, *Shipstead of Minnesota*, 52, 53; Naftalin, "History of the Farmer-Labor Party," 79, 80; undated campaign pamphlet [1922] (quotation), Shipstead Papers.

[8] Naftalin, "History of the Farmer-Labor Party," 78, 81–83; M[arion] H. Hedges, "Shipstead — Choice of a Third Party," in *Nation*, 115:543 (November 22, 1922); Preus interview, 47; Chester A. Rowell, "La Follette, Shipstead, and the Embattled Farmers," in *World's Work*, 46:415 (August, 1923); *Legislative Manual*, 1923, p. 452.

[9] Ross, *Shipstead of Minnesota*, 74.

[10] Ray Tucker and Frederick R. Barkley, *Sons of the Wild Jackass*, 171–173 (Boston, 1932); Creel, in *Collier's*, September 14, 1935, p. 26 (quotation).

[11] Ross, *Shipstead of Minnesota*, 89, 90, 92; George W. Garlid, "The Antiwar Dilemma of the Farmer-Labor Party," in *Minnesota History*, 40:369 (Winter, 1967).

[12] *Congressional Record*, 69 Congress, 1 session, 1963 (quotation), 4707 (quotation).

[13] *Congressional Record*, 69 Congress, 1 session, 8184 (quotation). Shipstead's antipathy to bankers, like Lindbergh's, was deep. He once overpaid a ninety-cent bill by ten cents to avoid writing a check that would allow a bank to profit from the ten-cent exchange charge. Shipstead to Dorothea A. McNab, November 21, 1946, Shipstead Papers.

[14] *Congressional Record*, 69 Congress, 1 session, 1963, 1964, 8184 (quotations).

[15] Article 231 states: "The Allied and Associated Governments affirm and Germany accepts the responsibility of Germany and her allies for causing all the loss and damage to which the Allied and Associated Governments and their nationals have been subjected as a consequence of the war imposed upon them by the aggression of Germany and her allies." 66 Congress, 1 session, *Senate Executive Documents*, no. 5, p. 249 (serial 7596). On Shipstead's reaction, see *Congressional Record*, 70 Congress, 1 session, 9321 (quotation); 71 Congress, 3 session, 4903 (quotation). His resolutions pertaining to Article 231 are in *Congressional Record*, 70 Congress, 2 session, 1521; 71 Congress, 2 session, 11073; 72 Congress, 1 session, 1126.

[16] Bailey, *A Diplomatic History*, 629.

[17] *Congressional Record*, 69 Congress, 1 session, 1957, 1958, 1964, 2820, 2821, 2825, 5986, 8182, 8184. Bailey, *A Diplomatic History*, 630, says: "The fifth reservation . . . provided that the Court should never entertain a request for an advisory opinion on a dispute affecting the United States, without the consent of the United States."

[18] *Congressional Record*, 68 Congress, 2 session, 3205. On the measures introduced, see *Congressional Record*, 68 Congress, 1 session, 10275; 2 session, 3205.

[19] *Congressional Record*, 68 Congress, 1 session, 1393; 2 session, 3205 (quotation); 69 Congress, special session, 247; 71 Congress, 2 session, 12034; special session of the Senate, 078. Bailey, *A Diplomatic History*, 648, 651, 652.

[20] On Knutson's position, see chapter 3, above; for a full discussion of the Kellogg-Briand Pact, see chapter 5, below. On the referendum, see *Congressional Record*, 70 Congress, 2 session, 1731. For the La Follette, Bone, and Nye resolutions, see *Congressional Record*, 76 Congress, 1 session, 1976, 3020; 77 Congress, 1 session, 2610.

[21] *Congressional Record*, 68 Congress, 2 session, 4427.

[22] *Congressional Record*, 68 Congress, 1 session, 4705–4707; 72 Congress, 1 session, 1099.

[23] *Congressional Record*, 72 Congress, 1 session, 14740; Henrik Shipstead, *et al*, "Should America Cancel Her Foreign War Debts?" in *Congressional Digest*, 10:247 (October, 1931).

[24] *Congressional Record*, 74 Congress, 1 session, 1633; 75 Congress, 2 session, *Appendix*, 575 (quotation).

[25] Bailey, *A Diplomatic History*, 505–507, 676–679.

[26] Henrik Shipstead, " 'Dollar Diplomacy' in Latin America," in *Current History*, 26:883, 886 (September, 1927).

[27] *Congressional Record*, 70 Congress, 1 session, 6689, 6756; 72 Congress, 1 session, 13156.

[28] *Congressional Record*, 70 Congress, 1 session, 6760; *New York Times*, April 12, 1927, p. 13 (quotation). In 1939 Shipstead reiterated his concern over wars fought

by the United States without benefit of congressional declaration listing Mexico in 1916, Russia in 1918, and the aforementioned interventions in Haiti, Nicaragua, and the Dominican Republic; see *Congressional Record*, 76 Congress, 1 session, 2198.

[29] Shipstead, in *Current History*, 26:887. In 1927 Shipstead introduced a Senate joint resolution authorizing the president to invite the Central American republics to a conference to consider plans for a Central American Confederation; *Congressional Record*, 69 Congress, 2 session, 3818. On the organization of a common market, see Joseph S. Nye, Jr., "Central American Regional Integration," in *International Conciliation*, 20 (March, 1967). On the Kellogg disavowal, see chapter 5, below.

[30] Lorentz, "Henrik Shipstead," 29; Charles B. Cheney, *The Story of Minnesota Politics: High Lights of Half a Century of Political Reporting*, 55 (Minneapolis, 1947). On Shipstead's endorsement, see *New York Times*, March 28, 1928, p. 3, and April 29, 1928, sec. III, p. 2.

[31] Malcolm C. Moos and E. W. Kenworthy, "Dr. Shipstead Come to Judgment," in *Harper's Magazine*, July, 1946, p. 23.

[32] Naftalin, "History of the Farmer-Labor Party," 152, 154, 155; *Legislative Manual*, 1929, p. 194. O. J. Kvale was the other successful candidate.

[33] Naftalin, "History of the Farmer-Labor Party," 243, 270, 271; Preus interview, 79. Shoemaker had been sentenced to a year and a day for "sending defamatory material (his own newspaper) through the mail." Although Shipstead had helped to get him released from prison, Shoemaker responded by saying, "I may not win . . . but I will wreck Shipstead and that is what I am out to do." He traversed the state comparing Shipstead to Judas Iscariot, but the senator won the primary by 198,951 to 71,172. See Lorentz, "Henrik Shipstead," 44, 45, 50; *Legislative Manual*, 1935, p. 201, 205.

[34] Karl E. Rolvaag, quoted in Blegen, *Minnesota*, 529. The decline of the Farmer-Labor party is well recorded in Naftalin, "History of the Farmer-Labor Party," 330.

[35] The article, dated August 1, 1940, is in the Shipstead Papers.

[36] *Legislative Manual*, 1941, p. 230.

[37] Bailey, *A Diplomatic History*, 695, 700–709.

[38] James MacGregor Burns, *Roosevelt: The Soldier of Freedom*, 42 (New York, 1970); Allen, *The Big Change*, 158.

[39] *Congressional Record*, 72 Congress, 1 session, 261, 15502, 15503; 74 Congress, 1 session, 1117; 77 Congress, 1 session, 1349; Ernest Lundeen and Millard Tydings, "How Big a Navy? A Debate," in *Forum and Century*, December, 1938, p. 293.

[40] Bailey, *A Diplomatic History*, 715; Carleton, in *Mississippi Valley Historical Review*, 33:385; Paul Seabury, *The Waning of Southern "Internationalism,"* 1 (Princeton, N.J., 1957); Smuckler, in *American Political Science Review*, 47:395; *Congressional Record*, 75 Congress, 1 session, 99, 2410. On Bernard's stand, see Barbara Stuhler, "The One Man Who Voted 'Nay': The Story of John T. Bernard's Quarrel with American Foreign Policy," in *Minnesota History*, 43:83–92 (Fall, 1972). For a tabulation of the twelve bills, see Rex Stout and Frank Sullivan, *The Illustrious Dunderheads*, 188–192 (New York, 1942).

[41] Stout and Sullivan, *The Illustrious Dunderheads*, 188–192; Elting E. Morison, *Turmoil and Tradition: A Study of the Life and Times of Henry L. Stimson*, 469 (Boston, 1960).

[42] *Minneapolis Journal*, November 6, 1935, p. 17; *Congressional Record*, 72 Congress, 1 session, 3574; 76 Congress, 2 session, 454.

[43] *Congressional Record*, 76 Congress, 2 session, 1024; 3 session, 10888, 11142; 77 Congress, 1 session, 1346 (quotation), 1347–1350, 2610. For the lend-lease law, see United States, *Statutes at Large*, 55:31.

[44] A copy of Shipstead's reply, filed with correspondence for January 5, 1941, is in the Shipstead Papers. See also *Congressional Record*, 76 Congress, 1 session, *Appendix*, 1316; 77 Congress, 1 session, 1530, *Appendix*, 1078. On the Norwegian-American attitude, see the Rev. Elias Rasmussen, executive secretary of the Norwegian Relief Committee of Minnesota, to Shipstead, October 13, 1941; Shipstead to Rasmussen, October 27, 1941, both in Shipstead Papers.

[45] George W. Garlid, "Minneapolis Unit of the Committee to Defend America by Aiding the Allies," in *Minnesota History*, 41:270 (Summer, 1969). On Ball and Stassen, see chapters 6 and 7, below. For information on the press in general, see William C. Rogers, "Isolationist Propaganda, September 1, 1939, to December 7, 1941," Ph.D. thesis, University of Chicago, 1945.

[46] For Shipstead's votes favoring various war measures, see *Congressional Record*, 77 Congress, 1 session, 9506, 9652, 9653; 2 session, 3275, 4854–4856; 78 Congress, 1 session, 1853; 2 session, 3683. On conscription, see *Congressional Record*, 76 Congress, 3 session, 11142; 77 Congress, 2 session, 8654.

[47] *Congressional Record*, 78 Congress, 1 session, 9179; 2 session, 3888, 6361; 79 Congress, 1 session, *Appendix*, 5416.

[48] *Congressional Record*, 79 Congress, 1 session, 8116–8118, 8190; Ruth Russell, *A History of the United Nations Charter*, 942 (Washington, D.C., 1958), maintains that had he not been ill, Senator Hiram T. Johnson of California would also have voted against the Charter.

[49] *Congressional Record*, 79 Congress, 1 session, 8123.

[50] *Congressional Record*, 78 Congress, 1 session, 4513; 2 session, 3888.

[51] *Congressional Record*, 79 Congress, 2 session, 5038–5040 (quotation); Bailey, *A Diplomatic History*, 765. On the Moscow Declaration, see chapter 6, note 39, below.

[52] See, for example, *Time*, 25, and *New York Times*, 14, both for July 8, 1946; Moos and Kenworthy, in *Harper's*, July, 1946, p. 24; *Nation*, 162:329 (March 23, 1946).

[53] Shipstead to Harry F. Klinefelter, March 28, 1953, and campaign literature, July 8, 1946, both in Shipstead Papers; *Legislative Manual*, 1947, p. 175; *Minneapolis Star-Journal*, July 9, 1946, p. 1, 6.

[54] Moos and Kenworthy, in *Harper's*, July, 1946, p. 23; Ross, *Shipstead of Minnesota*, 114–121; *Congressional Record*, 69 Congress, 1 session, 8184 (quotation); 70 Congress, 1 session, 5921; 71 Congress, 2 session, 12418. On the waterways, see Lorentz, "Henrik Shipstead," 104, 134; Mildred L. Hartsough, *From Canoe to Steel Barge* (Minneapolis, 1934).

[55] Campaign literature, 1922, 1946, Shipstead Papers; *Congressional Record*, 70 Congress, 1 session, 1380–1385; 71 Congress, 2 session, 6014; 77 Congress, 1 session, 8422; 79 Congress, 1 session, 6261–6264.

[56] Garlid, "Politics in Minnesota," 516.

[57] Moos and Kenworthy, in *Harper's*, July, 1946, p. 21; Mayer, *Floyd B. Olson*, 54, 55.

[58] *Pioneer Press*, 1, and *Minneapolis Star*, 8, both June 27, 1960; *New York Times*, June 27, 1960, p. 25; *Minneapolis Tribune*, June 28, 1960, p. 4.

Chapter 5 — FRANK B. KELLOGG — pages 99 to 122

[1] The opening quotation is from a speech by Kellogg before the World Alliance of International Friendship, New York City, November 11, 1928, in Frank B. Kellogg Papers, Minnesota Historical Society. See also Philip Harrison to Kellogg, March 7, 1912; Kellogg to Albert B. Cummins, June 28, 1912; to Theodore Christianson, January 31, 1916; to Edmund Pennington, May 25, 1916 (quotation); memorandum on state department letterhead, May 14, 1928, all in Kellogg Papers.

[2] Kellogg to Cushman K. Davis, May 3, 1898, Kellogg Papers.

[3] The Kellogg Papers contain a variety of sources giving biographical information. Typical is data gathered for the *Encyclopedia Britannica*, February 8, 1926. See also the authorized biography by David Bryn-Jones, *Frank B. Kellogg: A Biography*, 26 (New York, 1937).

[4] Bryn-Jones, *Frank B. Kellogg*, 46–48, 77, 83; clipping from the *Benson Times* reprinted in *St. Paul Dispatch*, December 7, 1910; Roosevelt to Kellogg, February 7, 1916, Kellogg Papers.

[5] Undated clipping, *Pioneer Press*; Borah to Kellogg, December 11, 1915; Kellogg to Dunn, February 23, 1916; to Mayo, March 11, 1916, all in Kellogg Papers. See also chapter 1, note 15, above. In a November 27, 1924, letter to Silas H. Strawn Kellogg wrote: "I am 68 years old this coming month. I have been in various positions of public service, more or less, for over twenty years. I should like to get back to look after my private affairs." On the 1916 election, see chapter 2, note 34, above.

[6] Kellogg to James M. Beck, March 3, 1916 (quotation); to C. A. Severance, March 4, 1916 (quotation); to Charles E. Hughes, September 18, 1924; Shipstead to Kellogg, April 4, 1916, Kellogg Papers.

[7] Kellogg to Hughes, June 30, 1916 (copy); to Lindbergh in an undated draft (the final letter was dated June 5, 1916); Roosevelt to Kellogg, June 21, 1916, Kellogg Papers. After losing the primary, Lindbergh supported Calderwood; he wrote his daughter on October 13, 1916, that "Kellogg has been a bad man for the U. S." Lindbergh Papers.

[8] In the primary, Kellogg had nearly a 19,000-vote margin over Eberhart. Clapp was third and Lindbergh fourth. In the general election he outpolled the Republican presidential candidate, Charles Evans Hughes, who beat Woodrow Wilson in Minnesota by less than 400 votes. Minnesota, *Legislative Manual*, 1917, p. 191, 509, 512. See also Chrislock, *Progressive Era in Minnesota*, 126.

[9] *Congressional Record*, 65 Congress, 1 session, 261, 6847 (quotation); 2 session, 107–112. On tariff and trade, see Kellogg to William Howard Taft, May 5, 1909; to Knute Nelson, May 15, 1909, Kellogg Papers. See also *Congressional Record*, 67 Congress, 1 session, 1291; 2 session, 8439–8445.

[10] Nelson to Kellogg, December 9, 1916; telegram (copy) from Theodore Roosevelt, March 15, 1917; memorandum from Charles J. Moos to Guy Chase, January 2, 1937; Kellogg to C. A. Severance, April 1, 1921, all in Kellogg Papers.

[11] *Congressional Record*, 65 Congress, 2 session, 680 (quotation). For background information on the League of Nations controversy here and below, see Bailey, *A Diplomatic History*, 596–632.

[12] On the round robin, see *Congressional Record*, 65 Congress, 3 session, 4974. See also Walter Johnson, *William Allen White's America*, 315 (New York, 1947).

[13] *Congressional Record*, 66 Congress, 1 session, 8786; 2 session, 4600; 67 Congress, 1 session, 3261, 3299.

[14] Robert H. Ferrell, ed., *Frank B. Kellogg — Henry L. Stimson*, 12, 14 (*The American Secretaries of State and Their Diplomacy*, vol. 11 — New York, 1963); *Congressional Record*, 65 Congress, 3 session, 73–79.

[15] Taft to Kellogg, June 10, 1919; Kellogg to Taft, July 21, 1919, Kellogg Papers.

[16] Kellogg to Butler, November 19, 1925 (copy), Kellogg Papers; Nicholas Murray Butler, *Across the Busy Years: Recollections and Reflections*, 2:197–202 (New York, 1939–40); *Congressional Record*, 66 Congress, 1 session, 3690.

[17] Charles G. Cleaver, "Frank B. Kellogg: Attitudes and Assumptions Influencing His Foreign Policy Decisions," 222, Ph.D. thesis, University of Minnesota, 1956, copy in the Minnesota Historical Society; Kellogg to Taft, July 21, 1919 (copy), Kellogg Papers; *Congressional Record*, 66 Congress, 1 session, 8780 (quotation), 8786.

[18] Kellogg to Taft, December 8, 1920; to Robert E. Olds, August 13, 1921, Kellogg Papers.

[19] Kellogg to Olds, February 28, April 19, July 1, 1922; to H. V. Jones, November 25, 1922, Kellogg Papers. In the primary Kellogg defeated Lundeen by 95,051 votes and Titus by 188,417; *Legislative Manual*, 1923, p. 281.

[20] *Congressional Record*, 65 Congress, 1 session, 7491; *Pioneer Press*, November 4, 1922, p. 1 (quotation).

[21] Ferrell, *Frank B. Kellogg*, 11:16, 17; Rodney Dutcher, "The Hardest Working Man in Washington," an unidentified clipping, 1927, Kellogg Papers. The combined votes for Shipstead and Anna D. Olesen were over 200,000 more than those cast for Kellogg; *Legislative Manual*, 1923, p. 453. On Kellogg's reaction to the election, see Kellogg to H. V. Jones, November 25, 1922; to John Uno Sebenius, December 8, 1922 (quotation), Kellogg Papers.

[22] Ferrell, *Frank B. Kellogg*, 11:17; Kellogg to Elbert H. Gary, December 10, 1924 (quotations), Kellogg Papers.

[23] Ferrell, *Frank B. Kellogg*, 11:19. On American reaction to the appointment, see C. A. Severance to C. Bascom Slemp, October 27, 1923, and a clipping from the *New York World*, October 29, 1923, both in Kellogg Papers. On opposition to and confirmation of the appointment, see clipping from the *Chicago Daily Tribune*, December 11, 1923, Kellogg Papers; *Congressional Record*, 68 Congress, 1 session, 235.

[24] Ferrell, *Frank B. Kellogg*, 11:21–23; Bailey, *A Diplomatic History*, 661.

[25] Kellogg to William H. Sanders, August 27, 1924; to L. M. Willcuts, October 21, 1924; to Hughes, January 3, 1925; to Walter H. Sanborn, January 23, 1925, Kellogg Papers.

[26] Kellogg to Strawn, November 27, 1924; Hughes to Kellogg, December 12, 1924, Kellogg Papers. Coolidge outran La Follette in Minnesota by over 80,000 votes; John Davis, the Democratic candidate, ran a poor third; *Legislative Manual*, 1925, p. 318.

[27] Kellogg to Frederick Hale, January 29, 1925; Gustave Schoole to Kellogg, January 11, 1925, Kellogg Papers.

[28] L. Ethan Ellis, *Frank B. Kellogg and American Foreign Relations, 1925–1929*, 21 (New Brunswick, N. J., 1961).

[29] Morison, *Turmoil and Tradition*, 271; Ellis, *Frank B. Kellogg*, 87–90, 95; Kellogg to Clara Kellogg, June 17, 1926, Kellogg Papers.

[30] For a full discussion of the Nicaraguan situation, see Ferrell, *Frank B. Kellogg*, 11:44–57; Morison, *Turmoil and Tradition*, 271–280.

[31] Ellis, *Frank B. Kellogg*, 48–57.

[32] Ferrell, *Frank B. Kellogg*, 11:25 (quotation), 62; Kellogg to Robert Woods Bliss, ambassador to Argentina, November 7, 1927, Kellogg Papers; "Official Statement of and Commentary upon the Monroe Doctrine by the Secretary of State," February 28, 1929, in U.S. Department of State, *Papers Relating to the Foreign Relations of the United States, 1929*, 1:698–719 (Washington, D.C., 1943).

[33] Ellis, *Frank B. Kellogg*, 96–101.

[34] Kellogg to William Phillips, minister to Canada, January 26, 1928, Kellogg Papers.

[35] Kellogg to Victor F. Ridder, March 10, 1928; to Phillips, January 26, March 19, 1928, Kellogg Papers.

[36] Kellogg to Strawn, November 2, 1926; to Alanson B. Houghton, ambassador to Great Britain, May 2, 1927 (quotation), Kellogg Papers.

[37] Draft of a letter from Kellogg to Calvin Coolidge, October 24, 1927, Kellogg Papers; Burns, *Roosevelt: The Soldier of Freedom*, 375.

[38] Barbara W. Tuchman, *Stilwell and the American Experience in China, 1911–45*, 103, 105 (New York, 1970).

[39] Kellogg to Coolidge, July 10, 1928, Kellogg Papers; Ellis, *Frank B. Kellogg*, 106; Ferrell, *Frank B. Kellogg*, 11:74–81.

[40] At the 1922 Washington Conference, Secretary of State Hughes had proposed a 10-year "holiday" in shipbuilding and a plan for scrapping over a million tons of existing ships. Bailey, *A Diplomatic History*, 638, 639–643, 648. See also Kellogg to Phillips, August 9, 1927; to Coolidge, August 10, 1927; to George W. Wickersham, April 19, 1928 (quotation), Kellogg Papers.

[41] *Congressional Record*, 69 Congress, 1 session, 2825; 74 Congress, 1 session, 1147.

[42] Kellogg to Norman H. Davis, March 11, 1929, Kellogg Papers. Information on the number of treaties is from a *New York Times* clipping, December 22, 1937, Kellogg Papers.

[43] Detailed studies of the Kellogg-Briand Pact may be found in Robert H. Ferrell, *Peace in Their Time: The Origins of the Kellogg-Briand Pact* (New Haven, 1952); David Hunter Miller, *The Peace Pact of Paris: A Study of the Briand-Kellogg Treaty*, 155–159 (New York, 1928). Briand is quoted in Ferrell, 71.

[44] Butler, *Across the Busy Years*, 2:203–206; Ferrell, *Peace in Their Time*, 73–75; Frank B. Kellogg, *Some Foreign Policies of the United States*, 2 (Washington, D.C., 1926).

⁴⁵ Herrick to Kellogg, June 10, 1927, Kellogg Papers.

⁴⁶ Ferrell, *Frank B. Kellogg*, 11:83; clipping from *Cleveland Plain Dealer*, May 28, 1927, filed under date of June 2, 1927, Kellogg Papers.

⁴⁷ U.S. Department of State, *The General Pact for the Renunciation of War: Text of the Pact as Signed, Notes and Other Papers*, 4 (Washington, D.C., 1928); memorandum from J. Theodore Mariner to Kellogg, William R. Castle, and Robert E. Olds, June 24, 1927 (quotations); Kellogg to Root, December 23, 1927, Kellogg Papers; Bryn-Jones, *Frank B. Kellogg*, 231.

⁴⁸ *General Pact*, 6 (quotation), 7, 15–21.

⁴⁹ Houghton to Olds, March 1, 1928; Kellogg to Coolidge, July 10, 1928, Kellogg Papers.

⁵⁰ Ferrell, *Frank B. Kellogg*, 11:118; *General Pact*, 36–38, 42–54. The six nations were France, Germany, Great Britain, Italy, and the United States. The treaties of Locarno, named for the Swiss town in which they were signed in 1925, ended the postwar diplomatic isolation of Germany and provided for mutual defense against aggression and for arbitration as a means of settling disputes. Kellogg interpreted the police action power of the treaties as applying only against a nation "which had resorted to war in violation of its solemn pledges thereunder." Ferrell, *Peace in Their Time*, 46–50; *General Pact*, 37 (quotation).

⁵¹ Kellogg to Lippmann, July 21, 1928; to Borah, August 2, 1928; to McCormick, July 21, 1928, Kellogg Papers.

⁵² Kellogg to Coolidge, July 13, August 2, 4, 8, 1928; Coolidge to Kellogg, August 7, 1928, Kellogg Papers. See also Ellis, *Frank B. Kellogg*, 209, 211; *General Pact*, 3.

⁵³ Kellogg to Henry P. Fletcher, ambassador to Italy, May 5, 1928; to Borah, December 13, 1928; S. O. Levinson to Kellogg, October 23, 29, 1928, Kellogg Papers. See also Ferrell, *Peace in Their Time*, 247; Franklin D. Roosevelt, "Our Foreign Policy: A Democratic View," in *Foreign Affairs*, 6:585 (quotation) (July, 1928); Ellis, *Frank B. Kellogg*, 211.

⁵⁴ *Congressional Record*, 70 Congress, 2 session, 1727, 1731; Coolidge to Kellogg, January 16, 1929, Kellogg Papers.

⁵⁵ Kellogg to Clara Kellogg, May 5, 1928; to Elisabeth M. (Mrs. Whitelaw) Reid, July 24, 1928; speeches by Kellogg in London, November 22, 1929, and New York, March 28, 1930, all in Kellogg Papers; Morison, *Turmoil and Tradition*, 300.

⁵⁶ Kellogg to William Hard, June 29, 1927; statement by Kellogg on the ninth anniversary of the Paris Peace Pact, August 27, 1937, Kellogg Papers; Frank H. Simonds, *American Foreign Policy in the Post-War Years*, 54 (Baltimore, 1935); Henry L. Stimson and McGeorge Bundy, *On Active Service in Peace and War*, 158 (New York, 1947).

⁵⁷ Kellogg to Clara Kellogg, May 12, 1928; to Beck, December 27, 1929; clippings from the *Lakeland* (Fla.) *Register*, *Nashville* (Tenn.) *Banner*, and *Scranton* (Pa.) *Times*, all dated November 28, 1930; copy of Nobel Prize acceptance speech by Kellogg, December 10, 1930, all in Kellogg Papers. See also Bryn-Jones, *Frank B. Kellogg*, 277, 279. On the World Court, see chapter 4, note 16, above.

⁵⁸ Clipping from the *New York Times*, December 22, 1937; from the *New York Evening World*, January 13, 1925, Kellogg Papers.

⁵⁹ An especially hostile critique of the Kellogg stewardship can be found in Adler, *The Isolationist Impulse*, 163, 164, 172. See also Ellis, *Frank B. Kellogg*, 232. Kellogg to Hard, August 17, 1927; to Henry Suydam, January 10, 1929; clipping from *Brooklyn Daily Eagle*, January 8, 1929; all in Kellogg Papers.

⁶⁰ *Pioneer Press*, December 22, 1937, p. 1; *Northfield News*, December 22, 1937, p. 1. Kellogg had once characterized a La Follette speech as "vicious and dangerous"; he railed against the radicals "who are advocating principles absolutely subversive of our government." See Kellogg to Severance, June 22, 1922, Kellogg Papers.

⁶¹ Undated copy of speech by Kellogg, "Napoleon and His Times" (quotation); copy of speech by Kellogg in London, November 22, 1929, both in Kellogg Papers; Frank B. Kellogg, *Address on the Pact of Paris and the Relationship of the United States*

to the World Community, a radio speech given October 30, 1935, at St. Paul, copy in Minnesota Historical Society library.

Chapter 6 — JOSEPH H. BALL — pages 123 to 144

[1] The opening quotation is from *Congressional Record*, 77 Congress, 1 session, *Appendix*, A682. On the background of internationalist organizations, see Robert A. Divine's excellent study, *Second Chance: The Triumph of Internationalism in America During World War II*, 18–23 (New York, 1967). See also Carnegie Corporation, *Annual Report, 1971*, [111] (New York, 1971); Garlid, in *Minnesota History*, 41:267–283 (Summer, 1969).

[2] Interview of the author with Lester A. Malkerson, Ball's campaign manager in 1942 and 1948 primaries, January 31, 1969, Stuhler Papers, Minnesota Historical Society.

[3] Carleton, in *Mississippi Valley Historical Review*, 33:387.

[4] Sevareid, *Not so Wild a Dream*, 198 (New York, 1946).

[5] Ball, "Isolationism is Far From Dead," in *New York Times Magazine*, October 29, 1944, p. 52.

[6] *Biographical Directory of the American Congress*, 510; Ivan Hinderaker, "Harold Stassen and Developments in the Republican Party in Minnesota, 1937–1943," p. 605, Ph.D. thesis, University of Minnesota, 1949.

[7] Concerning Lundeen and Shipstead, a columnist said in 1945 that Minnesota was "a state which seemed to be perfectly content to be represented by two of the country's most implacable isolationists"; Roscoe Drummond, "Senator Joe Ball of Minnesota," in *American Mercury*, 60:533 (May, 1945). On Ball's views, see Hinderaker, "Stassen," 610; Stassen to Garlid, February 3, 1965, quoted in Garlid, "Politics in Minnesota," 395n.

[8] *New Ulm Journal*, May 22, 1941, p. 2; Finney, "Joseph H. Ball: A Liberal Dose of Candor," in J. T. Salter, ed., *Public Men In and Out of Office*, 297 (Chapel Hill, N. C., 1946); Hinderaker, "Stassen," 615–619.

[9] *Minneapolis Star-Journal*, October 14, 1940, p. 6.

[10] Garlid, "Politics in Minnesota," 403, 409, 617.

[11] Ball to the author, April 11, 1967, Stuhler Papers; *St. Paul Sunday Pioneer Press*, May 18, 1941, sec. 1, p. 1, 11.

[12] *Sunday Pioneer Press*, May 18, 1941, p. 11; *Minneapolis Tribune*, May 19, 1941, p. 4; Harriet Webb Libby to Ball, May 28, 1941, Committee to Defend America by Aiding the Allies, Minneapolis Unit Papers, in the Minnesota Historical Society, hereafter cited as CDA Papers.

[13] *Pioneer Press*, May 18, p. 11, May 19, p. 3, 1941. Farmer-Labor Congressmen John T. Bernard of the eighth district and Henry G. Teigan of the third had taken internationalist stands in the 1930s. See Stuhler, in *Minnesota History*, 43:88 (Fall, 1972).

[14] Ball, "Notes from Washington," May 29, 1941 (quotation), a mimeographed newsletter to constituents, copies in the Minnesota Historical Society library. On Ball's possible opponents, see *Pioneer Press*, May 21, 1941, p. 1. Lindbergh recorded that in a visit with Congressman Knutson on January 9, 1942, Knutson "told me he thought I should run for the Senate in Minnesota, that I could be elected with no difficulty at all! I told Knutson I did not feel I was suited to political office and that I did not think I would make a good Senator. He was very insistent and kept on talking about it and trying to persuade me to take up residence in Minnesota." Lindbergh, *Wartime Journals*, 576.

[15] *Pioneer Press*, July 5, 1941, p. 1.

[16] Fred W. Welborn, *Diplomatic History of the United States*, 333 (Paterson, N. J., 1961); *Pioneer Press*, February 14, 1941, p. 1; special reprint of the *New York Times*, March 12, 1941, p. 1, with an undated editorial comment.

[17] Ball to A. C. Greenman, December 23, 1940, CDA Papers; *Pioneer Press*, February 14, 1941, p. 4; radio address in *Congressional Record*, 77 Congress, 1 session, *Appendix*, A682.

[18] *Congressional Record*, 77 Congress, 1 session, 815, 2097, 8680; Hinderaker, "Stassen," 647.

[19] Garlid, "Politics in Minnesota," 515, 594.

[20] Ball, "Notes from Washington," December 18, 1941 (quotation); Ball quoted in *Pioneer Press*, August 11, 1942, p. 1, 5; Ball to the author, April 11, 1967, Stuhler Papers; Ball, "How We Planned for the Postwar World," in Jack Goodman, ed., *While You Were Gone*, 558 (quotation) (New York, 1946).

[21] *Public Opinion Quarterly*, 6:661 (Winter, 1942). The poll also showed that the east central part of the country exceeded the west central in isolationist sentiment in 1937, and that the South was the most internationalist region in 1942.

[22] Interview with Malkerson, January 31, 1969, Stuhler Papers; *Minneapolis Star Journal*, September 9, 1942, p. 4, 18; Minnesota, *Legislative Manual*, 1943, p. 264.

[23] *Legislative Manual*, 1943, p. 272; *Minneapolis Star Journal*, September 9, p. 4, October 29, p. 17 (quotation), November 5, p. 12, 1942; Clapper, in *St. Paul Dispatch*, March 22, 1943, p. 4.

[24] In January, 1942, a declaration of the United Nations — the name was suggested by President Roosevelt — was signed by twenty-six allied countries at war with the Axis powers. The new name caught on, and the Allies were henceforth usually known as the United Nations. Russell, *United Nations Charter*, 51, 53. On the resolution and its sponsors, see Divine, *Second Chance*, 92, 93. Truman later commented that after he became president "Some congressmen were in doubt as to whether I would continue Roosevelt's foreign policy. A few senators wanted to know whether I intended to give strong support to the proposed international organization, and at the same time some of the old isolationists even imagined that I would go further than the late President had. This latter point of view, I suppose, was based on the fact that I had taken the lead, along with Senators Ball, Burton, Hatch, and Hill, in trying to get a resolution passed to encourage the administration in its efforts to set up a new international organization." Harry S Truman, *Memoirs: Year of Decisions*, 1:21 (New York, 1955).

[25] Divine, *Second Chance*, 92, 93; *Congressional Record*, 78 Congress, 1 session, 2030.

[26] *Congressional Record*, 78 Congress, 1 session, 2030, 2131.

[27] *New Republic*, 108:727–729 (May 31, 1943).

[28] Quoted in Arthur H. Vandenberg, Jr., ed., *The Private Papers of Senator Vandenberg*, 40 (Boston, 1952). See also Divine, *Second Chance*, 92.

[29] Russell, *United Nations Charter*, 125; Divine, *Second Chance*, 95 (quotation); Vandenberg, ed., *Private Papers*, 45.

[30] Vandenberg, ed., *Private Papers*, 44; interview with Malkerson, January 31, 1969, Stuhler Papers; Divine, *Second Chance*, 98, 99, 101.

[31] *Public Opinion Quarterly*, 7:334; Vandenberg, ed., *Private Papers*, 47.

[32] *Congressional Record*, 78 Congress, 1 session, 2939, 5934.

[33] Divine, *Second Chance*, 127–129.

[34] Vandenberg, ed., *Private Papers*, 55, 58.

[35] Ball, *Collective Security: The Why and How*, 11 (quotation), 13–19, 39–48 (World Peace Foundation, *America Looks Ahead*, no. 9 — Boston, 1943).

[36] *Congressional Record*, 78 Congress, 1 session, 7659 (quotation), 7728, 7729, 8028 (quotation).

[37] Quoted in Divine, *Second Chance*, 144.

[38] Quotations are from *Congressional Record*, 78 Congress, 1 session, 8294, 8609, 8650. On Vandenberg's attitude, see Divine, *Second Chance*, 145, and Vandenberg, ed., *Private Papers*, 62–65.

[39] *Congressional Record*, 78 Congress, 1 session, 8662, 8921. On the Moscow Declaration, see Russell, *United Nations Charter*, 127, 977 (quotation). For a fuller discus-

sion of the debate and the "willful fourteen," see Divine, *Second Chance*, 147–154; I. F. Stone, "Post-War Gold Brick," in *Nation*, 157:518 (November 6, 1943).

[40] *Congressional Record*, 78 Congress, 1 session, 9221.

[41] Ball, "It's Your Move, Mr. President," in *Saturday Evening Post*, February 19, 1944, p. 19, 86; Lippmann, in *Washington Post*, March 16, 1943.

[42] Ball, "Are We Losing the Peace," in *Collier's*, April 22, 1944, p. 24, 67; *Time*, November 8, 1943, p. 17.

[43] *Pioneer Press*, November 10, 1945, p. 2.

[44] Ball, "Liberalism Abroad and At Home," 7–9, 13, address, April 28, 1946, at Syracuse University, Syracuse, N.Y., copy in the Minnesota Historical Society library.

[45] Ball, address to the Philadelphia Foreign Policy Association, December 13, 1947, partially reprinted in *Congressional Digest*, 27:83 (March, 1948); Ball quoted in *Pioneer Press*, February 23, p. 1, 2, February 26, p. 17, 1948. On the Marshall Plan, see chapter 3, note 60, above.

[46] "Report from Washington by Senator Joseph H. Ball," March 13, 1948, a mimeographed news release, filed with Ball to James Ford Bell, March 31, 1948, Bell Papers, in the Minnesota Historical Society; interview with Malkerson, January 31, 1969, Stuhler Papers. The North Atlantic Treaty, which provided the military and political muscle to counter Russian aggression in Europe, was ratified by the Senate the year after Ball left office; it is likely that he would have supported the treaty as the missing link in the U.S. policy of containment. *Congressional Record*, 81 Congress, 1 session, 9916.

[47] On Shipstead's plan, see p. 84, above. See also *Congressional Record*, 80 Congress, 2 session, 2017; John Spanier, *American Foreign Policy Since World War II*, 44, 46 (Revised edition, New York, 1965); Henry Cabot Lodge, "Preface," in Pierre Uri, *Partnership for Progress*, xviii (New York, 1963); Arthur N. Holcombe, "An American View of European Union," in *American Political Science Review*, 47:417–430 (June, 1953).

[48] Interview with Malkerson, January 31, 1969, Stuhler Papers; Ball, "Liberalism Abroad and At Home," 4.

[49] *Pioneer Press*, October 13, 1944, p. 8; Divine, *Second Chance*, 236–238; *New York Times*, September 30, 1944, sec. 1, p. 2 (quotation).

[50] Divine, *Second Chance*, 237; *Pioneer Press*, October 13, p. 1, December 24, p. 4, 1944.

[51] *New York Times*, October 19, p. 12, October 22, p. 34, 1944.

[52] *St. Paul Dispatch*, October 23, p. 1, October 24, p. 4, October 29, p. 7, 1944.

[53] *Pioneer Press*, October 24, 1944, p. 3; *Minneapolis Tribune*, October 27, 1944, p. 1. The Dumbarton Oaks conference drafted the plan that became the Charter of the United Nations; Bailey, *A Diplomatic History*, 768.

[54] Finney, *Public Men In or Out of Office*, 307–309; Divine, *Second Chance*, 238; interview with Malkerson, January 31, 1969, Stuhler Papers.

[55] Notes of interview of the author with Marjorie J. Howard, former Minnesota Republican state chairwoman, May 1, 1967 (quotation), Stuhler Papers; *Pioneer Press*, December 12, 1946, p. 1, 2.

[56] Stassen to James Ford Bell, August 22, 1948, Bell Papers; interview with Malkerson, January 31, 1969, Stuhler Papers.

[57] *Minneapolis Tribune*, March 21, p. 23, April 25, p. 23, July 4, p. 11, 1948; *Legislative Manual*, 1949, p. 355.

[58] Interview with Malkerson, January 31, 1969, Stuhler Papers; for the poll results, see *Minneapolis Tribune*, April 11, 1948, p. 23.

[59] Albert Eisele in *Pioneer Press*, October 8, 1967, p. 1, 24.

Chapter 7 — HAROLD E. STASSEN — pages 145 to 168

[1] The opening quotation is from a transcript of a taped interview of Stassen by Russell W. Fridley and V. Arvid Johnson, May 9, 1963, p. 11, in the Minnesota Historical

Society. See also G. Theodore Mitau, *Politics in Minnesota*, 21 (Minneapolis, 1960); [Russell W. Fridley], *Governors of Minnesota, 1849–1971*, [2] (St. Paul, 1971).

[2] John Gunther, *Inside U.S.A.*, 293, 304 (New York, 1947).

[3] The senator was Charles A. Towne, 1900–01; the congressmen were John Lind, 1903–05; Winfield S. Hammond, 1907–15; Carl C. Van Dyke, 1915–19; Einar Hoidale, 1933–35; and Elmer J. Ryan, 1935–41. Minnesota, *Legislative Manual*, 1945, p. 61, 62. On Hagen, see Mitau, *Politics in Minnesota*, 115. See also Smuckler, in *American Political Science Review*, 47:398. For Ball's endorsement of FDR, see p. 141, above.

[4] Hinderaker, "Stassen," 40, 42; Rose Wilder Lane, "Minnesota Farm Boy," in *Woman's Day*, July, 1940, p. 18.

[5] Hinderaker, "Stassen," 42–46; typescripts of taped interviews of Stassen by Fridley and Johnson, May 9, 1963, p. 1, and of Edward J. Thye by Fridley, G. James Bormann, and Lucile M. Kane, June 27, 1963, p. 5, both in Minnesota Historical Society.

[6] Naftalin, "History of the Farmer-Labor Party," 329; *Legislative Manual*, 1939, p. 85.

[7] Hinderaker, "Stassen," 495; Mitau, *Politics in Minnesota*, 19 (quotation); *Legislative Manual*, 1941, p. 226; 1943, p. 272.

[8] Hinderaker, "Stassen," 559, 562; Willkie quoted in *Time*, May 20, 1940, p. 18.

[9] *Official Report of the Proceedings of the Twenty-second Republican National Convention*, 45, 51, 57 (Washington, D.C., [1940]).

[10] Hinderaker, "Stassen," 573; Bernard Weinraub, " 'The 1968 Nomination? I Do Not Rule It Out' — Harold Stassen," in *Esquire*, August, 1967, p. 99.

[11] Amos J. Peaslee, ed., *Man Was Meant To Be Free: Selected Statements of Governor Harold E. Stassen, 1940–1951*, 45, 47, 61 (Garden City, N.Y., 1951).

[12] Stassen, *A Proposal of a Definite United Nations Government*, [3-5] [Minneapolis, 1943?].

[13] On Lewis and Stassen, see Hinderaker, "Stassen," 533; for the quotation, see William F. McDermott, "Young Man with a Future," in *Coronet*, October, 1943, p. 82.

[14] Hinderaker, "Stassen," 668–670, 717; for Stassen's early announcement, see *Pioneer Press*, March 28, 1942, p. 1; interview with Thye, 9.

[15] Stassen, "We Need a World Government," in *Saturday Evening Post*, May 22, 1943, p. 17–26.

[16] *Time*, December 6, 1943, p. 17; Ellsworth Barnard, *Wendell Willkie: Fighter for Freedom*, 453 (Marquette, Mich., 1966); George H. Mayer, *The Republican Party, 1854–1964*, 463 (New York, 1964); *Life*, June 26, 1944, p. 21; Howard Y. Williams, "Harold Stassen: Fake Liberal," in *New Republic*, 110:756 (quotation) (June 5, 1944).

[17] Russell, *United Nations Charter*, 543; "Stassen's Creed," in *Time*, March 12, 1945, p. 19; Stassen, "The Cost of Lasting Peace," in *Collier's*, April 21, 1945, p. 11. Burns, *Roosevelt: The Soldier of Freedom*, 607, reveals that in 1944 Stassen lost out in a poll conducted by the president to determine the successor to Secretary of the Navy Frank Knox.

[18] Ill health precluded Hull's presence at San Francisco. Bailey, *A Diplomatic History*, 768; Gildersleeve, *Many a Good Crusade*, 321 (New York, 1954).

[19] Russell, *United Nations Charter*, 808–810; Gildersleeve, *Many a Good Crusade*, 337; Vandenberg, ed., *Private Papers*, 215.

[20] *Congressional Record*, 79 Congress, 1 session, *Appendix*, A3286.

[21] Peaslee, ed., *Selected Statements*, 60.

[22] "Midwest Trends in Voting," in *United States News*, July 19, 1946, p. 21; interview with Thye, 9–11; interview with Malkerson, January 31, 1969, Stuhler Papers. On the 1946 campaign, see chapter 4, above.

[23] Interview with Marjorie Howard, May 1, 1967, Stuhler Papers.

[24] Churchill is quoted in *Pioneer Press*, May 22, 1947, p. 8. For Stassen's proposal, see Peaslee, ed., *Selected Statements*, 116–118; for Shipstead's, see p. 84, above.

[25] *Pioneer Press*, May 22, 1947, p. 8. Other papers are quoted in Joseph Marion Jones, *The Fifteen Weeks*, 233, 234 (New York, 1964).

[26] Jones, *Fifteen Weeks*, 234, 281.

[27] Stassen, "Marshall Plan: Europe's Only Alternative to Communism," in *Vital Speeches*, 14:20–23 (October 15, 1947).

[28] Russell, *United Nations Charter*, 1036 (quotation), 1043; Peaslee, ed., *Selected Statements*, 147, 159–162 (quotation), 163. The Brussels Pact bound the signers to a fifty-year mutual defense agreement; the Atlantic Pact Treaty, signed April 4, 1949, gave rise to the North Atlantic Treaty Organization (NATO), a collective defensive arrangement to preserve peace in Europe. Bailey, *A Diplomatic History*, 807–810.

[29] Richard Wilson, "Can Stassen Win?" in *Look*, June 22, 1948, p. 56; John H. Runyon, Jennefer Verdini, Sally S. Runyon, comps. and eds., *Source Book of American Presidential Campaigns and Election Statistics, 1948–1968*, 8 (New York, 1971); interview with Thye, 9; *Minneapolis Sunday Tribune*, April 25, 1943, sec. 2, p. 1.

[30] Wilson, in *Look*, June 22, 1948, p. 56.

[31] Malcolm Moos, *The Republicans: A History of Their Party*, 437 (New York, 1956).

[32] Moos, *The Republicans*, 437, 439; "Dewey versus Stassen in Oregon," in *Public Opinion Quarterly*, 12:490 (Fall, 1948); Reston quoted in William L. Rivers, *The Opinion Makers*, 82 (Boston, 1967).

[33] *Public Opinion Quarterly*, 12:560 (Fall, 1948); *Minneapolis Tribune*, July 12, 1964, p. 1C. "Windom-10" became a legend, but in the end Windom lost to James A. Garfield, who later chose him to be secretary of the treasury; Robert P. Herrick, *Windom: The Man and the School*, 8 (Minneapolis, [1903]). On Stassen's move to Pennsylvania, below, see Weinraub, in *Esquire*, August, 1967, p. 100.

[34] Bailey, *A Diplomatic History*, 819 (quotation); Stassen's speech is reprinted in *Congressional Record*, 81 Congress, 2 session, *Appendix*, A5882.

[35] *Minneapolis Tribune*, January 24, 1948, p. 1, 2 (quotation), 8; Richard H. Rovere, *Affairs of State: The Eisenhower Years*, 4 (New York, 1956).

[36] Dwight D. Eisenhower, *Mandate for Change, 1953–1956*, 22 (London, 1963). The state chairman, J. Bradshaw Mintener, was later appointed by Eisenhower as assistant secretary of the department of health, education, and welfare.

[37] Mitau, *Politics in Minnesota*, 21. Breaking with tradition, a woman, Marjorie Howard, Minnesota state chairwoman and his long-time friend, was chosen to make the principal nominating address for Stassen at the national convention. Moos, *The Republicans*, 481.

[38] Sherman Adams, *Firsthand Report: The Story of the Eisenhower Administration*, 64 (New York, 1961); interview of the author with Elizabeth E. Heffelfinger, Republican national committeewoman, April 8, 1968, Stuhler Papers; *Minneapolis Tribune*, July 12, 1964, p. 1C (quotations).

[39] *Minneapolis Tribune*, November 26, 1967, p. 17A (quotation); interviews of the author with Marjorie Howard, May 1, 1967, and Elizabeth Heffelfinger, April 8, 1968, Stuhler Papers.

[40] Stassen claimed to have been "one of four men who suggested and brought the 'I will go to Korea' speech to General Eisenhower"; *Minneapolis Tribune*, November 26, 1967, p. 17A. See also Mayer, *The Republican Party*, 482 (quotation); *Legislative Manual*, 1953, p. 360.

[41] *Newsweek*, December 8, 1952, p. 25 (quotation); *U.S. News and World Report*, October 16, 1953, p. 58.

[42] *U.S. News and World Report*, October 16, 1953, p. 58, 60; *New Republic*, September 14, 1953, p. 4; *Wall Street Journal*, January 29, 1969.

[43] *Department of State Bulletin*, 29:213 (August 17, 1953), 29:384 (September 21, 1953), 30:333 (March 1, 1954), 30:674 (May 3, 1954). Judd's amendment provided for the sale of surplus food to developing countries in return for their local currencies; Judd to the author, June 6, 1967, Stuhler Papers.

[44] On the Stassen-McCarthy contretemps in this and the following paragraph, see Robert J. Donovan, *Eisenhower: The Inside Story*, 244, 245 (New York, 1956); *Minneapolis Tribune*, May 20, 1954, p. 8; *Time*, May 31, 1954, p. 12 (quotations).

[45] Donovan, *Eisenhower*, 388.

[46] *Department of State Bulletin*, 32:557 (April 4, 1955); Donovan, *Eisenhower*, 348; Rovere, *Affairs of State*, 265, 266 (quotation).

[47] For a general discussion of the disarmament problem, see William R. Frye, "The Quest for Disarmament Since World War II," in Louis Henkin, ed., *Arms Control: Issues for the Public*, 18–48 (Englewood Cliffs, N.J., 1961); *Arms Control and Disarmament Agreements, 1959–1972* (U.S. Arms Control and Disarmament Agency, *Publication*, no. 72 — Washington, D.C., 1972).

[48] Allan S. Names, "Disarmament: The Last Seven Years," in *Current History*, 42:267 (May, 1962).

[49] Adams, *Firsthand Report*, 177, 178 (quotation). The French delegate is quoted by Names, in *Current History*, 42:269.

[50] Frye, in *Arms Control*, 33–35, 38.

[51] Frye, in *Arms Control*, 35, 37–39.

[52] Frye, in *Arms Control*, 39; Adams, *Firsthand Report*, 328; John Robinson Beal, *John Foster Dulles: 1888–1959*, 324 (New York, 1959).

[53] *Newsweek*, January 13, 1958, p. 19; *Minneapolis Tribune*, January 9, 1958, p. 2 (quotation); *Christian Century*, 75:301 (March 5, 1958).

[54] Matteson's assessment appears in Chalmers M. Roberts, "The Case for Harold Stassen," in *New Republic*, March 10, 1958, p. 15. A more recent study of Dulles sheds light on his view of the Soviet system as atheistic; see Ole R. Holsti, "Cognitive Dynamics in Images of the Enemy," in *Journal of International Affairs*, 21:16–39 (January, 1967). For Stassen's appraisal, see Weinraub, in *Esquire*, August, 1967, p. 101.

[55] Roberts, in *New Republic*, March 10, 1958, p. 14, 16; Adams, *Firsthand Report*, 64. An illuminating episode in which Stassen alienated some party regulars appears in Adams, 238–241. It recounts Stassen's efforts to have Nixon replaced by Christian A. Herter as the vice-presidential nominee in 1956. See also Eisenhower, *Mandate for Change*, 67.

[56] On Stassen's career since 1958, see Weinraub, in *Esquire*, August, 1967, p. 100.

[57] *Minneapolis Tribune*, March 10, 1958, p. 7 (quotation); January 13, 1965, p. 35; *Minneapolis Star*, February 17, 1964, p. 10A.

[58] *Minneapolis Tribune*, August 23, 1963, p. 1; address by Stassen to the 1963 governors' conference, 4–6, May 4, 1963, copy in Stassen Papers, Minnesota Historical Society.

[59] "Questions and Answers Given in Correspondence in 1967 Between Republican Senators-Congressmen-Governors and Harold E. Stassen," and "Address of Harold Stassen to the Federal Bar Association," June 9, 1967, mimeographed copies, Stuhler Papers.

[60] Weinraub, in *Esquire*, August, 1967, p. 97; *Minneapolis Tribune*, June 13, p. 7, August 8, p. 3, 1968; *Wall Street Journal*, April 1, 1968.

[61] Address by Stassen to the United Nations Association of the United States, May 26, 1967, p. 2, mimeographed copy, Stuhler Papers; Stassen quoted in David Frost, *The Presidential Debate, 1968*, 69 (New York, 1968).

Chapter 8 — WALTER H. JUDD — pages 169 to 193

[1] The opening quotation is from a speech by Judd in *Congressional Record*, 83 Congress, 1 session, 6861. See also *Congressional Quarterly Fact Sheet*, July 15, 1960, p. 1; Dr. A. E. Benjamin to Judd, December 15, 1941, in Walter H. Judd Papers, Minnesota Historical Society.

[2] Interview of the author with Judd, June 28, 1967, Stuhler Papers.

[3] *Congressional Quarterly Fact Sheet*, July 15, 1960, p. 1; interview with Judd, June 28, 1967, Stuhler Papers.

[4] *Congressional Quarterly Fact Sheet*, July 15, 1960, p. 1.

[5] Tuchman, *Stilwell and the American Experience in China*, 189; *Congressional Quarterly Fact Sheet*, July 15, 1960, p. 1; undated biographical fact sheet sent by Judd to the author, Stuhler Papers.

[6] Judd, "Let's Stop Arming Japan!" in *Reader's Digest*, February, 1940, p. 41–44; Judd, "America's Stake in the Far East," 10, a speech given before the Chicago Rotary Club, October 3, 1939, copy in Stuhler Papers; Tuchman, *Stilwell and the American Experience in China*, 206 (quotation).

[7] Judd testimony, 76 Congress, 1 session, *Hearings before the Committee on Foreign Relations, United States Senate*, April 25, 1939, 305, 312 (Washington, D.C., 1939); Judd, "America's Stake in the Far East," 17, Stuhler Papers.

[8] Judd testimony, 76 Congress, 1 session, *Hearings before the Committee on Foreign Relations*, 316.

[9] Judd testimony, 76 Congress, 1 session, *Hearings before the Committee on Foreign Relations*, 298–300, 313; Judd, "America's Stake in the Far East," 18 (quotation), Stuhler Papers.

[10] Judd to the author, July 3, 1967; notes of the author's interview with Katherine D. Winton, August 2, 1967, both in Stuhler Papers.

[11] Richard P. Gale to W. J. Luyten, November 12, 1941, in CDA Papers.

[12] Interviews of the author with Marjorie Howard, May 1, 1967, Judd, June 28, 1967, and Lester Malkerson, January 31, 1969, Stuhler Papers. See also letter from Addison Lewis to Russell Bennett, June 3, 1942, CDA Papers: "I told him [Judd] . . . that . . . he would be waited upon by persons with sufficient authority and means to assist him." On his candidacy, see *Minneapolis Star-Journal*, June 26, 1942, p. 1.

[13] Interview with Judd, June 28, 1967; first platform draft, July, 1942, both in Stuhler Papers.

[14] A copy of Judd's reply to the question "What should our postwar policy be?" and Judd to the author, June 6, 1967, both in Stuhler Papers.

[15] Judd to the author, August 14, 1967 (quotation), Stuhler Papers; Minnesota, *Legislative Manual*, 1943, p. 256, 451; Judd to Harry A. Bullis, September 25, 1942, Harry A. Bullis Papers, Minnesota Historical Society.

[16] Judd, "Behind the Conflict in the Pacific," in American Association of School Administrators and the National Education Association Conventions, *Proceedings*, 1942, p. 198.

[17] *Congressional Record*, 78 Congress, 1 session, 1342–1347; Bailey, *A Diplomatic History*, 602.

[18] *Congressional Record*, 78 Congress, 1 session, 1345 (quotation); 82 Congress, 2 session, 4439; 83 Congress, 1 session, 10193, 10194.

[19] *Congressional Record*, 78 Congress, 1 session, 4223, 4225.

[20] On B2H2 and Fulbright, see chapter 6, above. See also *Congressional Record*, 78 Congress, 1 session, 7728.

[21] Judd, "After Victory — What?" 31, 36, a speech before the St. Louis Chamber of Commerce, August 11, 1943, Judd Papers; *Congressional Record*, 78 Congress, 2 session, *Appendix*, A1865 (quotation).

[22] On the Connally Resolution, see p. 135, above. *Congressional Record*, 79 Congress, 1 session, 5723; 80 Congress, 2 session, 6730, 6734; undated biographical fact sheet on Judd, Stuhler Papers. On his four points, see interview with Judd, June 28, 1967, Stuhler Papers.

[23] *Congressional Record*, 80 Congress, 1 session, 2554, 8567; *Congressional Quarterly*, IV (1948), p. 214; "Statement of the Honorable Walter H. Judd before the Committee on Foreign Affairs of the House of Representatives," May 4, 1948, p. 4 (quotation), mimeographed copy in Stuhler Papers.

[24] *Congressional Record*, 81 Congress, 2 session, 13529, 13567.

[25] *Congressional Record*, 80 Congress, 1 session, 4947. See also *Congressional Record*, 81 Congress, 1 session, 14163; 85 Congress, 1 session, 14158, and 2 session, 12840; 87 Congress, 2 session, 19486.

[26] *Congressional Record*, 80 Congress, 1 session, 4706 (quotation), 4818 (quotation), 4947.

[27] Judd testimony, 80 Congress, 1 session, *Hearings before the Committee on Foreign Affairs, House of Representatives, May 7, 8, 9, 1947,* 16; *Congressional Record,* 83 Congress, 1 session, 6861. The majority of Minnesota congressmen joined Judd in supporting aid to Greece and Turkey. O'Hara did not vote, and Knutson and John A. Blatnik, Jr., opposed the measure. See *Congressional Record*, 80 Congress, 1 session, 4706, 4710, 4975. On Knutson, see above, p. 73. Acheson, writing in the *Washington Sunday Star* of January 16, 1966, referred to Vietnam as "an Asian Greece." Judd commended the article, and Acheson acknowledged "What you said in 1947 is painfully pertinent twenty years later." Judd to the author, July 3, 1967, Stuhler Papers.

[28] *Congressional Record*, 80 Congress, 2 session, *Appendix*, A1337. On Stassen, see p. 159–161, above.

[29] *Congressional Record*, 83 Congress, 1 session, 6861 (quotation); 85 Congress, 1 session, 16750 (quotation). On Judd's other foreign aid positions, see, for example, *Congressional Record*, 83 Congress, 1 session, 9551, 9553, 9558, 2 session, 9113, 9207, 9232, 12284; 84 Congress, 1 session, 9620, 10231; 85 Congress, 2 session, 12840, 12948; 86 Congress, 2 session, 14790; 87 Congress, 1 session, 575, 6668. For opposing opinions on Judd, see statements by Republican Representatives Clare E. Hoffman and William S. Broomfield, both of Michigan, in *Congressional Record*, 87 Congress, 1 session, 6676, 16039.

[30] Judd to the author, June 6, 1967, Stuhler Papers; *Congressional Record*, 83 Congress, 2 session, 9238; John King Fairbank, *The United States and China*, 321, 322 (Cambridge, Mass., 1971).

[31] Judd to the author, June 6, 1967, Stuhler Papers; *Congressional Record*, 80 Congress, 2 session, 3727; 82 Congress, 2 session, 5835. On Ball, see p. 139, above. In 1952 Judd made a further effort to strengthen the unifying forces in Europe by offering an amendment to the Mutual Security bill which would provide for the distribution of not less than 75 per cent of American military assistance through the yet unborn European Defense Community. Judd argued that his amendment "throws the weight of our influence behind the real pioneers in Europe who realize clearly they will have to hang together or they will all hang separately." The amendment lost by a close margin, and the concept it offered was aborted by the French National Assembly's failure to approve the European Defense Community idea in 1954. See *Congressional Record*, 82 Congress, 2 session, 5834, 5858; Bailey, *A Diplomatic History*, 811.

[32] *Congressional Record*, 83 Congress, 1 session, 8694 (quotation); Judd to the author, June 6, 1967, Stuhler Papers.

[33] *Congressional Record*, 80 Congress, 1 session, 4947.

[34] *Congressional Quarterly Fact Sheet*, July 15, 1960, p. 1, 2.

[35] *Congressional Record*, 79 Congress, 1 session, 2294, 2302; 80 Congress, 1 session, 11108 (quotation); 2 session, *Appendix*, A4560 (quotation); 81 Congress, 2 session, 10554; Fairbank, *The United States and China*, 322.

[36] *Congressional Record*, 84 Congress, 2 session, 15575, 15576.

[37] Material here and in the paragraphs below is taken from Burns, *Roosevelt: The Soldier of Freedom*, 573–577, 588–592; Bailey, *A Diplomatic History*, 764–766, 785, 820, 826; A. Doak Barnett, *Our China Policy: The Need for Change*, 3–14 (Foreign Policy Association, *Headline Series*, no. 204 — New York, 1971). On extraterritoriality, see p. 113, above.

[38] *Congressional Record*, 81 Congress, 2 session, 10551; Truman, *Memoirs: Year of Decisions*, 411.

[39] *Congressional Record*, 79 Congress, 1 session, 2294; 83 Congress, 1 session, *Appendix*, A3982, A3983; 84 Congress, 1 session, 6861, 9579.

[40] Roger Hilsman, *To Move A Nation: The Politics of Foreign Policy in the Administration of John F. Kennedy*, 295, 296 (Garden City, N. Y., 1967).

[41] Hilsman, *To Move A Nation*, 299; Judd to Bullis, February 12, 1953, Bullis Papers.

[42] *Congressional Record*, 86 Congress, 1 session, 20012 (quotations), 20013–20015, 20017, 20019.

[43] *Congressional Quarterly Fact Sheet*, July 15, 1960, p. 2; *Congressional Record*, 84 Congress, 2 session, 13377 (quotation).

[44] A good example of the breakdown in 1959 appears in an exchange between Democratic Congressman Charles O. Porter and Judd; *Congressional Record*, 86 Congress, 1 session, 9921. For quotations, see *Congressional Record*, 81 Congress, 2 session, 10550; 87 Congress, 1 session, 6986, 16024, 17771.

[45] *Congressional Record*, 83 Congress, 2 session, 7360–7363; *Minneapolis Tribune*, April 22, 1954, p. 3.

[46] Judd testimony, 89 Congress, 2 session, *Hearings before the Committee on Foreign Relations, U.S. Senate, March 28, 1966*, 437–439, 451. On China in the United Nations, see *Minneapolis Star*, October 26, 1971, p. 1.

[47] Judd, "Where in the World Are We Going?" in New York State Horticultural Society, *News Letter*, 8, 9, 13, 14 (supplement, May, [1967]); interview with Judd, June 28, 1967, Stuhler Papers. The "Kennedy quarantine" refers to the 1962 blockade against Soviet ships carrying offensive weapons to Cuba. Bailey, *A Diplomatic History*, 883.

[48] *Congressional Record*, 87 Congress, 1 session, 11931; *Minneapolis Tribune*, September 8, 1963, Upper Midwest sec., p. 7.

[49] The questionnaires, entitled "What Do Minneapolis People Think on Major Issues?" are in *Congressional Record*, 84 Congress, 2 session, 9858–9860; 85 Congress, 2 session, 15870–15874; 87 Congress, 2 session, 12612–12614. On other polls, see "Minnesota Polls" in the *Minneapolis Tribune*, August, 1960, to September, 1961; William C. Rogers, Barbara Stuhler, and Donald Koenig, *A Comparative Study of Informed Opinion and General Public Opinion in Minnesota on Selected Issues of U.S. Foreign Policy* (University of Minnesota, General Extension Division, *Research Report No. 3* — Minneapolis, 1966).

[50] *Congressional Record*, 87 Congress, 2 session, 12614; *Minneapolis Tribune*, September 15, 1962, p. 5; *Minneapolis Star*, October 13, 1962, p. 10A (Rusk quotation).

[51] *Minneapolis Tribune*, July 26, 1960, p. 1, 3; *Minneapolis Star*, July 26, 1960, p. 2 (quotation). At the 1964 convention, Judd received 18 votes from Minnesota, 3 from North Dakota, and 1 from Alaska — a total of 22. In the final balloting, Minnesota cast its 26 votes for Senator Goldwater. See *Tribune*, July 16, 1964. p. 1, 12.

[52] On the 1948 vote, see *Legislative Manual, 1949*, n. 353; on Fraser, see *Biographical Directory of the American Congress*, 968.

[53] Interview with Malkerson, January 31, 1969; *Legislative Manual, 1963, p. 532*. On factors contributing to Judd's defeat, see *Time*, June 20, 1967, p. 11, and *Minneapolis Star*, November 7, 1962, p. 20A. On the Cuban crisis, see Bailey, *A Diplomatic History*, 882–884.

[54] Michael Amrine, *This is Humphrey: The Story of the Senator*, 150 (Garden City, N.Y., 1960); Eisenhower, *Mandate for Change*, 46; Beal, *John Foster Dulles*, 9.

[55] "Job for Judd?" in *New Republic*, January 12, 1963, p. 5; *Minneapolis Tribune*, January 12, 1963, p. 1 (quotation); *New York Times*, November 11, 1966, sec. 19, p. 4. See also Dodge, *Internationalism-Isolationism in Minnesota*, for foreign policy voting records of Judd and Humphrey.

[56] Interview with Judd, June 28, 1967, Stuhler Papers; Judd, in New York State Horticultural Society, *News Letter*, 4.

[57] Judd to the author, February 19, 1969, Stuhler Papers; Judd, in New York State Horticultural Society, *News Letter*, 3.

Chapter 9 — HUBERT H. HUMPHREY AND EUGENE J. McCARTHY — pages 194 to 220

[1] The opening quotations are from a typescript of a taped television speech, September 18, 1963, p. 7, in the Hubert H. Humphrey Papers, Minnesota Historical Society; Eugene J. McCarthy, *The Year of the People*, 23 (Garden City, N.Y., 1969). Many of McCarthy's papers may be found in the manuscripts department of the Minnesota Historical Society. For assessments of McCarthy's candidacy and President Johnson's decision, see William P. McDonald and Jerry G. Smoke, *The Peasants' Revolt: McCarthy 1968*, 1 (Mount Vernon, Ohio, 1969); Ben Stavis, *We Were the Campaign: New Hampshire to Chicago for McCarthy*, 199 (Boston, 1969). In *The Year of the People*, 248, McCarthy credits the rumor of Robert F. Kennedy's entrance into the primary contests as an influencing factor; Jeremy Larner, *Nobody Knows: Reflections on the McCarthy Campaign of 1968*, 62 (New York, 1970), asserts that Johnson was beaten by "McCarthy and his people, the shadow of Bobby, and the Tet offensive."

[2] Biographical data on both men appears in numerous biographies cited in this chapter. See also United States Congress, *Biographical Directory*, 1160, 1358. Albert Eisele, *Almost to the Presidency: A Biography of Two American Politicians* (Blue Earth, Minn., 1972) is the most recent and comprehensive study of the two men.

[3] Ludwig, "A Tale of Twin Cities," in *Holiday*, June, 1962, p. 54, 56.

[4] Humphrey's quandary is eloquently expressed in two books written about him. Allan H. Ryskind, *Hubert, An Unauthorized Biography of the Vice President* (New Rochelle, N.Y., 1968) is critical of Humphrey's dovelike tendencies; Robert Sherrill and Harry W. Ernst, *The Drugstore Liberal* (New York, 1968), as the title might imply, consider Humphrey a pseudoliberal. See also James Hitchcock, "The Other McCarthy and the Future," in *Continuum*, 6:362 (Autumn, 1968).

[5] Hubert H. Humphrey, *The Cause Is Mankind: A Liberal Program for Modern America*, 4 (New York, 1964); Humphrey, "My Father," in *Atlantic*, November, 1966, p. 81–89; Ryskind, *Hubert*, 25 (quotation); Amrine, *This Is Humphrey*, 76; Winthrop Griffith, *Humphrey: A Candid Biography*, 45 (quotation), 52–54 (New York, 1965). The latter is probably the best of the recent books on Humphrey. One knowledgeable reviewer termed it "no eulogy; it seeks not to expose but to balance, not to judge . . . but to appraise." G. Theodore Mitau, "Man from Minnesota," in *Minnesota History*, 39:258 (Summer, 1965).

[6] Quoted in Perry D. Hall, ed. and comp., *The Quotable Hubert H. Humphrey*, 92 (Anderson, S.C., 1967).

[7] On Judd's comment, see Ryskind, *Hubert*, 38. On the DFL merger, Millard Gieske is quoted in Sherrill and Ernst, *The Drugstore Liberal*, 36; other assessments of Humphrey's role appear in Eisele, *Almost to the Presidency*, 55. His achievements as mayor are recorded in *Congressional Quarterly Report*, 26:2349 (September 6, 1968).

[8] Griffith, *Humphrey*, 146–149 (quotation); G. Theodore Mitau, "The Democratic-Farmer-Labor Party Schism of 1948," in *Minnesota History*, 34:187–194 (Spring, 1955).

[9] *East Minneapolis Argus*, January 12, 1945, p. 8, quoted in Ryskind, *Hubert*, 51; *Minnesota Labor* (Minneapolis), December 7, 1945, p. 1. In 1954 Humphrey authored a bill which was passed unanimously by the Senate outlawing the Communist party. He came to regret the action, however, saying that it was "not one of the things I'm proudest of." See *Congressional Record*, 83 Congress, 2 session, 14209; Ryskind, 221.

[10] Griffith, *Humphrey*, 162–165; Amrine, *This Is Humphrey*, 129 (quotations); *Minneapolis Morning Tribune*, October 12, p. 1, October 19, p. 7, 1948; *Minneapolis Star-Journal*, October 19, 1948, p. 13. On Ball, see chapter 6, above.

[11] Ryskind, *Hubert*, 14–16; "Newsletter from the Desk of Senator Hubert H. Humphrey," January 19, 1953 (quotation), a series of newsletters issued irregularly and cited henceforth as "Humphrey Newsletter." Copies are in the Minnesota Historical Society library.

[12] Amrine, *This Is Humphrey*, 150.

[13] "Humphrey Newsletter," August 24, November 16, 1953 (quotation), July 5, 1954, January, 1957; 90 Congress, 2 session, *Background Information on the Committee of Foreign Relations*, 23; Griffith, *Humphrey*, 230. On Point Four, see Spanier, *American Foreign Policy since World War II*, 187.

[14] "Humphrey Newsletter," February, 1957, April 11, 1957 (quotation), May 15, 1958; *Congressional Record*, 85 Congress, 1 session, 3129. On the Eisenhower Doctrine, see Bailey, *A Diplomatic History*, 844.

[15] "Humphrey Newsletter," January 20, March 7, 1958, September 15, 1960.

[16] Amrine, *This Is Humphrey*, 193; "Humphrey Newsletter," June 26, 1959; Humphrey, *The Cause Is Mankind*, 142.

[17] Nelson W. Polsby, *The Citizen's Choice: Humphrey or Nixon*, 13 (quotation) (Washington, D.C., 1968); Griffith, *Humphrey*, 259, 260; Humphrey, *The Cause Is Mankind*, 123 (quotation); *Congressional Record*, 82 Congress, 1 session, 10303; "Humphrey Newsletter," August 12, 1955. Interestingly, Stassen seemed more annoyed than pleased with the establishment of a legislative counterpart. It became apparent that he lacked congressional rapport, a condition Humphrey's willingness to help could have remedied. Jerome H. Spingarn, "The Humphrey Subcommittee: Was it Worthwhile?" in *Bulletin of Atomic Scientists*, 13:224 (June, 1957).

[18] Griffith, *Humphrey*, 261; Frye, in *Arms Control*, 43.

[19] Jerome H. Spingarn, "Disarmament: The Washington Scene," in *Bulletin of Atomic Scientists*, 14:385 (November, 1958).

[20] "Humphrey Newsletter," June 26, October 14, 1959. An effort to give some substance to long-range planning prompted a study in 1960 by the Senate foreign relations subcommittee on disarmament. See *Congressional Record*, 87 Congress, 2 session, 22558–22562.

[21] Arthur M. Schlesinger, Jr., *A Thousand Days: John F. Kennedy in the White House*, 455 (Boston, 1965).

[22] *Congressional Record*, 87 Congress, 1 session, 11680, 18721, 18755. The other three sponsors were fellow-Democrat John J. Sparkman of Alabama and Republicans Alexander Wiley of Wisconsin and John Sherman Cooper of Kentucky.

[23] Theodore C. Sorensen, *Kennedy*, 727 (New York, 1965); Alton Frye, "Congress: The Virtues of Its Vices," in *Foreign Policy*, Summer, 1971, p. 113 (quotation); *Congressional Record*, 88 Congress, 1 session, 17832.

[24] Griffith, *Humphrey*, 265, 266.

[25] Griffith, *Humphrey*, 272, 276; *Congressional Record*, 83 Congress, 2 session, 2226 (quotation); Schlesinger, *A Thousand Days*, 108.

[26] *Congressional Record*, 86 Congress, 1 session, 6119, 18081–18107, 18347–18380; Amrine, *This Is Humphrey*, 236; Schlesinger, *A Thousand Days*, 169, 170; Griffith, *Humphrey*, 273 (quotation). Professor Willard W. Cochrane, director of agricultural economics in the department of agriculture from 1961 to 1964, credited Humphrey's fellow Minnesotan, Secretary of Agriculture Orville Freeman, with implementing the decision to use surpluses and described Humphrey as more a "food giver" than an "agricultural developer." Notes of an interview of the author with Cochrane, May 26, 1971, Stuhler Papers.

[27] Griffith, *Humphrey*, 275, 276; *Congressional Record*, 86 Congress, 2 session, 12634, 12635; "Humphrey Newsletter," April, 1961 (quotation). An amendment to the Mutual Security Act of 1961 introduced by Representative Henry S. Reuss of Wisconsin and Senator Richard L. Neuberger of Oregon call for a study of the Peace Corps idea.

[28] Humphrey, "U.S. Policy in Latin America," in *Foreign Affairs*, 42:585 (July, 1964). On the Alliance for Progress, see *Congressional Record*, 88 Congress, 2 session, 5843–5845; Bailey, *A Diplomatic History*, 870.

[29] *Congressional Quarterly Weekly Report*, 26:2349; Eric Sevareid, ed., *Candidates 1960: Behind the Headlines in the Presidential Race*, 153–155 (New York, 1959); Theodore H. White, *The Making of the President, 1960*, 88 (New York, 1961).

[30] Theodore H. White, *The Making of the President, 1964*, 270, 273, 285, 288, 289 (New York, 1965).

[31] For biographical information about McCarthy see note 2, above; his early years in politics are amusingly reported in an article by Marshall Smelser, a former colleague at St. Thomas, entitled "Senator McCarthy: How to succeed by ignoring your well-wishers," in *Harper's*, June, 1964, p. 76–78.

[32] Congressional Quarterly Service, *Candidates 1968*, 130 (Revised edition, Washington, D.C., 1968). On the DFL friction, see note 8, above. On the elections, see Minnesota, *Legislative Manual*, 1949, p. 355.

[33] Smelser, in *Harper's*, 76; "Report from the Office of Eugene J. McCarthy, M.C.," March, 1954, a sporadic, mimeographed information sheet sent to his constituents and henceforth cited as "McCarthy Reports." Copies are in the Minnesota Historical Society library.

[34] Arthur Herzog, *McCarthy for President*, 52 (New York, 1969).

[35] "McCarthy Reports," March, 1955; Eugene J. McCarthy, *Frontiers in American Democracy*, 125–127 (Cleveland and New York, 1960); *Congressional Record*, 85 Congress, 2 session, 12965; *Life*, November 24, 1967, p. 39. On Point Four, see note 13, above.

[36] *Legislative Manual*, 1959, p. 474. An account of the senatorial race appears in Abigail McCarthy, *Private Faces / Public Places*, 217–220 (Garden City, N.Y., 1972).

[37] *Life*, November 24, 1967, p. 38; Herzog, *McCarthy for President*, 51, 59; *Candidates 1968*, 132; National Broadcasting Company, *Meet the Press*, 10 (August 23, 1964), a published transcript of the radio and television program. On the Goldwater amendment, see *Congressional Record*, 87 Congress, 1 session, 18721.

[38] Herzog, *McCarthy for President*, 51; *Candidates 1968*, 131 (quotation).

[39] *Congressional Record*, 85 Congress, 1 session, 1199; 89 Congress, 1 session, 25620–25623 (quotation). The 1947 Treaty of Rio de Janiero was the first regional defense pact and served as a model for the North Atlantic Treaty of 1949; Bailey, *A Diplomatic History*, 807. On McCarthy's defense and foreign aid postures, see Larner, *Nobody Knows*, 73; McCarthy, "The U.S.: Supplier of Weapons to the World," in *Saturday Review*, July 9, 1966, p. 13–15.

[40] McCarthy, *Frontiers in American Democracy*, 31; McCarthy, *A liberal answer to the conservative challenge*, 123, 127 (New York, 1964).

[41] Lewis Chester, Godfrey Hodgson, and Bruce Page, *An American Melodrama: The Presidential Campaign of 1968*, 24 (New York, 1969). An opposing view is held by Henry Fairlie, "We knew what we were doing when we went into Vietnam," in *Washington Monthly*, May, 1973, p. 7–26.

[42] According to Neil Sheehan in *The Pentagon Papers*, 247, 248 (New York, 1971), a team of defense and state department officials wrote a "scenario" as early as May 23, 1964, for a full-scale bombing of the North and a plan to elicit a joint congressional resolution "authorizing whatever is necessary with respect to Vietnam." Although the plan was not then put into effect, it reveals that a larger escalation of the war was under consideration before the Tonkin Gulf incident occurred. See also *Congressional Record*, 88 Congress, 2 session, 18132 (quotation), 18471; Chester, *et al*, *An American Melodrama*, 65.

[43] Eugene J. McCarthy, *The Year of the People*, 17–21, 49, 257; *Candidates 1968*, 132; *Time*, March 22, 1968, p. 14.

[44] A full account of the effort to find a challenger within the Democratic party appeared in Chester, *et al*, *An American Melodrama*, 65–75. Jerry Eller, quoted in *Minneapolis Tribune*, August 8, 1971, p. 13A, listed boredom as a principal reason; Paul R. Wieck, "McCarthy in '72 — Are the Troops There?" in *New Republic*, August 7, 14, 1971, p. 13, 15, suggested his disaffection with the "claptrap of campaigning." Other reasoning may be found in Joseph Roddy, "The Prime Mover," in *Look*, June 25, 1968, p. 87; Herzog, *McCarthy for President*, 29–32; McCarthy, "Why I'm Battling LBJ," in *Look*, February 6, 1968, p. 24.

[45] McDonald and Smoke, *The Peasants' Revolt*, 40; Larner, *Nobody Knows*, 45, 52; David Frost, *The Presidential Debate, 1968*, 26 (New York, 1968).

[46] *Time*, April 5, 1968, p. 23, July 26, 1968, p. 21.

[47] Herzog, *McCarthy for President*, 290; *Time*, September 6, 1968, p. 20, 25.

[48] McCarthy, *The Year of the People*, 253; Tom Wicker, "Report on the Phenomenon Named McCarthy," in *New York Times Magazine*, August 25, 1968, p. 80.

[49] *Minneapolis Tribune*, November 10, 1968, p. 1A, 14A; Chester, *et al*, *An American Melodrama*, 832–833, McCarthy reportedly doubted that his influence would have made a difference in the outcome of the election and later insisted that it was up to Humphrey to accommodate himself more precisely to the antiwar feeling represented by the McCarthy movement. *Minneapolis Tribune*, August 8, 1971, p. 13A.

[50] Humphrey speech, August 22, 1969, before the American Association for State and Local History, St. Paul, typescript of a taped speech, in the Minnesota Historical Society; Geri Joseph, in *Minneapolis Tribune*, August 13, 1972, p. 16A; *Washington Post*, reprinted in *Pioneer Press*, June 18, 1971, p. 13C (quotations). A Humphrey aide said the vice-president was "systematically excluded" from policy talks after expressing his opposition. For an account of the differences between Humphrey and Johnson, see David Halberstam, *The Best and the Brightest*, 534–536, 662 (New York, 1972). Following publication of the Pentagon papers, Humphrey confirmed that he had taken issue with the president on February 17, 1965, concerning the escalation of the war. Disclaiming any real influence, he said, "To tell the truth, I didn't have a hell of a lot to say." *Minneapolis Tribune*, June 27, 1971, p. 1A, 8A. *The Pentagon Papers*, 519, seem to substantiate these assessments of Humphrey's minimal role.

[51] Eisele, *Almost to the Presidency*, 423, 425–427.

[52] Eisele, *Almost to the Presidency*, 431; *Congressional Record*, 92 Congress, 1 session, 8015–8022.

[53] *Minneapolis Tribune*, January 11, p. 1, March 15, p. 1, April 5, p. 1, June 8, p. 1, 4, 1972.

[54] McCarthy did not accept the UN offer because Minnesota's Republican Governor Harold LeVander would not appoint a Democrat to succeed him; Eisele, *Almost to the Presidency*, 398, 413; *Minneapolis Tribune*, July 25, 1969, p. 1. In January, 1973, McCarthy became a senior editor at Simon & Schuster, Inc., New York. *St. Paul Dispatch*, February 13, 1973, p. 3.

[55] *Minneapolis Tribune*, May 24, 1971, p. 1, April 4, 1972, p. 1; Reston, in *Tribune*, May 30, 1971, p. 6A; interview of the author with Elizabeth A. Salisbury, cochairman of the Bipartisan Caucus to Stop the War, May 9, 1972, Stuhler Papers.

[56] Polsby, *The Citizen's Choice*, 9.

[57] McCarthy, *The Year of the People*, 30; *Minneapolis Tribune*, September 27, 1968, p. 1, 12; Eisele, *Almost to the Presidency*, 446.

[58] For discussions of the comparison, see Jonas, *Isolationism in America, 1935–1941*, 284; Selig Adler, "The Ghost of Isolationism," in *Foreign Service Journal*, November, 1969, p. 35; Seabury, *The Waning of Southern "Internationalism"*, 26, 29; Gabriel A. Almond, *The American People and Foreign Policy*, 131 (New York, 1960). Historian Richard H. Miller, in his study of *American Imperialism in 1898: The Quest for National Fulfillment*, 13, warned against historical analogies and emphasized that "historical time and circumstances are seldom, if ever, twice the same." Issues of *Fortune* and the *Wall Street Journal*, respected barometers of business opinion, substantiate the business community's concerns with respect to the war. See for example, *Fortune*, August 1, 1969, whole issue; *Wall Street Journal*, December 17, 1969, p. 16. The quotation may be found in Marion J. Levy, Jr., "Our Ever and Future Jungle," in *World Politics*, 22:315 (January, 1970).

[59] Graham T. Allison, "Cool It: The Foreign Policy of Young America," in *Foreign Policy*, Winter, 1970–71, p. 158.

INDEX